W9-BWH-201

ISRAEL

OPPOSING VIEWPOINTS®

Other Books of Related Interest in the Opposing Viewpoints Series:

American Foreign Policy
Central America
China
Latin America & U.S. Foreign Policy
The Middle East
Problems of Africa
The Soviet Union
Terrorism

Additional Books in the Opposing Viewpoints Series:

Abortion
AIDS
American Government
The American Military
American Values
America's Elections
America's Prisons
The Arms Race
Biomedical Ethics
Censorship
Chemical Dependency
Civil Liberties
Constructing a Life Philosophy
Crime & Criminals
Criminal Justice
Death and Dying
The Death Penalty
Drug Abuse
Economics in America
The Environmental Crisis
The Health Crisis
Male/Female Roles
The Mass Media
Nuclear War
The Political Spectrum
Poverty
Religion in America
Science & Religion
Sexual Values
Social Justice
Teenage Sexuality
The Vietnam War
War and Human Nature

ISRAEL

OPPOSING VIEWPOINTS®

David L. Bender and Bruno Leone, *Series Editors*

Bob Anderson and Janelle Rohr, *Book Editors*

OPPOSING VIEWPOINTS SERIES ®

Greenhaven Press, Inc.   San Diego, CA

Library of Congress Cataloging-in-Publication Data

Israel : opposing viewpoints / Janelle Rohr & Robert Anderson, book editors.
    p.   cm. — (Opposing viewpoints series)
    Bibliography: p.
    Includes index.
    ISBN 0-89908-435-4 : $13.95. ISBN 0-89908-410-9
    (pbk.) : $6.95
    1. Israel. 2. Zionism. 3. Palestinian Arabs—Israel.
4. Israel—Ethnic relations. 5. West Bank. I. Rohr,
Janelle, 1963-   . II. Anderson, Robert, 1950-   . III.
Series.
DS126.5.I793 1989
956.94—dc19   88-24432
                                                        CIP

"Congress shall make no law . . .
abridging the freedom of speech,
or of the press."

First Amendment to the US Constitution

The basic foundation of our democracy is the first amendment guarantee of freedom of expression. The *Opposing Viewpoints Series* is dedicated to the concept of this basic freedom and the idea that it is more important to practice it than to enshrine it.

Contents

Why Consider Opposing Viewpoints?

> *"It is better to debate a question without settling it than to settle a question without debating it."*
>
> Joseph Joubert (1754-1824)

The Importance of Examining Opposing Viewpoints

The purpose of the Opposing Viewpoints books, and this book in particular, is to present balanced, and often difficult to find, opposing points of view on complex and sensitive issues.

Probably the best way to become informed is to analyze the positions of those who are regarded as experts and well studied on issues. It is important to consider every variety of opinion in an attempt to determine the truth. Opinions from the mainstream of society should be examined. But also important are opinions that are considered radical, reactionary, or minority as well as those stigmatized by some other uncomplimentary label. An important lesson of history is the eventual acceptance of many unpopular and even despised opinions. The ideas of Socrates, Jesus, and Galileo are good examples of this.

Readers will approach this book with their own opinions on the issues debated within it. However, to have a good grasp of one's own viewpoint, it is necessary to understand the arguments of those with whom one disagrees. It can be said that those who do not completely understand their adversary's point of view do not fully understand their own.

A persuasive case for considering opposing viewpoints has been presented by John Stuart Mill in his work *On Liberty*. When examining controversial issues it may be helpful to reflect on this suggestion:

> The only way in which a human being can make some approach to knowing the whole of a subject, is by hearing what can be said about it by persons of every variety of opinion, and studying all modes in which it can be looked at by every character of mind. No wise man ever acquired his wisdom in any mode but this.

Analyzing Sources of Information

The Opposing Viewpoints books include diverse materials taken from magazines, journals, books, and newspapers, as well as statements and position papers from a wide range of individuals, organizations and governments. This broad spectrum of sources helps to develop patterns of thinking which are open to the consideration of a variety of opinions.

Pitfalls To Avoid

A pitfall to avoid in considering opposing points of view is that of regarding one's own opinion as being common sense and the most rational stance and the point of view of others as being only opinion and naturally wrong. It may be that another's opinion is correct and one's own is in error.

Another pitfall to avoid is that of closing one's mind to the opinions of those with whom one disagrees. The best way to approach a dialogue is to make one's primary purpose that of understanding the mind and arguments of the other person and not that of enlightening him or her with one's own solutions. More can be learned by listening than speaking.

It is my hope that after reading this book the reader will have a deeper understanding of the issues debated and will appreciate the complexity of even seemingly simple issues on which good and honest people disagree. This awareness is particularly important in a democratic society such as ours where people enter into public debate to determine the common good. Those with whom one disagrees should not necessarily be regarded as enemies, but perhaps simply as people who suggest different paths to a common goal.

Developing Basic Reading and Thinking Skills

In this book carefully edited opposing viewpoints are purposely placed back to back to create a running debate; each viewpoint is preceded by a short quotation that best expresses the author's main argument. This format instantly plunges the reader into the midst of a controversial issue and greatly aids that reader in mastering the basic skill of recognizing an author's point of view.

A number of basic skills for critical thinking are practiced in the activities that appear throughout the books in the series. Some of the skills are:

Evaluating Sources of Information   The ability to choose from among alternative sources the most reliable and accurate source in relation to a given subject.

Separating Fact from Opinion   The ability to make the basic distinction between factual statements (those that can be demonstrated or verified empirically) and statements of opinion (those that are beliefs or attitudes that cannot be proved).

Identifying Stereotypes   The ability to identify oversimplified, exaggerated descriptions (favorable or unfavorable) about people and insulting statements about racial, religious or national groups, based upon misinformation or lack of information.

Recognizing Ethnocentrism   The ability to recognize attitudes or opinions that express the view that one's own race, culture, or group is inherently superior, or those attitudes that judge another culture or group in terms of one's own.

It is important to consider opposing viewpoints and equally important to be able to critically analyze those viewpoints. The activities in this book are designed to help the reader master these thinking skills. Statements are taken from the book's viewpoints and the reader is asked to analyze them. This technique aids the reader in developing skills that not only can be applied to the viewpoints in this book, but also to situations where opinionated spokespersons comment on controversial issues. Although the activities are helpful to the solitary reader, they are most useful when the reader can benefit from the interaction of group discussion.

Using this book and others in the series should help readers develop basic reading and thinking skills. These skills should improve the readers' ability to understand what they read. Readers should be better able to separate fact from opinion, substance from rhetoric and become better consumers of information in our media-centered culture.

This volume of the Opposing Viewpoints books does not advocate a particular point of view. Quite the contrary! The very nature of the book leaves it to the reader to formulate the opinions he or she finds most suitable. My purpose as publisher is to see that this is made possible by offering a wide range of viewpoints which are fairly presented.

David L. Bender
Publisher

Legend:
- Israel 1949-1967
- Occupied

LEBANON

SYRIA

Nazareth

Nablus

Tel-Aviv

Jericho

•Amman

Jerusalem

Gaza

Hebron

Beersheba

ISRAEL

EGYPT

JORDAN

Eilat

Apaba

Reprinted from *Multinational Monitor*, April 1988.

Introduction

"Israel was born in strife and has continued to live in strife for 40 years."

Glenn Frankel, *The Washington Post National Weekly Edition,* April 25/May 1, 1988.

Israel was founded in response to centuries of oppression of Jews, culminating in the horrors of the Nazi Holocaust. To partially correct this heinous wrong, the United Nations (UN) in 1948 recognized Israel as a Jewish homeland, a place where Jews would be safe from persecution. Ironically, Israel today is the focus of heated debate about whether its policies toward its minority population, the Palestinians, are oppressive.

While Israel has faced many controversies since its founding, conflict with the Palestinians has been perhaps the most persistent. Much of the Israeli-Palestinian conflict is centered in the West Bank and Gaza Strip. Not originally part of the United Nations-established Israel, these two territories were won by Israel in the Six-Day War in 1967. After twenty years of Israeli military administration, it is still unclear what will be the political future of the over one million Palestinians living in these occupied territories. Israel's occupation sparks debate about whether its policies are humane.

To many people, including a sizable number of Israelis, no occupation is humane. While occupation by its very nature denies self-determination, the Palestinians should not lose the basic human rights stipulated in the UN charter. Palestinians living in occupied territories are not afforded the same civil rights as those living freely in their own countries. For example, when Palestinians are suspected of committing terrorist acts, their families' homes can be demolished. In contrast, an Israeli citizen suspected of a crime is entitled to the same rights of due process as citizens have in the US. No retaliation is made against a suspect's relatives.

Furthermore, critics argue that Palestinians are an exploited class lacking economic rights. To find jobs, many Palestinians must work illegally in Israel, thus losing the protection of fair labor laws. Israeli author David Grossman visited Palestinians who worked and lived in a factory during the week. One man told Grossman of the dehumanizing conditions: "We are like living dead here. I work thirteen hours a day. I have two breaks, each one for half an hour. . . . I don't get paid for breaks." Another worker said he goes home once a week. "I get there at five in the evening on Friday and go to sleep. I sleep until twelve on Saturday. Afterwards, I fix things at home and look at my [three-month-old] daughter to see how she's grown. She still doesn't know me. . . . On Sunday at seven in the morning I'm already back at my machine."

Israel's critics conclude that it is appalling that a people that has experienced great suffering throughout its history is responsible for such suffering of the Palestinians.

There are many who disagree with this view. They believe that Israel's occupation policies have been relatively benign, especially given the omnipresent threat of Palestinian violence. Far from denying Palestinians' civil rights, say these people, Israel's security policies are necessary to safeguard *all* who live in the occupied territories—Palestinians as well as Israelis. Strict policies are motivated by fears caused by repeated Palestinian terrorist attacks. *New York Times* correspondent David Shipler interviewed Brett Goldberg, an American Jew who had emigrated to Israel. Goldberg talked about having to identify a friend's body, a custodian who had been stabbed by West Bank Arabs. "I was full of outrage simply because he was so defenseless. . . . He was stabbed over one hundred twenty times." As a result, Goldberg said contact with Arabs was physically and psychologically unpleasant for him, and "even if all of a sudden [Palestinian leader Yassir] Arafat were to sit down with [Jewish rabbi] Meir Kahane and terror were to be forsworn for generations, I think these fears would be very hard to eradicate."

Israel's supporters point out that despite such violence, Israel has respected Palestinians' economic rights by providing services that have improved their living standards. According to Israel's Information Service, the per capita income of residents in the occupied territories has increased by eleven percent each year and people can more easily buy consumer goods. In addition, four universities for West Bank students have opened since 1967, while the number of Palestinian children attending school has increased by 175,000.

Many Israelis argue that while an occupation certainly is not pleasant, the Israeli commitment to democracy has meant that Palestinians' civil and economic rights have been reasonably protected.

The Israeli-Palestinian conflict, and specifically, the impact of occupation, are important factors in several of the questions debated in *Israel: Opposing Viewpoints.* The five chapters are as follows: Historical Debate: Is a Homeland for the Jews Necessary? Does Israel Treat the Palestinians Fairly? Should the US Support Israel? What Is Israel's International Role? and What Is the Future of Israel? Given the turbulence of Israel's first forty years, it is clear that these questions will not be easily resolved.

Historical Debate: Is a Homeland for the Jews Necessary?

Chapter Preface

The year 135 A.D. marked the defeat of the last Jewish nation in the Holy Land. Jews then began a thousand-year period of diaspora; they resided in other countries and frequently suffered persecution. How this millennium of exile affected the Jewish people and their culture is one basis of an important question that early twentieth-century Zionists faced—must a homeland for the Jewish people be predominantly Jewish?

Most Zionist leaders looked back on this diaspora and concluded that Jews must be a majority in their own state. Despite being a productive and highly literate populace, Jews had been victims of the medieval Crusades, the notorious Spanish Inquisition, pogroms in late nineteenth-century Russia, and many other devastating anti-Semitic episodes. Zionists concluded that Jews would be truly safe only when they were a majority in their own country.

A small dissident group of Jews held a different view of the diaspora and the question of a Jewish state. While acknowledging the persecution Jews had experienced, they argued that as the Old Testament prophesied, suffering had uplifted the Jews. As an oppressed people, Jews had developed an empathic sense of justice. To become a majority in a Jewish state in Palestine, these dissidents argued, would require displacing or establishing dominion over the Arabs already living there. Either course of action would corrupt Jewish ethics and turn Jews into oppressors, a people no better than the Gentiles who had persecuted them for centuries.

The viewpoints in the following chapter present both responses to Jewish history as they examine the question, is a homeland for the Jews necessary?

"The Jews who will it shall achieve their State."

A Separate Jewish State Is Necessary

Theodor Herzl

Theodor Herzl (1860-1904) is considered the founder of modern Zionism. He was instrumental in convening the first Zionist Congress, in Basle, Switzerland, in August 1897, where it was declared that Palestine should be a homeland for the Jews. The following viewpoint is an excerpt from *The Jewish State*, a pamphlet Herzl wrote in Vienna in 1895. In it, he argues that Jews remain a persecuted minority in most countries. By designating territory as a Jewish homeland, Herzl believed, Jews could protect their rights and maintain their cultural identity.

As you read, consider the following questions:

1. In Herzl's opinion, why would it be dangerous for Jews to remain exiled from their homeland?
2. What steps should Jewish emigrants take in developing their homeland, according to the author?
3. How does Herzl argue that a Jewish state will benefit its Arab neighbors?

Theodor Herzl, *The Jewish State*, 1896.

The idea which I have developed in this pamphlet is an ancient one: It is the restoration of the Jewish State.

The world resounds with clamor against the Jews, and this has revived the dormant idea. . . .

The Jewish question still exists. It would be foolish to deny it. It is a misplaced piece of medievalism which civilized nations do not even yet seem able to shake off, try as they will. They proved they had this high-minded desire when they emancipated us. The Jewish question persists wherever Jews live in appreciable numbers. Wherever it does not exist, it is brought in together with Jewish immigrants. We are naturally drawn into those places where we are not persecuted, and our appearance there gives rise to persecution. This is the case, and will inevitably be so, everywhere, even in highly civilized countries—see, for instance, France—so long as the Jewish question is not solved on the political level. The unfortunate Jews are now carrying the seeds of anti-Semitism into England; they have already introduced it into America.

One People

Anti-Semitism is a highly complex movement, which I think I understand. I approach this movement as a Jew, yet without fear or hatred. I believe that I can see in it the elements of cruel sport, of common commercial rivalry, of inherited prejudice, of religious intolerance—but also of a supposed need for self-defense. I consider the Jewish question neither a social nor a religious one, even though it sometimes takes these and other forms. It is a national question, and to solve it we must first of all establish it as an international political problem to be discussed and settled by the civilized nations of the world in council.

We are a people—*one* people.

We have sincerely tried everywhere to merge with the national communities in which we live, seeking only to preserve the faith of our fathers. It is not permitted us. In vain are we loyal patriots, sometimes superloyal; in vain do we make the same sacrifices of life and property as our fellow citizens; in vain do we strive to enhance the fame of our native lands in the arts and sciences, or her wealth by trade and commerce. In our native lands where we have lived for centuries we are still decried as aliens, often by men whose ancestors had not yet come at a time when Jewish sighs had long been heard in the country. The majority decide who the "alien" is; this, and all else in the relations between peoples, is a matter of power. I do not surrender any part of our prescriptive right when I make this statement merely in my own name, as an individual. In the world as it now is and will probably remain, for an indefinite period, might takes precedence over right. It is without avail, therefore, for us to be loyal patriots, as were the Huguenots, who were forced to emigrate. If we were left in

18

peace . . .

But I think we shall not be left in peace.

Oppression and persecution cannot exterminate us. No nation on earth has endured such struggles and sufferings as we have. Jew-baiting has merely winnowed out our weaklings; the strong among us defiantly return to their own whenever persecution breaks out. This was most clearly apparent in the period immediately following the emancipation of the Jews. Those Jews who rose highest intellectually and materially entirely lost the sense of unity with their people. Wherever we remain politically secure for any length of time, we assimilate. I think this is not praiseworthy. . . .

The Power of the State Idea

No human being is wealthy or powerful enough to transplant a people from one place of residence to another. Only an idea can achieve that. The State idea surely has that power. The Jews have dreamed this princely dream throughout the long night of their history. "Next year in Jerusalem" is our age-old motto. It is now a matter of showing that the vague dream can be transformed into a clear and glowing idea.

Viewed with Favour

His Majesty's Government view with favour the establishment in Palestine of a national home for the Jewish people, and will use their best endeavours to facilitate the achievement of this object, it being clearly understood that nothing shall be done which may prejudice the civil and religious rights of existing non-Jewish communities in Palestine, or the rights and political status enjoyed by Jews in any other country.

Arthur James Lord Balfour, letter to Lord Rothschild, November 2, 1917.

For this, our minds must first be thoroughly cleansed of many old, outworn, muddled, and shortsighted notions. The unthinking might, for example, imagine that this exodus would have to take its way from civilization into the desert. That is not so! It will be carried out entirely in the framework of civilization. We shall not revert to a lower stage; we shall rise to a higher one. We shall not dwell in mud huts; we shall build new, more beautiful, and more modern houses, and possess them in safety. We shall not lose our acquired possessions; we shall realize them. We shall surrender our well-earned rights for better ones. We shall relinquish none of our cherished customs; we shall find them again. We shall not leave our old home until the new one is available. Those only will depart who are sure thereby to improve their lot; those who are now desperate will go first, after them the poor, next the well

19

to do, and last of all the wealthy. Those who go first will raise themselves to a higher grade, on a level with that whose representatives will shortly follow. The exodus will thus at the same time be an ascent in class. . . .

No one can deny the gravity of the Jewish situation. Wherever they live in appreciable number, Jews are persecuted in greater or lesser measure. Their equality before the law, granted by statute, has become practically a dead letter. They are debarred from filling even moderately high offices in the army, or in any public or private institutions. And attempts are being made to thrust them out of business also: "Don't buy from Jews!"

Attacks in parliaments, in assemblies, in the press, in the pulpit, in the street, on journeys—for example, their exclusion from certain hotels—even in places of recreation are increasing from day to day. The forms of persecutions vary according to country and social circle. In Russia, special taxes are levied on Jewish villages; in Romania, a few persons are put to death; in Germany, they get a good beating occasionally; in Austria, anti-Semites exercise their terrorism over all public life; in Algeria, there are traveling agitators; in Paris, the Jews are shut out of the so-called best social circles and excluded from clubs. The varieties of anti-Jewish expression are innumerable. But this is not the occasion to attempt the sorry catalogue of Jewish hardships. We shall not dwell on particular cases, however painful.

A Model State

I do not aim to arouse sympathy on our behalf. All that is nonsense, as futile as it is dishonorable. I shall content myself with putting the following questions to the Jews: Is it not true that, in countries where we live in appreciable numbers, the position of Jewish lawyers, doctors, technicians, teachers, and employees of every description becomes daily more intolerable? Is it not true that the Jewish middle classes are seriously threatened? Is it not true that the passions of the mob are incited against our wealthy? Is it not true that our poor endure greater suffering than any other proletariat? I think that this pressure is everywhere present. In our upper economic classes it causes discomfort, in our middle classes utter despair.

The fact of the matter is, everything tends to one and the same conclusion, which is expressed in the classic Berlin cry: *"Juden 'raus!"* ("Out with the Jews!").

I shall now put the question in the briefest possible form: Shouldn't we "get out" at once, and if so, whither?

Or, may we remain, and if so, how long?

Let us first settle the point of remaining. Can we hope for better days, can we possess our souls in patience, can we wait in pious resignation till the princes and peoples of this earth are more mercifully disposed toward us? I say that we cannot hope for the current to shift. And why not? Even if we were as near to the hearts of princes as are their other subjects, they could not protect us. They would only incur popular hatred by showing us too much favor. And this "too much" implies less than is claimed as a right by any ordinary citizen or ethnic group. The nations in whose midst Jews live are all covertly or openly anti-Semitic. . . .

We are one people—our enemies have made us one whether we will or not, as has repeatedly happened in history. Affliction binds us together, and thus united, we suddenly discover our strength. Yes, we are strong enough to form a State, and, indeed, a model State. We possess all the requisite human and material resources.

This would, accordingly, be the appropriate place to give an account of what has been somewhat crudely termed our "human material." But it would not be appreciated till the broad outlines of the plan, on which everything depends, have first been marked out.

Nazi Germany, 1933: Persecution of the Jews. Jewish boy is forced to cut his father's beard while German soldiers watch jeeringly.

The whole plan is essentially quite simple, as it must necessarily be if it is to be comprehensible to all.

Let sovereignty be granted us over a portion of the globe adequate to meet our rightful national requirements; we will attend to the rest.

To create a new State is neither ridiculous nor impossible. Haven't we witnessed the process in our own day, among nations which were not largely middle class as we are, but poorer, less educated, and consequently weaker than ourselves? The governments of all countries scourged by anti-Semitism will be keenly interested in obtaining sovereignty for us.

The plan, simple in design but complicated in execution, will be executed by two agencies: the Society of Jews and the Jewish Company. . . .

We must not visualize the exodus of the Jews as a sudden one. It will be gradual, proceeding over a period of decades. The poorest will go first and cultivate the soil. They will construct roads, bridges, railways, and telegraph installations, regulate rivers, and provide themselves with homesteads, all according to predetermined plans. Their labor will create trade, trade will create markets, and markets will attract new settlers—for every man will go voluntarily, at his own expense and his own risk. The labor invested in the soil will enhance its value. The Jews will soon perceive that a new and permanent frontier has been opened up for that spirit of enterprise which has heretofore brought them only hatred and obloquy.

The founding of a State today is not to be accomplished in the manner that a thousand years ago would have been the only possible one. It is silly to revert to older levels of civilization, as many Zionists propose. Supposing, for example, we were obliged to clear a country of wild beasts, we should not set about it in the fashion of the fifth-century Europeans. We should not take spear and lance and go out individually in pursuit of bears; we would organize a grand and glorious hunting party, drive the animals together, and throw a melinite bomb into their midst.

If we planned to erect buildings, we should not drive a few shaky piles in a marsh like the lake dwellers, but should build as men build now. Indeed, we shall build in bolder and more stately style than has ever been done before; for we now possess means which heretofore did not exist.

Emigrants

The emigrants standing lowest in the economic scale will be gradually followed by those of the next grade. Those now in desperate straits will go first. They will be led by the intellectual mediocrities whom we produce so abundantly and who are oppressed everywhere. . . .

Who would go with us, let him fall in behind our banner and fight for the cause with word and pen and deed.

Those Jews who agree with our State idea will rally around the Society. Thereby they will give it the authority in the eyes of governments to confer and treat on behalf of our people. The Society will be recognized as, to put it in terminology of international law, a State-creating power. And this recognition will, in effect, mean the creation of the State.

A Work of Wisdom

The Zionists know that they have undertaken a work of unparalleled difficulty. . . .

What gives Zionists the courage to begin this labor of Hercules is the conviction that they are performing a necessary and useful task, a work of love and civilization, a work of justice and wisdom. They wish to save eight to ten million of their kin from intolerable suffering. They desire to relieve the nations among whom they now vegetate of a presence which is considered disagreeable. They wish to deprive anti-Semitism, which lowers the morals of the community everywhere and develops the very worst instincts, of its victim. They wish to make the Jews, who are nowadays reproached with being parasites, into an undeniably productive people. They desire to irrigate with their sweat and to till with their hands a country that is today a desert, until it again becomes the blooming garden it once was. Zionism will thus equally serve the unhappy Jews and the Christian peoples, civilization and the economy of the world.

Max Nordau, *Zionism*, 1902.

Should the powers show themselves willing to grant us sovereignty over a neutral land, then the Society will enter into negotiations for the possession of this land. Here two regions come to mind: Palestine and Argentina. Significant experiments in colonization have been made in both countries, though on the mistaken principle of gradual infiltration of Jews. Infiltration is bound to end badly. For there comes the inevitable moment when the government in question, under pressure of the native populace— which feels itself threatened—puts a stop to further influx of Jews. Immigration, therefore, is futile unless it is based on our guaranteed autonomy.

The Society of Jews will treat with the present authorities in the land, under the sponsorship of the European powers, if they prove friendly to the plan. We could offer the present authorities enormous advantages, assume part of the public debt, build new thoroughfares, which we ourselves would also require, and do many other things. The very creation of the Jewish State would be beneficial to neighboring lands, since the cultivation of a strip of land increases the value of its surrounding districts.

Is Palestine or Argentina preferable? The Society will take whatever it is given and whatever Jewish public opinion favors. The Society will determine both these points. . . .

Palestine is our unforgettable historic homeland. The very name would be a marvelously effective rallying cry. If His Majesty the Sultan were to give us Palestine, we could in return undertake the complete management of the finances of Turkey. We should there form a part of a wall of defense for Europe in Asia, an outpost of civilization against barbarism. We should as a neutral state remain in contact with all Europe, which would have to guarantee our existence. . . .

Let me repeat once more my opening words: The Jews who will it shall achieve their State.

We shall live at last as free men on our own soil, and in our own homes peacefully die.

The world will be liberated by our freedom, enriched by our wealth, magnified by our greatness.

And whatever we attempt there for our own benefit will redound mightily and beneficially to the good of all mankind.

"Judaism . . . does not need an independent State."

A Separate Jewish State Is Not Necessary

Ahad Ha-am

Rabbi Ahad Ha-am (1856-1927) was the pen name of Asher Zvi Ginsberg, an author and agnostic. Born in Ukrainia, Ha-am supported the Hibbat Zion movement, founded in 1881, which advocated sending Jews to Palestine. Unlike Theodor Herzl, the author of the opposing viewpoint, Ha-am believed that Jewish culture and teachings must be revived before a state was created. Without this revival, a Jewish state would have little meaning. The following viewpoint is Ha-am's response to the August 1897 Zionist Congress meeting in Basle, Switzerland, which had advocated establishing a Jewish state in Palestine.

As you read, consider the following questions:

1. According to the author, what was the motivation behind the Zionist Congress's call for a Jewish state?
2. What does Ha-am mean when he draws a distinction between "political Zionists" and Zionists inspired by the "spiritual problem"?
3. Why does Ha-am think it would be dangerous to create a Jewish state prematurely?

Ahad Ha-am (Asher Zvi Ginsberg), *The Jewish State and the Jewish Problem.* 1897.

Some months have passed since the Zionist Congress, but its echoes are still reverberating in daily life and in the press. All kinds of gatherings—small and large, local and regional—are taking place. Since the delegates returned home, they have been calling public meetings and repeatedly regaling us with tales of the wonders that were enacted before their very eyes. The wretched, hungry public is listening, becoming ecstatic, and hoping for salvation. It is inconceivable to them that "they"—the Jews of the West—can fail to succeed in what they propose. Heads grow hot and hearts beat fast, and many "leaders" who had for years—until [the Congress]—lived only for Palestinian settlement, and for whom a penny donation in aid of Jewish labor in Palestine or the Jaffa School was worth the world, have now lost their bearings and ask one another: "What's the good of this sort of work? The days of the Messiah are near at hand, and we busy ourselves with trifles! The time has come for great deeds, for great men, men of the West, have enlisted in the cause and march before us."

A Name from the West

There has been a revolution in their world, and, to emphasize it, they have given the cause itself a new name: It is no longer "Love of Zion", but "Zionism" (Zioniyuth). Indeed, there are even "precisionists" who, being determined to leave no loophole for error, use only the European form of the name ("Zionismus")— thus announcing to all and sundry that they are not talking about anything so antiquated as Hibbat Zion, but about a new, up-to-date movement, which comes, like its name, from the West, where people are innocent of the Hebrew language. . . .

There is no doubt that, even when the Jewish State is established, Jewish settlement will be able to advance only by small degrees, as permitted by the resources of the people themselves and by the progress of the economic development of the country. Meanwhile the natural increase of Jewish population both within the Palestinian settlement and in the Diaspora, will continue, with the inevitable result that, on the one hand, Palestine will have less and less room for the new immigrants, and, on the other hand, despite continual emigration, the number of those remaining outside Palestine will not be appreciably diminished. In his opening speech at the Congress, Dr. Theodor Herzl, wishing to demonstrate the superiority of his State idea to the previous form of Palestinian colonization, calculated that by the latter method it would take nine hundred years before all the Jews could be settled in their land. The members of the Congress applauded this as a conclusive argument. But is was a cheap victory. The Jewish State itself, do what it will, will find no way to make a more favorable calculation.

The truth is bitter, but with all its bitterness it is better than illusion. We must admit to ourselves that the "ingathering of the exiles" is unattainable by natural means. We may, by natural means, someday establish a Jewish State; it is possible that the Jews may increase and multiply within it until the "land is filled with them"—but even then the greater part of our people will remain scattered on foreign soils. "To gather our scattered ones from the four corners of the earth" (in the words of the Prayer Book) is impossible. Only religion, with its belief in a miraculous redemption, can promise such a consummation.

But if this is so, if the Jewish State, too, means not an "ingathering of the exiles" but the settlement of a small part of our people in Palestine, then how will this solve the material problem of the Jewish masses in the lands of the Diaspora?

Freeing the Jewish Soul

We must revitalize the idea of the national renascence, and use every possible means to strengthen its hold and deepen its roots, until it becomes an organic element in the Jewish consciousness and an independent dynamic force. Only in that way, as it seems to me, can the Jewish soul be freed from its shackles and regain contact with the broad stream of human life without having to pay for its freedom by the sacrifice of its individuality.

Ahad Ha-am, *The Law of the Heart*, 1894.

The material problem will not be ended by the establishment of a Jewish State, and it is, indeed, beyond our power to solve it once and for all. (Even now there are various means at our disposal to alleviate this problem to a greater or lesser degree, e.g., by increasing the proportion of farmers and artisans among our people *in all lands*, etc.) Whether or not we create a Jewish State, the material situation of the Jews will always basically depend on the economic condition and the cultural level of the various nations among which we are dispersed.

Zionism's Real Basis

Thus we are driven to the conclusion that the real and only basis of Zionism is to be found in another problem, the spiritual one.

But the spiritual problem appears in two differing forms, one in the West and one in the East, which explains the fundamental difference between western "Zionism" and eastern "Hibbat Zion." Nordau dealt only with the western form of the problem, apparently knowing nothing about the eastern; and the Congress as a whole concentrated on the first, and paid little attention to the second.

The western Jew, having left the ghetto and having sought acceptance by the gentile majority, is unhappy because his hope of an open-armed welcome has been disappointed. Perforce he returns to his own people and tries to find within the Jewish community that life for which he yearns—but in vain. The life and horizon of the Jewish community no longer satisfy him. He has already grown accustomed to a broader social and political life, and on the intellectual side the work to be done for our Jewish national culture does not attract him, because that culture has played no part in his earliest education and is a closed book to him. In this dilemma he therefore turns to the land of his ancestors and imagines how good it would be if a Jewish State were re-established there—a State and society organized exactly after the pattern of other States. Then he could live a full, complete life within his own people, and he could find at home all that he now sees outside, dangled before his eyes but out of reach. Of course, not all the Jews will be able to take wing and go to their State; but the very existence of the Jewish State will also raise the prestige of those who remain in exile, and their fellow citizens will no longer despise them and keep them at arm's length, as though they were base slaves, dependent entirely on the hospitality of others. As he further contemplates this fascinating vision, it suddenly dawns on his inner consciousness that even now, before the Jewish State is established, the mere idea of it gives him almost complete relief. It provides an opportunity for communal work and political excitement; his emotions find an outlet in a field of activity which is not subservient to non-Jews; and he feels that, thanks to this ideal, he stands once more spiritually erect and has regained his personal dignity, without overmuch trouble and purely by his own efforts. So he devotes himself to the ideal with all the ardor of which he is capable; he gives rein to his fancy and lets it soar as it will, beyond reality and the limitations of human power. For it is not the attainment of the ideal that he needs; its pursuit alone is sufficient to cure him of his spiritual disease, which is that of an inferiority complex, and the loftier and more distant the ideal, the greater its power to exalt.

Eastern Zionism

This is the basis of western Zionism and the secret of its attraction. But eastern Hibbat Zion originated and developed in a different setting. It, too, began as a political movement; but, being a result of material evils, it could not be content with an "activity" consisting only of outbursts of feeling and fine phrases, which may satisfy the heart but not the stomach. Hibbat Zion began at once to express itself in concrete activities—in the establishment of colonies in Palestine. This practical work soon clipped the wings of fancy and demonstrated conclusively that Hibbat Zion could not lessen the material woe of the Jews by one iota. One might, there-

28

fore, have thought that, when this fact became patent, the Hovevei Zion would give up their effort and cease wasting time and energy on work which brought them no nearer their goal. But, no: they remained true to their flag and went on working with the old enthusiasm, though most of them did not understand, even in their own minds, why they did so. . . .

The eastern form of the spiritual problem is absolutely different from the western. In the West it is the problem of the Jews; in the East, the *problem of Judaism.* The first weighs on the individual; the second, on the nation. The one is felt by Jews who have had a European education; the other, by Jews whose education has been Jewish. The one is a product of anti-Semitism, and is dependent on anti-Semitism for its existence; the other is a natural product of a real link with a millennial culture, and it will remain unsolved and unaffected even if the troubled of the Jews all over the world attain comfortable economic positions, are on the best possible terms with their neighbors, and are admitted to the fullest social and political equality. . . .

The Biblical Palestine

A word to the Jews in Palestine. I have no doubt that they are going about in the wrong way. The Palestine of the Biblical conception is not a geographical tract. It is in their hearts. . . .

Let the Jews who claim to be the chosen race prove their title by choosing the way of non-violence for vindicating their position on earth. Every country is their home including Palestine not by aggression but by loving service.

Mohandas K. Gandhi, *My Non-Violence,* 1960.

Judaism is, therefore, in a quandry: It can no longer tolerate the *Galut* form which it had to take on, in obedience to its will-to-live, when it was exiled from its own country; but, without that form, its life is in danger. So it seeks to return to its historic center, where it will be able to live a life developing in a natural way, to bring its powers into play in every department of human culture, to broaden and perfect those national possessions which it has acquired up to now, and thus to contribute to the common stock of humanity, in the future as it has in the past, a great national culture, the fruit of the unhampered activity of a people living by the light of its own spirit. For this purpose Judaism can, for the present, content itself with little. It does not need an independent State, but only the creation in its native land of conditions favorable to its development: a good-sized settlement of Jews working without hindrance in every branch of civilization, from agriculture and handicrafts to science and literature. This Jewish settlement, which will be a gradual growth, will become in course of time the center of the nation, wherein its spirit will find pure expression and develop in all its aspects to the highest degree of perfection of which it is capable. Then, from this center, the spirit of Judaism will radiate to the great circumference, to all the communities of the Diaspora, to inspire them with new life and to preserve the over-all unity of our people. When our national culture in Palestine has attained that level, we may be confident that it will produce men in the Land of Israel itself who will be able, at a favorable moment, to establish a State there—one which will be not merely a State of Jews but a really Jewish State.

This Hibbat Zion, which concerns itself with the preservation of Judaism at a time when Jewry is suffering so much, is something odd and unintelligible to the "political" Zionists of the West. . . . And so political Zionism cannot satisfy those Jews who care for Judaism; its growth seems to them to be fraught with danger to the object of their own aspiration.

The Secret of Our People

The secret of our people's persistence is that at a very early period the Prophets taught it to respect only the power of the spirit and not to worship material power. Therefore, unlike the other nations of antiquity, the Jewish people never reached the point of losing its self-respect in the face of more powerful enemies. As long as we remain faithful to this principle, our existence has a secure basis, and we shall not lose our self-respect, for we are not spiritually inferior to any nation. But a political ideal which is not grounded in our national culture is apt to seduce us from loyalty to our own inner spirit and to beget in us a tendency to find the path of glory in the attainment of material power and political dominion, thus breaking the thread that unites us with the past and undermining our historical foundation. Needless to say, if the political ideal is not attained, it will have disastrous consequences, because we shall have lost the old basis without finding a new one. But even if it is attained under present conditions, when we are a scattered people not only in the physical but also in the spiritual sense—even then, Judaism will be in great danger. Almost all our great men—those, that is, whose education and social position have prepared them to be at the head of a Jewish State—are spiritually far removed from Judaism and have no true conception of its nature and its value. Such men, however loyal to their State and devoted to its interests, will necessarily envisage those interests by the standards of the foreign culture which they themselves have imbibed; and they will endeavor, by moral persuasion or even by force, to implant that culture in the Jewish State, so that in the end the Jewish State will be a State of Germans or Frenchmen of the Jewish race. We have even now a small example of this process in Palestine.

History teaches us that in the days of the Herodian house Palestine was indeed a Jewish State, but the national culture was despised and persecuted. The ruling house did everything in its power to implant Roman culture in the country and frittered away the resources of the nation in the building of heathen temples, amphitheaters, and so forth. Such a Jewish State would spell death and utter degradation for our people. Such a State would never achieve sufficient political power to deserve respect, while it would be estranged from the living inner spiritual force of Judaism. The puny State, being "tossed about like a ball between its powerful neighbors, and maintaining its existence only by diplomatic shifts and continual truckling to the favored of fortune," would not be able to give us a feeling of national glory; the national culture, in which we might have sought and found our glory, would not have been implanted in our State and would not be the principle of its life. So we should really be then—much more than we are now—"a small and insignificant nation," enslaved in spirit to "the favored of fortune," turning an envious and covetous eye on the armed force of our "powerful neighbors"; our existence in such terms, as a sovereign State would not add a glorious chapter to our national history. . . .

Jewish National Culture

In sum: Hibbat Zion, no less than "Zionism," wants a Jewish State and believes in the possibility of the establishment of a Jewish State in the future. But while "Zionism" looks to the Jewish State to furnish a remedy for poverty and to provide complete tranquillity and national glory, Hibbat Zion knows that our State will not give us all these things until "universal Righteousness is enthroned and holds sway over nations and States"—it looks to a Jewish State to provide only a "secure refuge" for Judaism and a cultural bond to unite our nation. "Zionism," therefore, begins its work with political propaganda; Hibbat Zion begins with national culture, because only *through* the national culture and *for its sake* can a Jewish State be established in such a way as to correspond with the will and the needs of the Jewish people.

"For our future's sake, let us put forth the will, the faith and power to reconstruct the basis of our existence and establish a sovereign, self-governing Jewry in Israel."

Palestine Is the Jewish Birthright

David Ben Gurion

The following viewpoint is an excerpt from a speech David Ben Gurion made before a Zionist meeting in Basle, Switzerland, in 1931. In 1929 Palestinian Arabs had rioted against Jewish settlements. Ben Gurion's speech is a response to the fighting. He maintains that only when Jews are a majority in a Jewish state will they be truly safe and free from discrimination. Ben Gurion was born in Poland and emigrated to Palestine in 1906. Long an important figure in Israeli politics, he founded the national labor union, Histadrut, and was its general secretary from 1921 to 1935. In 1948, he became the first prime minister of the newly-created state of Israel.

As you read, consider the following questions:

1. Why does hostility toward the idea of a Jewish state persist, according to Ben Gurion?
2. Why does the author argue that Jews must not be a minority in their homeland?
3. According to Ben Gurion, what rights do Arabs have in the Jewish homeland?

David Ben Gurion, *Rebirth and Destiny of Israel.* Copyright © 1954 by Philosophical Library. Reprinted with permission.

We appear from the battlefront of 'Zionism on the way,' sent to you by the Army of Fulfillment, linked in destiny, for life or death, with the realization of Zionism. For more than twenty-five years, first a tiny platoon, then in companies and battalions, and now in brigades and divisions, that Army stands guard, firm and fast, over our agricultural development, our educational advances, our political progress in the Land. It is as such that we face you here, swayed by a profound sense of responsibility and solicitude for the position of the Zionist Movement and all its works. . . .

We were murderously attacked, we are exposed to systematic and continuous incitement, to the libels and provocation of effendis [upper-class Arabs] of the Comintern's agents, of Government officers. The essence of our right to be in Palestine is wantonly assailed, and not just by this officer or that but by a Great Britain governed today by the British Labor party. Even our civic status is disputed at every turn. . . .

Persistent Gentile Hostility

We saw that international testimony and recognition did not dispel the universal unfriendliness, the atmosphere of hostility, suspicion and misunderstanding, which surround our eternal people. The Gentiles cannot yet stomach our strangeness, nor comprehend our longings and lament, cannot register consciously our basic, natural right to be independent again in our Homeland. In the global upset of a World War the foundations of all the earth are shaken, the great Powers fight for their lives and the least external succor is worthwhile. That succor our small nation gave, and, in return, a right was given it. But to the public opinion of Great Britain and the world it is not yet an ironclad, unappealable right. Unpleasant, perhaps, to say so, but we should be purblind, playing ostrich-politics, not to see exactly where we stand with the nations. The Balfour Declaration, the Mandate and fifty years of proudest construction in Palestine are behind us, and still it is gallingly necessary to tell an incredulous world of our rights and works, to make it see we come neither to extort nor exploit, but in equity to remodel our lives. It is the worst kind of self-deception to preach that if we possess a scrap of paper furbished with the seals of Britain and the League, a Jewish State on both banks of Jordan is safe in our hands and all we need do is elect a new leader and all will be well. . . .

Avoiding Further Exile

If we are to be few amongst many in Palestine, as in every other land we are, trusting to the magic of superior intellect unsupported by moil and toil, or by husbandry and independent living, and if you think that the air of Israel and its ancient memories will then spare us an exilic fate, you will be tragically mistaken. If we are a minority, out of touch with creativity and labor, landless and

33

Jewish immigrants from war-ravaged Europe are shown at the port of Tel Aviv. They disembarked from ships which had been waiting for the British Mandate to expire.

denied all earthy livelihoods, in short—unless we become an autonomous nation, the Galuth [exile] malady, the plague of cultural assimilation and physical decline, will never quit us, not even in Palestine. For our future's sake, let us put forth the will, the faith and power to reconstruct the basis of our existence and establish a sovereign, self-governing Jewry in Israel. If we do not, we only make a second Galuth.

Achad Ha'am once dreamed of a new Jewish type in Palestine, a pattern to pilgrims who would enjoy the brilliance of this invention and tell the Diaspora of the marvels it did. Except we are a working people, that lovely dream will not come true.

What he saw in Palestine twenty years ago led him to conclude that the only invention was an upper-class of precocious Jewish landowners employing Arab labor. He did not then believe that the great proletariat that would do the rough chores of colonization would be Jews. He made two mistakes. First, a Jewish landowner without Jewish labor would be not a pattern but a pest. Second, lacking faith in the possibility of undiluted Jewish labor, Achad Ha'am could not grasp that, adrift in a great non-Jewish sea, we can create nothing, and that it will not take long in present circumstances of Palestine to turn a Jewish minority into what we were in Galuth: middlemen of foreign cultures and economies. On the fringes of our intelligentsia in Palestine signs of British coloring already emerge; if we continue a negligible minority, there will be Arab assimilation as well. Freedom and nationhood alone are the antidote.

As one who has lived and worked in Palestine many years, who came as a Zionist, I want to say that my faith in its promise was never so buoyant. Mine own eyes have seen the unfolding of infinite, hidden riches of dunes, of swamps and boulders. They saw the greater miracle, the creativeness of young workers aflame with vision and burning to resurrect Land and folk—in the Emek, in Sharon and Tel Aviv, in the trenches of Haganah, in industry and in organized labor. Labor and soul—if they bind the Jew in faith to his Land, then assuredly there is room in Palestine, there are prospect and capacity yet unrevealed. All we need is that the will of a few should grow into the will of a whole people. . . .

Arab Rights

We are not blind, withal, to the fact that Palestine is no void. Some million Arabs inhabit both sides of Jordan, and not since yesterday. Their right to live in Palestine, develop it and win national autonomy is as incontrovertible as is ours to return and, by our own means and merit, uplift ourselves to independence. The two can be realized. We must, in our work in Palestine, respect Arab rights, and if our first contact was unhappy, we were not in the wrong. Nor, perhaps, were the Arabs, for there are historic imponderables. We knew we lived at the edge of the desert, that our neighbors still kept largely to its ways; so we quickly raised a posse for self-protection, and many of our finest men paid the price of insecurity with their lives. Before the World War, and after, we declared roundly that we should always be unsafe, till we were so numerous that we could defend ourselves. . . .

The moral content of Zionism and its necessary practical objects demand a policy of rapprochement and mutual understanding towards the Palestinian Arabs, in economics, enlightenment and politics.

We endorse constitutional changes designed to give the inhabitants a share in administration. . . . Here, to Jewry, to Labor, and to the Arab nation, we vow that we shall never agree to one national group in Palestine dominating the other, now or evermore. If we do not accept the idea of a Jewish State wherein Jews rule over Arabs, neither do we accept bi-nationalism as in Switzerland or Canada. The political problem of Israel is sui generis. The rights to Palestine do not, as in those countries they do, belong to the existing settlers, whether it be Jews or Arabs. The crux is the Right of Return of Jewry dispersed, a prerogative of rebuilding and development, of freedom and sovereignty, yet not to infringe the prerogatives of others or hold sway over them. To be impervious to that conception, is to vitiate our title to Israel. . . .

Jewish Survival Must Be Guaranteed

We are an ancient race, we have survived thousands of years, we have made a substantial contribution to the treasury of human thought and human civilisation. These people have a right to live, they have a right to survive in normal conditions. They are as good as anybody else. It is this that prompted me to say that the Jewish State is the only guarantee of survival.

Chaim Weizmann, statement to the Anglo-American Committee of Inquiry on Palestine, 1947.

We dissent from dominion of present majority over present minority, for that minority is but the nucleus of a returning nation. So, too, shall we dissent from Jewish dominion over Arabs when the dynamism of Aliyah [immigration] alters the balance of power in our favor. We scorn the plea that, while we are a minority, a British High Commissioner be empowered to prevent majority domination, but, as soon as we reverse the roles, he hand authority to us. It is playing with political fire to interpret messianic redemption and liberation as a lust to govern behind the bayonets of imperial Britain, condemning the right of those who are citizens of Palestine as much as we are.

A Free Nation

In our view, the form of government should be so modified as to associate both national groups in it, together with Britain, on a basis of parity and without regard to numbers. But we shall never let ourselves become 'protected Jews' in Palestine, and never a ruling race. We shall be a free and self-sufficing nation, honoring Arab rights in an accord of equality, and living in peace with neighbor countries.

*"The rights of the Arabs are derived
from actual and long-standing possession. . . .
Their connexion with Palestine goes back
uninterruptedly to the earliest historic times."*

Palestine Is the Arab Birthright

George Antonius

In a 1915 letter to the Arab leader Sharif Husain, British official Sir Henry McMahon promised that Palestine would become an independent Arab state. In the following viewpoint, written in 1939, George Antonius argues that the British should fulfill this promise. He maintains that Palestine should be an Arab state because Arabs are the indigenous population and have a long heritage in Palestine. Antonius was an Arab historian and a senior civil servant in the Palestine Mandate government.

As you read, consider the following questions:

1. What two reasons does Antonius offer for his agrument that Palestine should be an Arab state?
2. How does Antonius respond to the issue of Arabs using violent tactics against Jews?
3. What will be the role of Jews in an Arab state, according to the author?

George Antonius, *The Arab Awakening: The Story of the Arab National Movement.* Philadelphia: J.B. Lippincott Company, 1939.

There is in existence already a considerable body of literature in English and other European languages on the history of the British mandate in Palestine. But it has to be used with care, partly because of the high percentage of open or veiled propaganda, and partly because the remoteness of the indispensable Arabic sources has militated against real fairness, even in the works of neutral and fair-minded historians. A similar inequality vitiates the stream of day-to-day information. Zionist propaganda is active, highly organised and widespread; the world Press, at any rate in the democracies of the West, is largely amenable to it; it commands many of the available channels for the dissemination of news, and more particularly those of the English-speaking world. Arab propaganda is, in comparison, primitive and infinitely less successful: the Arabs have little of the skill, polyglottic ubiquity or financial resources which make Jewish propaganda so effective. The result is, that for a score of years or so, the world has been looking at Palestine mainly through Zionist spectacles and has unconsciously acquired the habit of reasoning on Zionist premisses. . . .

Perhaps the best approach to the problem is to begin with a review of the rights, claims and motives of each of the three parties concerned, as they stood at the end of the [First World] War.

The Rights of the Arabs

The rights of the Arabs are derived from actual and long-standing possession, and rest upon the strongest human foundation. Their connexion with Palestine goes back uninterruptedly to the earliest historic times, for the term 'Arab' denotes nowadays not merely the incomers from the Arabian Peninsula who occupied the country in the seventh century, but also the older populations who intermarried with their conquerors, acquired their speech, customs and ways of thought and became permanently arabised. The traditions of the present inhabitants are as deeply rooted in their geographical surroundings as in their adoptive culture, and it is a fallacy to imagine that they could be induced to transplant themselves, even to other Arab surroundings, any more than the farmers of Kent or Yorkshire could be induced to go and settle in Ireland. It may seem superfluous to point this out, but the fallacy is one on which the Palestine Royal Commission have raised a new edifice of false hopes; and the fact needs stressing, therefore, that any solution based on the forcible expulsion of the peasantry from the countryside in which they have their homesteads and their trees, their shrines and graveyards, and all the memories and affections that go with life on the soil, is bound to be forcibly resisted.

In addition to those natural rights, the Arabs had acquired specific political rights derived from the Sharif Husain's compact with Great Britain and the help they gave her, in Palestine amongst other theatres. The thesis that Palestine west of the Jordan was excluded from the British pledges can no longer be maintained. The texts now available show that the Sharif Husain was given a general promise relating to its independence in the McMahon Correspondence and a specific promise securing the political and economic freedom of its Arab population in the message conveyed to him by the late Commander Hogarth. There is also the pledge contained in the Declaration to the Seven. Taken together, these undertakings amount to a binding recognition of Arab political rights. . . .

An Alien State

The whole Arab people is unalterably opposed to the attempt to impose Jewish immigration and settlement upon it, and ultimately to establish a Jewish State in Palestine. Its opposition is based primarily upon right. The Arabs of Palestine are descendants of the indigenous inhabitants of the country, who have been in occupation of it since the beginning of history; they cannot agree that it is right to subject an indigenous population against its will to alien immigrants, whose claim is based upon a historical connection which ceased effectively many centuries ago. Moreover they form the majority of the population; as such they cannot submit to a policy of immigration which if pursued for long will turn them from a majority into a minority in an alien state; and they claim the democratic right of a majority to make its own decisions in matters of urgent national concern.

The Arab Office, evidence submitted to the Anglo-American Committee of Inquiry, March 1946.

In other words, the Arab claims rest on two distinct foundations: the natural right of a settled population, in great majority agricultural, to remain in possession of the land of its birthright; and the acquired political rights which followed from the disappearance of Turkish sovereignty and from the Arab share in its overthrow, and which Great Britain is under a contractual obligation to recognise and uphold.

Respect for Jewish Minorities

Thus in their opposition to the British mandate, the Arabs are animated by the motive of self-preservation as well as that of self-determination. Their attitude is not dictated by any hostility to the Jewish race. Both in the Middle Ages and in modern times, and thanks mainly to the civilising influence of Islam, Arab history remained remarkably free from instances of deliberate persecution and shows that some of the greatest achievements of the

Jewish race were accomplished in the days of Arab power, under the aegis of Arab rulers, and with the help of their enlightened patronage. Even to-day, in spite of the animosity aroused by the conflict in Palestine, the treatment of Jewish minorities settled in the surrounding Arab countries continues to be not less friendly and humane than in England or the United States, and is in some ways a good deal more tolerant. . . .

The rights of the Jews are of a different order. In the minds of many people in the West, and more particularly in the Protestant countries, Zionism appears as a new embodiment of the old Jewish yearning for the Holy Land, and one that is destined to bring about the fulfillment of the Biblical prophecies. That is only one more of the prevalent misconceptions. There does exist a school of 'spiritual' Zionists, sponsored by some of the most eminent names in Jewry, whose aims are primarily cultural and whose mainsprings are to be found in the idealistic and religious sentiments which had hitherto inspired Judaism in its affection for Palestine. But their influence in international politics has become relatively insignificant. The real power is wielded by the exponents of 'political' Zionism which is not a religious but a nationalist movement aiming at the establishment of a Jewish state in Palestine on a basis of temporal power backed by the usual attributes of possession and sovereignty. It is against that school of Zionism that the Arab resistance in Palestine is directed. . . .

The Zionists base their claims on the historic connexion of Jewry with Palestine, which they represent as entitling the Jews to return to their ancient homeland. The connexion is too well-known to need recapitulation; but what does need stressing, in view of the widespread misconceptions that prevail, is that an historic connexion is not necessarily synonymous with a title to possession, more particularly when it relates to an inhabited country whose population claims, in addition to an ancient historic connexion of their own, the natural rights inherent in actual possession. Ever since the Dispersion, the Jews have been a minority—and most of time a very small minority—in Palestine, living mainly in the cities sacred to Judaism and enjoying no distinctive rights other than those enjoyed from time to time by the other minorities. At the end of the War, they numbered barely 55,000 souls, that is to say less than 8% of the total population of which the Arabs formed over 90%. . . .

Moral Violence

No lasting solution of the Palestine problem is to be hoped for until the injustice is removed. Violence, whether physical or moral, cannot provide a solution. It is not only reprehensible in itself: it also renders an understanding between Arabs, British and Jews increasingly difficult of attainment. By resorting to it, the Arabs have certainly attracted an earnest attention to their grievances, which all their peaceful representations in Jerusalem, in London and in Geneva had for twenty years failed to do. But violence defeats its own ends; and such immediate gains as it may score are invariably discounted by the harm which is inseparable from it. Nothing but harm can come of the terror raging in Palestine; but the wise way to put an end to it is to remove the causes which have brought it about. The fact must be faced that the violence of the Arabs is the inevitable corollary of the moral violence done to them, and that it is not likely to cease, whatever the brutality of the repression, unless the moral violence itself were to cease.

A Sacred Right

I am an Arab, and I believe that the Arabs constitute one nation. The sacred right of this nation is to be sovereign in her own affairs. Her ardent nationalism drives her to liberate the Arab homeland, to unite all its parts, and to found political, economic, and social institutions more sound and more compatible than the existing ones.

Manifesto of the First Arab Students' Congress, December 1938.

To those who look ahead, beyond the smoke-screen of legend and propaganda, the way to a solution is clear: it lies along the path of ordinary common sense and justice. There is no room for a second nation in a country which is already inhabited, and inhabited by a people whose national consciousness is fully awakened and whose affection for their homes and countryside is obviously unconquerable. The lesson to be drawn from the efforts hitherto made to lay the foundations of a Jewish state in Palestine is that they have turned the country into a shambles—not because of any inherent Arab hatred of Jews or lack of feeling for their plight, but because it is not possible to establish a Jewish state in Palestine without the forcible dislodgement of a peasantry who seem readier to face death than give up their land. On that ground alone, and without taking the political issues into account, the attempt to carry the Zionist dream into execution is doomed to failure; and the first step along the road to a solution is to face that fact objectively and realise its implications.

An Arab State

Once the fact is faced that the establishment of a Jewish state in Palestine, or of a national home based on territorial sovereignty, cannot be accomplished without forcibly displacing the Arabs, the way to a solution becomes clearer. It is not beyond the capacity of British, Jewish and Arab statesmanship to devise one. There seems to be no valid reason why Palestine should not be constituted into an independent Arab state in which as many Jews as the country can hold without prejudice to its political and economic freedom would live in peace, security and dignity, and enjoy full rights of citizenship. Such an Arab state would naturally be tied to Great Britain by a freely-negotiated treaty which should contain provisions for the safeguarding of British strategic and economic interests, for ensuring the safety and the inviolability of the Holy Places of all faiths, for the protection of all minorities and minority rights, and for affording the Jewish community the widest freedom in the pursuit of their spiritual and cultural ideals.

A solution on those lines would be both fair and practicable. It would protect the natural rights of the Arabs in Palestine and satisfy their legitimate national aspirations. It would enable the Jews to have a national home in the spiritual and cultural sense, in which Jewish values could flourish and the Jewish genius have the freest play to seek inspiration in the land of its ancient connexion. It would secure Great Britain's interests on a firm basis of consent. And it would restore Palestine to its proper place, as a symbol of peace in the hearts of Judaism, Christianity and Islam.

---

*"It is possible to say that the Jews are right
and the Arabs are right."*

Palestine Should Be a Binational State

Judah L. Magnes

Judah L. Magnes was a San Francisco native who went to Palestine in 1922. He founded Hebrew University in Jerusalem and became its chancellor in 1925. Part I of the following viewpoint is an excerpt from a pamphlet he published in 1930, after serious fighting had broken out between Arabs and Jews. Magnes believed the fighting showed that trying to establish Jewish dominion over Arabs was futile and violated Jewish ethics. He advocated a binational state in which both groups shared power. Part II is an addendum to the pamphlet, written in 1937.

As you read, consider the following questions:

1. Why is Magnes willing to give up a Jewish majority in Palestine?
2. How has the dispersion of Jews throughout the world benefited Judaism, according to the author?
3. Why does Magnes believe that even a small, poor Jewish community in Palestine is better than a community which rules over a hostile Arab population?

"Like All The Nations" by Judah L. Magnes from THE ZIONIST IDEA: A HISTORICAL ANALYSIS AND READER edited by Arthur Hertzberg. Copyright © 1959 by Arthur Hertzberg. Reprinted by permission of Doubleday, a division of Bantam, Doubleday, Dell Publishing Group, Inc.
Excerpted by permission of the publishers from *Dissenter in Zion: From the Writings of Judah L. Magnes*, edited by Arthur Goren. Cambridge: Harvard University Press. Copyright © 1982 by the President and Fellows of Harvard College.

I

The discussion concerning the future political regime in Palestine is now happily beginning to take on a more or less objective character and the searching question is being asked as to what we want here. What is our Zionism? What does Palestine mean for us?

As to what we should want here I can answer for myself in almost the same terms that I have been in the habit of using many years:

Immigration.

Settlement on the land.

Hebrew life and culture.

If you can guarantee these for me, I should be willing to yield the Jewish state, and the Jewish majority; and on the other hand I would agree to a legislative assembly together with a democratic political regime so carefully planned and worked out that the above three fundamentals could not be infringed. Indeed, I should be willing to pay almost any price for these three, especially since this price would in my opinion also secure tranquillity and mutual understanding. If the Jews really have an historical connection with Palestine, and what student of history will deny it, and if the Jewish people is to be in Palestine not on sufferance (as during the days of the Turks) but as of right—a right solemnly recognized by most governments and by the League of Nations, and also by thinking Arabs—then surely these three rights are elemental and hardly to be contested.

Without Palestine

Whether through temperament or other circumstances I do not at all believe, and I think the facts are against believing, that without Palestine the Jewish people is dying out or is doomed to destruction. On the contrary it is growing stronger; and what is more, it should grow stronger, for Palestine without communities in the dispersion would be bereft of much of its significance as a spiritual center for the Judaism of the world. To me it seems that there are three chief elements in Jewish life, in the following order of importance: the living Jewish people—now some sixteen million; the Torah, in the broadest sense of this term, i.e., all our literature and documents and history, as also the great religious and ethical and social ideals the Torah contains for use and development in the present and the future; and third, the Land of Israel. My view is that the people and the Torah can exist and be creative as they have existed and have been creative without the Land; that, however, the Land is one of the chief means, if not the chief means, of revivifying and deepening the people and the Torah.

The living Jewish people is primary. It is the living carrier and

44

vessel of Judaism, the Jewish spirit. It has used even its Exile for spreading light and learning. Palestine can help this people to understand itself, to give an account of itself, to an intensification of its culture, a deepening of its philosophy, a renewal of its religion. Palestine can help this people perform its great ethical mission as a national-international entity. But this eternal and far-flung people does not need a Jewish state for the purpose of maintaining its very existence. The Jewish community throughout the world is a wondrous and paradoxical organism. It participates in the life of many nations, yet in spite of numberless predictions in the past and the present, it is not absorbed by them. It is patriotic in every land, yet it is international, cosmopolitan. Palestine cannot solve the Jewish problem of the Jewish people. Wherever there are Jews there is the Jewish problem. It is part of the Jewish destiny to face this problem and make it mean something of good for mankind.

Both Sides Love the Land

We could not and cannot renounce the Jewish claim; something even higher than the life of our people is bound up with this land, namely its work, its divine mission. But we have been and still are convinced that it must be possible to find some compromise between this claim and the other, for we love this land and we believe in its future; since such love and such faith are surely present on the other side as well, a union in the common service of the land must be within the range of possibility.

Martin Buber, letter to Mahatma Gandhi, 1939.

Nor are the Jews dying out, despite their weaknesses, their mixed marriages, their ignorance of Judaism, and the deterioration that has laid hold of many a limb. I see them in America growing healthier and stronger in numbers and intellectual power. Their hearts respond generously to every Jewish call. They are multiplying their communities, their synagogues, schools, societies, libraries, unions. They are acquiring economic independence, and their sons and daughters are getting what the universities and colleges can give them. They are ignorant of Judaism. But they are asking eagerly, mostly in vain, to know what Judaism is. Perhaps it is not the fault of the teachers that the answers take so long in coming. Judaism is a complex phenomenon. It is and it is not religion, philosophy, ethics, politics, ceremonies, life. The answer as to what it is and may mean to a new generation cannot come overnight. . . .

But if I have thus exalted the Diaspora, what is Palestine to us? It is the Land of Israel, our Holy Land. It is holy for us in a practi-

45

cal and a mystic sense. . . .

Three great things this poor little land has already given Israel in two generations. Hebrew has become a living possession and has thus restored to us and our children the sources of our history and our mind, and has thus given us the medium again for classic, permanent Jewish expression. The second great thing is the return of Jews to the soil, not only for the sake of a living from the soil but also for the sake of their love of this particular soil and its indissoluble connection with the body of the Jewish people. Third, the brave attempt on the part of city-bred, school-bred young Jews—moderns of the modern—to work out in life, in the cities and on the land, a synthesis between the radicalism of their social outlook and their ancestral Judaism. It is problems of the same nature that a whole world in travail is laboring to solve; and among Jewry no more splendid attempt at a synthesis has been made than here, in everyday life and not in theory alone.

The beginnings of all this, and much more than the beginnings, were made under the Turks; and Palestine is of such moment to us that it is capable of giving us much even though our community here be poor and small. I have indicated above that I do not want it to be poor and small. But poor and small and faithful to Judaism, rather than large and powerful like all the nations. . . .

Our theories may differ as to the purposes Palestine may or may not serve. But there is no question that it is now serving as a testing ground, a dangerous frontier land for the lovers of peace in Israel. Much of the theory of Zionism has been concerned with making the Jews into a normal nation in Palestine like the gentiles of the lands and the families of the earth. The desire for power and conquest seems to be normal to many human beings and groups, and we, being the ruled everywhere, must here rule; being the minority everywhere, we must here be in the majority. There is the *Wille zur Macht* [Will through power], the state, the army, the frontiers. We have been in exile; now we are to be masters in our own Home. We are to have a Fatherland, and we are to encourage the feelings of pride, honor, glory that are part of the paraphernalia of the ordinary nationalistic patriotism. In the face of such danger one thinks of the dignity and originality of that passage in the liturgy which praises the Lord of all things that our portion is not like theirs and our lot not like that of all the multitude.

The Danger of Seeking Power

We are told that when we become the majority we shall then show how just and generous a people in power can be. That is like the man who says that he will do anything and everything to get rich, so that he may do good with the money thus accumulated. Sometimes he never grows rich—he fails. And if he does grow rich under those circumstances his power of doing good has been atrophied from long lack of use. In other words, it is not only the end which for Israel must be desirable, but what is of equal importance, the means must be conceived and brought forth in cleanliness. If as a minority we insist upon keeping the other man from achieving just aims, and if we keep him from this with the aid of bayonets, we must not be surprised if we are attacked and, what is worse, if moral degeneration sets in among us. . . .

What I am driving at is to distinguish between two policies. The one maintains that we can establish a Jewish Home here through the suppression of the political aspirations of the Arabs, and therefore a Home necessarily established on bayonets over a long period—a policy which I think bound to fail because of the violence against us it would occasion, and because good opinion in Britain and the conscience of the Jewish people itself would revolt against it. The other policy holds that we can establish a Home here only if we are true to ourselves as democrats and internationalists, thus being just and helpful to others, and that we ask for the protection of life and property the while we are eagerly and intelligently and sincerely at work to find a *modus vivendi et operandi* [method of living and operating] with our neighbors. The world—not in Palestine alone—may be bent upon violence and bloodshed. But will not my opponent agree that there is a better chance of averting this tendency to bloodshed if we make every possible effort politically as well as in other ways to work hand in hand—as teachers, helpers, friends—with this awakening Arab world?

Arab and Jewish Rights

We have the Arab natural rights, on the one hand, and the Jewish historical rights on the other. The question therefore is, "How can an honourable and reasonable compromise be found?" There are those, we know, who reject the very idea of compromise. But no answer can be found for this complicated situation, except through compromise, that may be reasonable and feasible.

Judah L. Magnes, speech delivered to the United Nations Special Committee on Palestine, Jerusalem, July 14, 1947.

You ask me, Do I want to quit? No, I do not. The Jew will not abandon the Land of Israel. He cannot abandon it. Palestine is of value by and of itself—its rocks, its hills, its ruins, its beauty—and that it is of value to Judaism even if our community here be small and poor. I am afraid the first of the quitters will be those who say it is useless except we be in the majority. But I also know that we cannot establish our work as it should be established if it be against the determined will of the Arab world, and if we have not the good will of the good European world on our side. . . .

Palestine is holy to the Jew in that his attitude toward this Land is necessarily different from his attitude toward any other land. He may have to live in other lands upon the support of bayonets, but that may well be something which he, as a Jew, cannot help. But when he goes voluntarily as a Jew to repeople his own Jewish Homeland, it is by an act of will, of faith, of free choice, and he should not either will or believe in or want a Jewish Home that can be maintained in the long run only against the violent opposition of the Arab and Moslem peoples. The fact is that they are here in their overwhelming numbers in this part of the world, and whereas it may have been in accord with Israelitic needs in the time of Joshua to conquer the land and maintain their position in it with the sword, that is not in accord with the desire of plain Jews or with the long ethical tradition of Judaism that has not ceased developing to this day.

II

Not nearly enough stress has been laid upon the fact that Palestine is a Holy Land for three great religions.

No one should expect to have his maximalist aspirations fulfilled in such a land. The presence here of so many differing sects and peoples requires moderation, concession, compromise, so that they may live together in peace without at the same time giving up their peculiarities and the differentiae to safeguard which they may have come here. . . .

Palestine is no place for maximalist Jewish aspirations. That this is so, is also part of the Jewish tragedy. There are those who speak of a Jewish National Home containing many millions of Jews—present-day Palestine, Transjordan, the Hauran, and Sinai as far as the Suez Canal. Such aspirations are due in large measure to the pressure of Jewish life, the persecution to which Jews are being subjected in all too many parts of the world. When Israel Zangwill said: "Give the land without a people to the people without a land," neither he nor many other Jews realized that there was a people here. The Jews are justified in seeking the active support of Government for settlement possibilities for as large a number of Jews as is in any way possible; but this must always be compatible with the natural rights of the Arabs. If the Jews could come to a political understanding with the Arabs as to Palestine, there would doubtless be an opportunity for the settlement of large number of oppressed Jews in other Arab lands. These would not, to be sure, be part of the Jewish National Home, but they would be contiguous and helpful to it.

Palestine is no place for maximalist Arab aspirations. The whole world knows that Palestine is not just an Arab land. It belongs in the spiritual sense to millions of people scattered throughout the world; and in a real sense not only to the Arabs but also to those Jews and Christians who, coming here and living here, are trying through their devotion to make of it a land worthy of being called holy. Palestine may some day become a member of an Arab federation and/or of the League of Nations, but not just as an Arab land. Rather as a bi-national land, entrusted to the two peoples who are the sole actual descendants of the Semites of antiquity; a Holy Land, entrusted to these two peoples, from whom these religions are derived, and entrusted also to the League of Nations and to Great Britain, the representatives of the European mind and the Christian conscience. . . .

A Tragic History

It is possible to say that the Jews are right and that the Arabs are right. Such a situation has within it the elements of tragedy. The whole history of Palestine has been one of tragedy. But the question is, must the tragedy again march to its appointed end? Is there perhaps no solution to the problem?

Two Peoples

Neither the history nor the present conditions in Palestine can justify any one-sided solution of the Palestine problem, either in favour of the creation of an independent Arab state, ignoring the lawful rights of the Jewish people, or in favour of the creation of an independent Jewish state, ignoring the lawful rights of the Arab population. Neither of these extreme solutions would bring about a just settlement of this complex problem, first and foremost since they both fail to guarantee the regulations of the relations between Arabs and Jews, which is the most important task of all. A just settlement can be found only if account is taken in sufficient degree of the lawful interests of both peoples.

Andrei Gromyko, speech delivered to the United Nations, New York, May 1947.

Yet those of us who are not willing to accept fate without an effort to influence it, must make our choice. There are those on all sides who say that there is no way out of the impasse except through sword and blood, because that is the history of conquest and that the history of Palestine. Yet there is another way that must be tried: through a moderation of ambitions, through concession and compromise, to find the way of life.

a critical thinking activity

Understanding Words
In Context

Readers occasionally come across words which they do not recognize. And frequently, because they do not know a word or words, they will not fully understand the passage being read. Obviously, the reader can look up an unfamiliar word in a dictionary. However, by carefully examining the word in the context in which it is used, the word's meaning can often be determined. A careful reader may find clues to the meaning of the word in surrounding words, ideas, and attitudes.

Below are excerpts from the viewpoints in this chapter. One word is printed in italics. Try to determine the meaning of each word by reading the excerpt. Under each excerpt you will find four definitions for the italicized word. Choose the one that is closest to your understanding of the word.

Finally, use a dictionary to see how well you have understood the words in context. It will be helpful to discuss with others the clues which helped you decide on each word's meaning.

1. Public opinion in Great Britain and the world does not yet recognize the rights of Jews. Unpleasant, perhaps, to say so, but we would be *PURBLIND*, playing ostrich-politics, not to acknowledge this fact.

   PURBLIND means:
   a) international   c) blind
   b) pure   d) flightless bird

2. Jews will be welcomed as a new frontier opens for that spirit of enterprise which has heretofore brought them only hatred and *OBLOQUY*.

   OBLOQUY means:
   a) abuse   c) sleep
   b) compassion   d) revenge

3. The man who says he will do anything and everything, no matter how immoral, to get rich, soon loses the ability to do good. It has been *ATROPHIED* from long lack of use.

ATROPHIED means:

a) reorganized
b) awarded
c) ignored
d) worn away

4. Zionist propaganda is active, translated into many languages, and found all over the world. Arab propaganda is far less successful; Arabs have little of the skill and their propaganda lacks the *UBIQUITY* which makes Jewish propaganda so effective.

UBIQUITY means:

a) forgotten
b) widespread
c) stupid
d) average

5. The moral teachings of Zionism demand a policy of *RAP-PROCHEMENT* and mutual understanding toward the Palestinian Arabs.

RAPPROCHEMENT means:

a) neglect
b) realism
c) ill will
d) friendly relations

6. Months have passed since the Zionist Congress, but its effects are still being felt, its echoes still *REVERBERATING* in daily life and the press.

REVERBERATING means:

a) resounding
b) learning
c) closing
d) weeping

7. Is it not true that our poor endure greater suffering than any other *PROLETARIAT?*

PROLETARIAT means:

a) upper class
b) nationality
c) lower class
d) religion

8. We are murderously attacked and subjected to libel. Our right to be in Palestine is *WANTONLY* assailed.

WANTONLY means:

a) intelligently
d) cruelly
c) happily
d) needlessly

Does Israel Treat the Palestinians Fairly?

Chapter Preface

The first months of 1988 were marked by serious rioting in the Palestinian-populated territories Israel has ruled since 1967. The rioters were young—most of them were teenagers but some were as young as ten years old. These riots reveal a tragic truth about Israel: Conflict will undoubtedly persist, as children perpetuate the fighting that has preoccupied their ancestors for decades.

Three out of four inhabitants of the Palestinian-populated West Bank and Gaza Strip are under age 25. The majority of Palestinian teenagers have spent their entire lives in refugee camps. They feel oppressed and riot against the Israelis because they do not have a country to call their own. The Israeli government has responded: Thousands of Palestinians have been imprisoned in Israeli jails for political reasons, spurring further Palestinian bitterness.

Against these angry young Palestinians stands the Israeli army—consisting of Jewish youths who are drafted into military service at age 18. Longstanding fears influence the political views of many of these Jewish teenagers. They cite attacks on Jews walking in Arab neighborhoods in Jerusalem and other West Bank cities. Furthermore, they have been raised with the war stories of their parents and grandparents. Since its founding, Israel has been involved in a war against Arabs every decade. From this forty-year history of hostility, a majority of Jewish teenagers conclude that Israel cannot safely compromise with Palestinians.

As Israeli and Palestinian teenagers participate in a conflict decades older than they themselves are, debate continues on whether the Palestinians have been treated fairly. The following viewpoints consider this challenging question.

"Israel has from the beginning systematically violated the human rights of the Palestinian people."

Israel Has Treated the Palestinians Unfairly

Edward W. Said, Ibrahim Abu-Lughod, Janet L. Abu-Lughod, Muhammad Hallaj, and Elia Zureik

The Palestinian position is that their people were denied their national rights when Israel was created as a Jewish homeland. Five well-known Palestinians explain this position in the following viewpoint. Edward W. Said, a widely-published author, is Parr Professor of English and Comparative Literature at Columbia University in New York City. Ibrahim Abu-Lughod teaches political science at Northwestern University in Evanston, Illinois. Janet L. Abu-Lughod is a sociology professor at Northwestern University. Muhammad Hallaj directs the Palestine Research and Educational Center in Fairfax, Virginia. Elia Zureik teaches sociology at Queen's University in Kingston, Ontario. Three of the authors, Said, Ibrahim Abu-Lughod, and Hallaj, are members of the Palestine National Council, which is considered the Palestinians' parliament in exile.

As you read, consider the following questions:

1. Why do the authors believe that Zionists have tried to dehumanize the Palestinians?
2. What are the two goals of Palestinian political activity, according to the authors?

Edward W. Said, Ibrahim Abu-Lughod, Janet L. Abu-Lughod, Muhammad Hallaj, and Elia Zureik, *A Profile of the Palestinian People*, revised second edition. Chicago: Palestine Human Rights Campaign, 1987. Reprinted with permission of the publisher.

The land of Palestine gave rise to one of the most ancient of all civilizations. Centuries before the first Hebrew tribes migrated to the area, [according to Emmanuel Anati], "Palestine gave birth to a unique culture. In this period in Palestine, as far as we know, the earliest permanent villages in the world were built." Palestine is also the birthplace of urban life. It is "the only place in the world where a town is known to date back nine thousand years." Jericho is the oldest continuously inhabited city in the world, being "four thousand years older than any other urban settlement known at present." It is one of the greatest ironies of history that in the middle of the twentieth century—in the Golden age of peoples' rights to self-determination—Palestine was dropped from the map of the world.

A Fertile Land

Palestine became predominantly Arab and Islamic by the end of the seventh century. Its boundaries and its characteristics—including its name in Arabic, Filastin—soon became known to the entire Islamic world, as much for its fertility and beauty as for its religious significance. . . .

Despite the steady arrival in Palestine of Jewish colonists after 1882, it is important to realize that not until the few weeks immediately preceding the establishment of Israel in the spring of 1948 was there ever anything other than a large Arab majority. For example, the Jewish population in 1931 was 174,606 against a total of 1,033,314; in 1936, Jewish numbers had gone up to 384,078 and the total to 1,366,692; in 1946 there were 608,225 Jews in a total of 1,912, 112. In all these statistics, "natives" were easily distinguishable from the arriving colonists. But who were these natives?

Most of them were Sunni Muslims, although a minority among them were Christians, Druzes, and Shi'ite Muslims. All of them spoke Arabic and considered themselves Arabs. Approximately 65 percent of the Palestinian Arabs were agriculturalists, living in some five hundred villages where grains as well as fruits and vegetables were grown. The principal Palestinian cities—Nablus, Jerusalem, Nazareth, Acre, Jaffa, Jericho, Ramlah, Hebron, and Haifa—were built in the main by Palestinian Arabs who continued to live in them, even after the expanding Zionist colonies encroached upon them. Also in existence by that time were: a respectable Palestinian intellectual and professional class, the beginnings of modern industry, and a highly developed national consciousness. . . .

This Palestinian society was dismantled and dispersed. Even the historic fact of Palestine's prior existence as an entity and of the Palestinians as a people was questioned and portrayed as an apparition of doubtful authenticity.

It is often forgotten how recent the destruction of Palestine has been. Professor Janet Abu-Lughod has described both the uniqueness and recency of this tragedy. Of the dismantlement of Palestinian society she writes:

> Except for the extermination of the Tasmanians, modern history knows no cases in which the virtually complete supplanting of the indigenous population of a country by an alien stock has been achieved in as little as two generations. Yet this, in fact, is what has been attempted in Palestine since the beginning of the twentieth century.

She warns against the danger of forgetting the "startling recency" of the destruction of Palestine: "Our natural tendency to assume that what exists today has always been, may afford us psychic peace but only at the terrible cost of denying reality. And once historic reality has been denied, our capacity to understand and react meaningfully to the present is similarly destroyed."

Zionism

The destruction of Palestine was not the unintended consequence of unforeseen events. It was, and still is, an essential part of the Zionist plan to transform Palestine into "Eretz Yisrael." When a young Israeli soldier participating in the invasion of Lebanon in the summer of 1982 said "I would like to see all the Palestinians dead because they are a sickness wherever they go," he was giving crude expression to a long-standing theme within the Zionist movement. This attitude was widely shared, as was reported by the King-Crane Commission, whose investigations in Palestine in 1919 led it to conclude that "the Zionists look forward to a practically complete dispossession" of the Palestinian people.

A New Diaspora

Today, the whole of Palestine is under Israeli control, together with other Arab territories in Syria and Lebanon. The Palestinians are now victims of a new diaspora. They are either under Israeli military occupation or having been forcibly expelled by them, they are refugees in the four corners of the earth, dispossessed, dispersed, denied and deprived of their inalienable rights.

Muhammad El-Farra, *Years of No Decision*, 1987.

Most histories of the question of Palestine focus on the Zionist effort to create a Jewish presence in Palestine. For that reason, they leave a misleading impression of a totally constructive effort. There is no question that Zionist immigrants brought to Palestine in the interwar period skilled manpower and capital, and built villages and factories. What is equally true, but less familiar, is the fact that because the Zionist movement was committed to the transformation of Palestine into a "mono-religious" Jewish state, its success required it to be as intent on the destruction of the indigenous Arab society as it was on the construction of a Jewish life in Palestine. . . .

Someone Else's Homeland

The Zionist leaders realized from the beginning that the biggest obstacle to the objective of transforming Palestine into "Eretz Yisrael" would be the fact that it was already someone else's homeland. The reality of the situation hampered the Zionist effort to mobilize Jewish and non-Jewish support. Ahad Ha-am (Asher Ginsberg), one of the best known Jewish literary figures in the early part of this century, who traveled to Palestine and witnessed the destructive impact of Zionist colonization on Arab society, remarked that the Zionists "treat the Arabs with hostility and cruelty, deprive them of their rights, offend them without cause, and even boast of these deeds." He was so repelled that he said of Zionism: "If this is the 'Messiah', then I do not wish to see his coming."

Similarly, when the Zionists sought the endorsement and support of Asian nationalist leaders in the 1930s and 1940s, they were rebuffed precisely because of the destructive impact of Zionism on Palestinian society. Mahatma Gandhi told a Zionist emissary who sought his support that "you want to convert the Arab majority into a minority." And Jawaharlal Nehru was driven by Zionist disregard for the rights and well-being of the indigenous Arab community to observe that the Zionists "neglected one not unimportant fact . . . Palestine was not a wilderness or an empty, uninhabited place. It was already somebody else's home."

What the Zionists Knew

Recent research utilizing early Zionist archives makes it clear that members of the Zionist movement were not unaware of the existence of the Palestinian people and were in fact preoccupied with what was referred to as the Arab question. Palestine was not only an ancient land, but the populous homeland of a contemporary society as well. In 1922, at the outset of serious Zionist colonization, "the population density in Palestine was 72 persons per square mile—a high figure if compared with the countries of the region and those outside of it." Neither was Palestine a neglected land. Lawrence Oliphant visited Palestine in 1887 and wrote in his book *Haifa, or Life in Modern Palestine* that the valley of Esdraelon was "a huge green lake of waving wheat, with its village-crowned mounds rising from it like islands; and it presents one of the most striking pictures of luxuriant fertility which it is possible to conceive." It served Zionist purposes to deny this reality and, as Professor John Ruedy argues, "it was convenient for

OCCUPATION

Seymour Joseph/*People's Daily World.*

Zionists and their supporters to picture Palestine as a wasteland before they came.''. . .

When Zionists found it untenable to maintain the myth of Palestinian non-existence in its crude and literal meaning, they sought to diminish the significance of Palestinian existence. When asked by a journalist in 1969 if he did not agree that the Palestinians, like the Israelis, were entitled to a homeland, Levi Eshkol responded: ''What are Palestinians? When I came here—there were 250,000 non-Jews—mainly Arabs and Bedouins. It was desert—more than underdeveloped. Nothing.'' Vladimir Jabotinsky, Menachem Begin's mentor, described the Arabs as ''a yelling rabble dressed up in gaudy, savage rags." And Ber Borochov, an early Zionist theoretician, believed that the Palestinian Arabs "lacked any culture of their own and did not have any outstanding national characteristics."

By denying the existence of the Palestinian people, and by dehumanizing them, Zionists meant to hide from the world the intended victims of their colonization. They paraded before world public opinion as the national liberation movement of the Jewish people, but they could not do so if the fact were known that they were destroying an indigenous Asian community struggling to be free. . . .

Political Status of Palestinians Today

In the world today there are slightly more than 4.5 million Palestinians—those born in Palestine and their offspring born there or in other areas after dispersion. Nowhere do these people enjoy or exercise any political rights as Palestinians. Yet they are deeply committed to attainment of a normal political status. They are committed to a struggle for national self-determination, including the right to independence and sovereignty in Palestine, the right of return, and the right to national identity. Over the past three decades, the Palestinians have largely succeeded in maintaining that identity and in designating their own representative, the Palestine Liberation Organization, despite concerted attempts to obliterate both. . . .

Political activity specifically designed to enhance Palestinian social, economic, or cultural rights is proscribed in most states where Palestinians reside. Because of these external constraints, Palestinians, when wishing to organize themselves for national Palestinian endeavor, have had to do so in semi-legal or illegal fashion. Today, the Palestinian movements comprehended by the Palestine National Council and generally identified as the constituting elements of the Palestine Liberation Organization are primarily organized for the specific purpose of liberating Palestine. Of necessity, they exist on the margin of legality in the states wherein they function. In Israeli-occupied Palestine any association with a specifically Palestinian organization or national goal conforming to the Palestine National Charter is contrary to Israeli law or to the decrees of the Israeli military occupation of the West Bank and the Gaza Strip.

These difficulties have not prevented the Palestinians from engaging in political activity, activity primarily motivated by two broad imperatives: first, to continue the struggle to regain national rights; second, to direct existing political opportunities toward improvement of social, economic and educational conditions. . . .

While the ultimate intention of Israel with regard to the West Bank and Gaza is still debated, it is virtually certain that, with or without *de jure* annexation, Israel intends to expel Palestinians and transform those remaining under its control into a permanently subordinate population.

Israel and Human Rights

Towards that end, Israel has from the beginning systematically violated the human rights of the Palestinian people under its occupation. It has exercised strict controls over cultural institutions, has refused to observe the various provisions of the Geneva convention on occupied areas, and has disregarded all UN resolutions that call for such observance. Thousands of Palestinians have been arrested, charged with opposition to the military occupation; thousands of their homes have been demolished. The violation of Palestinian human rights culminated in the dismissal, by Israel's military governor of the West Bank and Gaza, of the elected mayors of practically all major Palestinian towns and cities, in an attempt to forestall any expression of political support for Palestinian self-determination. . . .

A Basic Human Right

Short of total obliteration, the Palestinians will continue to resist occupation and demand their right to self-determination. As a native Palestinian and a social scientist, my personal and professional experience tells me that the fundamental need and right of self-determination is at the crux of the conflict, and it will have to be addressed on all sides by honest, brave people with vision. Hapless and spineless politicians need not apply.

In an age when the right to self-determination was upheld for 1,800 Falklanders, who could really quarrel with the right to self-determination for the Palestinians? No human being should be discriminated against because of his religion, race or ethnic background. No one should be deported from his or her homeland. No human being should be deprived of his national identity or culture. This basic human right should apply equally to the Tibetans, the Soviet refuseniks and the Palestinians.

Tawfic Farah, *Los Angeles Times*, January 4, 1988.

The present situation of the Palestinian people then is fundamentally and seriously anomalous. The Palestinians have all the attributes of nationhood—a common history, language, and set of traditions, a national culture, national institutions, a national representative, the Palestine Liberation Organization, recognized universally by every segment of the Palestinian population as well as by a large majority of the world's states, a common framework of aspirations and values—but they do not control Palestine, the natural site of their projected independent state. The United

Nations has been very clear on the imperatives for Palestinian national self-determination, and so too have the Islamic Conference, the Movement of the Non-Aligned, the Organization of African Unity, as well as various important European, Asian and Latin American states. Yet, the inexorable processes continue by which the Palestinian people have been alienated both from their natal territory and their cultural patrimony. Today, more Palestinians than ever before are born in exile and face the prospect of continued exile. In the Occupied Territories, more Israeli settlements, more Israeli violence and collective punishment attempt to break the Palestinian national will: the aims of Israel are clear, for, as Zionist and Israeli leaders have been saying candidly for several generations, Palestinian national claims are neither admissable nor valid. . . .

The Sufferings Are Legion

The sufferings consequently imposed upon a people in their dispersion and political difficulties are legion. All these sufferings derive, however, from the absolute *inability* of every Palestinian man, woman, and child to exercise a fundamental set of inalienable rights. No Palestinian has a Palestinian passport, no Palestinian has Palestinian nationality, no Palestinian can vote in a national election as a Palestinian, no Palestinian can voluntarily return to Palestine and take up residence there. In most places, the very word "Palestine" is either denied or in some way made the object of particular (usually injurious) juridical, political, social and cultural discrimination. Thus, for example, there has never been a Palestinian census, nor, for that matter, a referendum. The anomaly of course is that, as a people, the Palestinians are among the most advanced in the world so far as their political consciousness is concerned. Every Palestinian shares with all other Palestinians a history of dispossession and, no less important, a history of determined struggle. The profoundest truth about the Palestinians today is not that they are exiled, dispersed and punished, but that they have advanced so far beyond these negative attributes as to have articulated a positive vision of the future. Unmistakably and collectively, the Palestinian people have formulated their own sense of themselves and of their future as intending the establishment of an independent Palestinian state on their historical national soil.

"The assertion of . . . Palestinian Arab identity is merely one more subterfuge designed to bring about the destruction of the State of Israel."

Israel Has Treated the Palestinians Fairly

Yehuda Z. Blum

Yehuda Z. Blum holds the Hersch Lauterpacht Chair in International Law at Hebrew University in Jerusalem. The following viewpoint is an excerpt from a collection of speeches Blum made before the United Nations, when he was the Israeli ambassador and permanent representative from 1975 to 1982. In this viewpoint, Blum presents the basic Israeli response to the Palestinian case: Israel has always been the homeland of the Jews. He contends that Arab nations should settle and integrate their fellow Arabs—the Palestinians.

As you read, consider the following questions:

1. Why does Blum not agree that there is a national group of people called "Palestinians"?
2. What effect did Jewish immigrants have on the land of Israel in the early part of the twentieth century, according to the author?
3. How does Blum believe the Arab countries have used the Palestinians?

Yehuda Z. Blum, *For Zion's Sake*. Cranbury, NJ: Cornwall Books, 1987. Reprinted with permission of the publisher.

The United Nations has been discussing the Arab-Israel conflict for over thirty years. Had this Organization encouraged the Arab states to live up to their commitments under the United Nations Charter, this conflict could have been resolved peacefully long ago through dialogue and negotiation. The Organization, however, has long permitted itself to be exploited by those opposed to peace in the Middle East. These forces set out not only to block any progress on this issue, but have sought also to inflate the conflict, by adding an ever-increasing number of features to their Middle East repertoire. . . .

The UN's approach to the issue now before us is very different from what it was when first brought before this Organization in 1947. When it was first discussed then, virtually everybody recognized the right of the Jewish people to self-determination and its right to sovereignty in its homeland. It was also evident at that time that the core of the Arab-Israel conflict was the unwillingness of the Arab world to come to terms with the rights of the Jewish people. Nowadays, those rights are scarcely, if ever, mentioned. Today, all the emphasis is put on the claims of the Palestinian Arabs, and the empty charge is trotted out by speaker after speaker from various quarters that the Palestinian Arabs are, as it were, a people uprooted from its land, a nation denied its rights.

Crude Myths

The crude repetition of these falsities does not make them any truer—or more accurately—any less false.

The first myth which has to be dispelled is that at any time prior to the British Mandate there was an Arab political entity called Palestine. Throughout history there has never been a kingdom, a principality, let alone a state, called Palestine. The term "Palestine" was given currency by the Romans in an attempt to obliterate the Jewish character of the Land of Israel. Until this century, it was purely a geographical concept referring to an area of undefined expanse. Indeed, throughout the centuries that area was governed in the main from distant capitals of successive empires.

Only after World War I was Palestine created as a separate political entity, for the specific purpose of reconstituting therein a national home for the Jewish people. In so doing, the League of Nations recognized that only one people in history has, for three-thousand years and more, preserved and maintained its unbroken links with the Holy Land. That people is the Jewish people. For that reason it has been known throughout the annals of mankind as the Land of Israel, which is the translation of its name in Hebrew—Eretz Yisrael.

The association of the Jewish people with the Land of Israel, unique in its circumstances, has become part and parcel of the history of mankind, inextricably entwined in the fabric and texture of world culture. Here at the United Nations, constant attempts have been made over the past thirty years to obscure the inseparable bond between the Jewish people and the Jewish homeland. But no amount of distortion and fabrication in this building can undo so central a fact of the political, spiritual, cultural and religious history of the world. . . .

Economic Benefits

Zionist settlement in Palestine began to stimulate an economic revival from which the Arab inhabitants also benefited. . . . There was a marked rise in Arab standards of income, health and education—partly through the direct impact of Zionist activity, partly through tax revenues collected by the Administration, mainly from the Jewish community, and spent on public services directed largely to the more backward and less self-reliant Arab community.

Michael Comay, *Zionism, Israel, and the Palestinian Arabs*, 1983.

The passionate yearnings of return finally gave birth to the practical ideas and political organizations which, amid the storms of the nineteenth and twentieth centuries, launched the mass movement for the return to Zion and for restored Jewish national independence. Upheld and fortified in dispersion and adversity by the vision of an ultimate return, the Jewish people did not forsake its homeland or forgo its links with it.

The Jews were never a people without a homeland. Having been robbed of their land, Jews never ceased to give expression to their anguish at their deprivation and to pray for and demand its return. Throughout the nearly two millennia of dispersion, the Land of Israel remained the focus of the Jewish national culture. Every single day, in all those seventy generations, Jews gave voice to their attachment to Zion. . . .

Arab Attitudes Toward Zionism

There was a time when this fundamental truth was acknowledged also by the Arabs themselves. Thus for example, on 23 March 1918, there appeared in the Mecca newspaper *Al-Qibla* an article written or inspired by Sherif Hussein, the leader of the Arab national movement at that time, the great-grandfather of the present King of Jordan. The article was written two months after Hussein had been officially informed of the British Government's Balfour Declaration, promising the Jewish people a national home in Palestine. The article notes:

The resources of the country (Palestine) are still virgin soil and will be developed by the Jewish immigrants. One of the most amazing things until recent times was that the Palestinian used to leave his country, wandering over the high seas in every direction. His native soil could not retain its hold on him. . . .At the same time we have seen the Jews from foreign countries streaming to Palestine from Russia, Germany, Austria, Spain, America. The cause of causes could not escape those who had the gift of a deeper insight. They knew that the country was for its original sons, for all their differences, a sacred and beloved homeland. The return of these exiles to their homeland will prove materially and spiritually an experimental school for their brethren who are with them in the fields, factories, trades, and in all things connected with toil and labor. . . .

In February 1947, nine months after the establishment of that Arab state in Palestine, the question of what remained of Mandated Palestine was brought before the United Nations. In an attempt to resolve the claims of the Jewish and Arab communities living in what can only be called the rump of Mandated Palestine, the General Assembly adopted the partition resolution 181 (II) of 29 November 1947 that recommended a further truncation of the area west of the River Jordan. In its desire to achieve a peaceful solution, the Jewish people expressed its readiness to make this concession and to reconcile itself to the painful sacrifice involved, despite the fact that the projected Jewish state would have extended over only one eighth of the Palestine Mandate originally designated for a Jewish national home. That acceptance, however, was contingent on reciprocity, that is, a similar acceptance also by the Arab side.

Arab Rejection

No such readiness was forthcoming from the Arab side. The Arabs in Palestine and all the members of the Arab League categorically rejected the resolution. At the United Nations, the Arab states formally announced on the record that they reserved to themselves complete freedom of action, and then set out to thwart the resolution of the General Assembly by the illegal use of force from the moment of its adoption.

With the termination of the mandate over Palestine on 14 May 1948, the armies of the seven Arab states illegally crossed the international boundaries, in clear violation of the Charter of the United Nations. Their armed aggression was aimed at crushing the newly established State of Israel. . . .

Everything that we have witnessed in the Middle East since 1947 flows from this fundamental fact—the unwillingness of Arab governments to accept, and coexist with, a sovereign Jewish state. This is the core of the Arab-Israel conflict, and everything else is pretext or subterfuge. This is the reason why the Arab states have launched four major wars against Israel, with the express purpose of destroying it. This is the reason why they have developed a ramified series of battlefronts and a variety of weapons

MIKE

Mike, printed with permission of Cartoonists & Writers Syndicate.

against Israel. . . .

Within this context, but with even uglier intent, the Arab states also created the terrorist organization which came to be known as the PLO. This murder organization was founded in 1964, three years before the Six Day War of 1967, at a time when Judea, Samaria and the Gaza District were under Jordanian and Egyptian occupation, respectively. In other words, it is evident that the PLO was created by the Arab states merely as another weapon in their serried arsenal for the destruction of Israel, even within the 1949 Armistice Lines.

The PLO operative in Saudi Arabia, Rafiq Natshe, confirmed this on 13 November 1979, in the Saudi newspaper *al-Riad,* when he explained that:

> The Palestinian revolution was born in 1965 from a strategic concept of liberating all Palestine, and the revolution will not change this, whatever the pressures put on it. The best solution is for the Palestinians to return to their homeland and the Jewish foreigner to the country of his birth. . . . Any Palestinian entity to be established on any part of the Palestinian territories will be a starting-point for the liberation of the Palestinian territories in all of Palestine. . . .

Until 1967 the problem of the Palestinian Arabs had been viewed by all as a refugee problem, as it essentially was and is. Before 1967 Israel did not control Judea, Samaria and the Gaza District. Yet there was no demand then for the establishment of a so-called Palestinian state in those areas. The explanation for this is very simple: the entire world knew that the Kingdom of Jordan—on the territory of 80 percent of the Palestine Mandate—is the Palestinian Arab state, just as the State of Israel is the Palestinian Jewish state. The entire world also knew that the vast majority of Palestinian Arabs are Jordanian citizens and that the majority of Jordanian citizens are Palestinian Arabs. . . .

However, from that point on, Arab strategists appreciated that, given the general political climate which had developed in the world by the late 1960s, they stood more to gain by promoting the alleged existence of a *second* Palestinian Arab people, entitled to a *second* Arab state in the area of the former Palestine Mandate. The advantages of that tactical sleight-of-hand were obvious: it would enable the Arab states to claim that there was still a Palestinian Arab people deprived of the rights to self-determination and independence. The implementation of those claims would clearly be at the expense of Israel.

Leading spokesmen of the PLO admit that this bogus thesis was invented to work toward the destruction of the State of Israel. For instance, Zuhair Muhsin, the head of the PLO's so-called 'military department' until his death in 1979, was quoted in the Dutch daily newspaper *Trouw*, on 31 March 1977:

> There are no differences between Jordanians, Palestinians, Syrians and Lebanese. . . . We are one people.
>
> It is only for political reasons that we carefully stress our Palestinian identity, for it is in the national interest of the Arabs to encourage a separate Palestinian identity to counter Zionism. Yes, the existence of a separate Palestinian identity serves only tactical purposes.
>
> The founding of a Palestinian state is a new tool in the continuing battle against Israel and for Arab unity.
>
> Jordan is a state with defined borders. It cannot claim Haifa or Jaffa, whereas I have a right to Haifa, Jaffa, Jerusalem or Beersheba. After we have attained all our rights in the whole of Palestine, we must not postpone, even for a single moment, the reunification of Jordan and Palestine.

The meaning could not be clearer. The assertion of a second Palestinian Arab identity is merely one more subterfuge designed to bring about the destruction of the State of Israel. . . .

Extremist Leadership

One of the tragedies of the Palestinian Arabs has been that for over fifty years they have been dominated by an extremist leadership. Starting with the notorious Mufti of Jerusalem, who was wanted by the Allies as a war criminal for his complicity in the Nazi genocide of European Jewry, that leadership had no compunction about terrorizing and assassinating its political rivals. It was totally lacking in political realism and obstinately opposed to compromise. It led those whom it claimed to represent from one disaster to another. The Palestinian Arabs in Judea, Samaria and the Gaza District, who are prepared to live in peace with

Israel, have been steadily terrorized and intimidated by the PLO, which has been conducting without let-up a campaign of political assassination against them. To quote from *The Times* of London of 27 November 1981:

> The Palestinian people . . . ever since the birth of Israel have paid dearly for the extremism and intrigue of the Arab radicals who destroyed the Lebanon, nearly destroyed Jordan and will not rest, they say, until they have destroyed Israel. The Arab radicals . . . cannot deliver anything except what they have delibered in the past: bloodshed and futility.

PLO terrorism has been used to intimidate Palestinian Arabs willing to coexist peacefully with Israel. . . .

Let me try to define the true nature and scope of the problem today. For this we have to return again to 1947. Immediately after the adoption of General Assembly resolution 181(II), the Arabs resorted to the illegal use of force, with a view to destroying that resolution. Subsequently the armies of seven Arab states marched against the fledgling State of Israel on the day it was established, on 14 May 1948.

As a result of those acts of aggression in 1948, the Arab states created two refugee problems—not just one, as is commonly supposed.

The Destruction of Israel

The "heart of the matter" is not the Arab refugees or the "Palestinian Arab refugees" or the "rights" of the "Palestinians"—or even Palestine. . . .

The Arabs believe that by creating an Arab Palestinian identity, at the sacrifice of the well-being and the very lives of the "Arab refugees," they will accomplish politically and through "guerrilla warfare" what they failed to achieve in military combat: the destruction of Israel—the unacceptable independent state. That is the "heart of the matter."

Joan Peters, *From Time Immemorial*, 1984.

By the time Arab aggression against Israel was successfully thwarted in 1949, some six hundred thousand Palestinian Arabs had become refugees and found themselves in areas—including Judea, Samaria and the Gaza District—controlled by Arab governments. Instead of absorbing and integrating their Palestinian brethren, who speak the same language, share the same cultural, historical and religious heritage and frequently even have family relations in the Arab host countries, those countries forced them to remain in camps and exploited them callously as a political weapon against Israel.

A much larger refugee problem was caused by Arab hostility toward the ancient Jewish communities in Arab lands. From 1948 to the present day more than eight hundred thousand Jews have been forced to leave Arab countries. About six hundred fifty thousand of them came to Israel—in most cases with only their clothes on their backs. Hence, in effect, a *de facto* exchange of populations has taken place between the Arab states and Israel, triggered by Arab aggression in 1947-1948.

These Jewish refugees integrated themselves into Israel's society, and today Jews from Arab lands and from other Muslim countries, as well as their offspring born in Israel, form the majority of the Jewish population of Israel.

Not a Major Problem

On the other hand, the world continues to hear much clamor about the Arab refugees, who are still at the center of the Palestinian problem as we know it today. But when one takes a closer look at that group of refugees, it can readily be seen that it is not a problem of major dimensions. According to United Nations figures, there have been anything between 60 million and 100 million refugees and displaced persons since the end of World War II. Even if one accepts the more conservative figure, the Arab refugees in 1948 constituted no more than 1 percent of the total. The vast majority of the other refugee problems in the world, including that of the Jewish refugees, has been solved by their absorption and rehabilitation into their new countries or places of residence. To be sure, this has already been done as regards most of the Arab refugees and their offspring, at least two-thirds of whom continue to live in the territory of the former Palestine Mandate and are nationals of Jordan, the Palestinian Arab state created on the bulk of that territory.

3

"The opening of Israel's labour market to residents of the [Judea-Samaria and Gaza] areas has greatly improved employment opportunities, bringing virtually full employment."

Israel Has Improved Palestinian Living Standards

Israel Information Centre

Since 1967 Israel has governed the Gaza Strip and the West Bank (called Judea-Samaria by the Israeli government). These two territories have a combined Palestinian population of over one million people. The following viewpoint is taken from a pamphlet published by the Jerusalem-based Israel Information Centre. The author contends that Israel has administered the territories fairly. Israel has allowed Palestinians from the territories to take jobs in Israel and Israeli social programs have improved living standards.

As you read, consider the following questions:

1. What is the legal status of Judea-Samaria and the Gaza district, according to the author?
2. How does the author believe Israeli influence has improved agriculture in the territories?
3. What examples does the author cite to show that Israel has taken steps to improve health in Judea-Samaria and the Gaza district?

Judea-Samaria and the Gaza District Since 1967. Jerusalem: Israel Information Centre, 1986. Used with permission.

Judea-Samaria is a mostly mountainous region, about 70 miles long and 30 miles wide, west of the Jordan River; the Gaza district is a narrow strip of flat shoreline that extends some 20 miles along the Mediterranean coast to the Egyptian border. Historically part of the ancient Land of Israel, both areas were included in the territory temporarily mandated to Great Britain after World War I. This territory, lying east and west of the Jordan River, was divided in 1922 by Britain into two districts. In the eastern part, on 77 percent of the total area, a new Arab entity was set up which, in 1946, became the independent Hashemite Kingdom of Transjordan. In the western portion, the remaining 23 percent, the Jewish national home was being developed, in accordance with Britain's commitment to the terms of the Mandate, which recognized the historical connection of the Jewish people with the Land of Israel and "the grounds for reconstituting their national home in that country." . . .

Upon termination of the British Mandate on 14 May 1948, Israel proclaimed its independence. The following day, the armies of Egypt, Syria, Transjordan, Lebanon and Iraq invaded the new state, compelling Israel to fight its War of Independence, as a result of which the Gaza district came under Egyptian military rule and Judea-Samaria was occupied by Transjordan. In 1950, the Transjordanian king annexed Judea-Samaria, an act recognized only by Britain and Pakistan, and renamed his country the Hashemite Kingdom of Jordan.

The administration of Judea-Samaria, as well as of the Gaza district, came under Israel's control after the war waged against Israel by Egypt, Jordan and Syria in 1967.

Civil Administration

Judea-Samaria and the Gaza district are being administered by Israel pending the final determination of their status in a peace treaty among the parties concerned. Apart from the eastern section of Jerusalem, which is regarded by Israeli law as an integral part of the territory of Israel, neither the status of the areas, nor that of their inhabitants, has been altered.

Israel's policy in Judea-Samaria and the Gaza district, which is determined by the government and carried out by the Minister of Defence, is based on maintaining security and ensuring the functioning of civil affairs in all spheres of life. The senior Israeli official in each area is the military commander of that region, who deals with security matters. Civil affairs are the responsibility of the head of the civil administration in each area, who coordinates the activities of various Israeli ministries operating there. Both civil administrations are under the direction of the Coordinator of Government Activities in the Ministry of Defence.

The civil administrations aim to maintain normal life for the population, ensure public order, promote economic growth and facilitate the expansion of infrastructure and the development of public services. Local participation and responsibility are encouraged at every level; out of about 17,000 persons working in the civil administrations, some 98 percent are Arab residents of the areas. Most municipal affairs are conducted by the residents themselves, including service in the local police.

The legal systems in Judea-Samaria and the Gaza district are based on the laws and regulations that were in effect before 1967. To meet changing needs and circumstances, some modifications

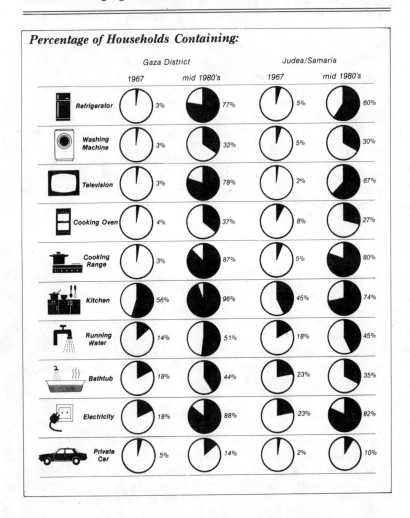

Percentage of Households Containing:

	Gaza District		Judea/Samaria	
	1967	mid 1980's	1967	mid 1980's
Refrigerator	3%	77%	5%	60%
Washing Machine	3%	32%	5%	30%
Television	3%	78%	2%	67%
Cooking Oven	4%	37%	8%	27%
Cooking Range	3%	87%	5%	80%
Kitchen	56%	96%	45%	74%
Running Water	14%	51%	18%	45%
Bathtub	18%	44%	23%	35%
Electricity	18%	88%	23%	82%
Private Car	5%	14%	2%	10%

Israel Information Centre. Reprinted with permission.

have been introduced and new laws enacted, usually in line with existing legislation. Although Israel's legal system does not have jurisdiction beyond the country's borders, provisions were made to enable the residents of the areas to apply to the Israel Supreme Court, sitting as a High Court of Justice, for redress of grievances against the administration. Since such petitions are heard by the Supreme Court, the inhabitants of Judea-Samaria and the Gaza district are thus assured the safeguards of Israeli administrative law.

Guaranteed Freedoms

Freedom of speech, press, assembly and movement of the population, as well as academic freedom, are respected, and principles of the Hague Regulations and the humanitarian provisions of the Fourth Geneva Convention of 1949 are fully applied. Since the Israeli authorities functioning in the areas are bound by international, local and Israeli administrative law, local residents benefit from a comprehensive system of guarantees and controls.

The lack of an independent economic base in Judea-Samaria and the Gaza district, coupled with a near-total absence of investment, severely restricted the areas' development prior to 1967. Interaction with Israel's economy since 1967, continued access to Arab markets via the Open Bridges across the Jordan River and the retention of Jordanian currency as legal tender have stimulated economic development in Judea-Samaria and the Gaza district, and have brought their inhabitants a steadily rising standard of living.

Agricultural Production Doubled

Agriculture continues to be the chief economic activity in Judea-Samaria and the Gaza district. The introduction of modern farming methods and increased use of mechanized equipment (3,000 tractors in the areas today represent a 6-fold increase since 1970), after 1967, has doubled agricultural production per unit of land and water and brought its rate of growth to about 10 percent a year. The sharing of Israel's expertise with local farmers has resulted in widespread use of modern irrigation, effective application of fertilizers, better pest control, the planting of upgraded seed varieties and the expansion of veterinary services, among other improvements in crop and livestock raising.

Little interest on the part of the Jordanian and Egyptian governments, combined with a lack of raw materials, infrastructure and skilled workers, limited industry in Judea-Samaria and the Gaza district to small workshops and factories. Since 1967, new industrial enterprises have been established and productivity in existing ones has risen, primarily due to increased investment and the upgrading of the labour force through extensive vocational training programmes. New initiatives by local residents are encouraged, as are those carried out by international organizations and foreign countries.

Judea-Samaria and the Gaza district were previously characterized by a very low labour force participation rate and chronic unemployment (10% in Judea-Samaria, over 40% in the Gaza district). New sources of employment were not being developed, and no provisions existed for helping people to find work, thus forcing many to seek jobs abroad. Since 1967, the opening of Israel's labour market to residents of the areas has greatly improved employment opportunities, bringing virtually full employment to both areas for the first time in their history. A network of 38 employment offices, staffed by residents of the areas, has been established to direct workers to job vacancies in Israel and to ensure that these workers receive the pay and benefits prescribed by law. Today, about one third of the areas' total labour force is employed in Israel. As a result, more capital has become available for investment, generating economic growth and the demand for more manpower. More and better employment possibilities, together with the upgrading of the labour force through extensive vocational and technical training, have helped to stem the large-scale emigration of those seeking work abroad. . . .

More Purchasing Power

It is clear that considerable economic gains have been achieved in Judea, Samaria and Gaza over the past 15 years. This rapid growth has been stimulated in no small measure by contacts established with the economy of Israel. Employment in Israel, and the subsequent increase in real wages and other income, has served to lessen appreciably the effect of one of the classic constraints on development in regions such as Judea, Samaria and Gaza—namely, limited market size or the very low purchasing power of the local population. . . .

The partial opening of Israel's markets for goods and labour to the residents of these areas has served to enlarge the markets for local products and expand incomes and purchasing power, thereby stimulating the growth of local output.

Israeli Ministry of Labour and Social Affairs, *Labour and Employment in Judea, Samaria and the Gaza District*, March 1985.

In the early 1970's, about half of the adult population of Judea-Samaria and the Gaza district had never attended school, and only 19 percent had nine or more years of education. A decade later, those without any schooling had declined to 28 percent, while 38 percent had completed nine or more years. This rise in educational levels has resulted from substantial expansion of the school systems in both areas since 1967, more girls attending school with the society's growing acceptance of education for women, more pupils continuing their studies in the upper grades, and more and better-qualified teachers being available.

Education in both areas is free and compulsory for all children at primary and intermediate levels, and free through secondary school. The entire education network, from kindergarten onwards, has continued to operate in line with pre-existing structures and standards, following Jordanian and Egyptian curricula in Judea-Samaria and the Gaza district, respectively. . . .

There were no universities in Judea-Samaria and the Gaza district in 1967. Since then, five universities have been established, with the authorization and encouragement of the administration. They are coeducational and accept local students as well as applicants from Gaza, Israel and other countries. Existing professional and technological institutes, as well as various colleges, have been expanded and upgraded in recent years, and a number of new ones have been opened.

From Charity to Rehabilitation

The focus of social service activities in Judea-Samaria and the Gaza district has changed since 1967, from distribution of food and money to destitute people to an emphasis on occupational and physical rehabilitation, designed to help the recipients to help themselves. A wide range of new services has been introduced, including programmes for school drop-outs, the physically and mentally disabled and the aged. Minimum income is assured to those in need. The 27 social service bureaus operating in the areas today represent more than double the number that existed in 1967.

Community development projects have been initiated, particularly in the Gaza district where, to date, some 8,000 families have been enabled to leave refugee camps and relocate in new residential areas. Through organized community committees, local residents are encouraged to take the initiative in identifying their neighbourhood's needs and to play an active role in developing facilities and services to meet them. . . .

Inadequate environmental control and poor administration of medical facilities and services were the main causes of high morbidity and mortality rates in Judea-Samaria and the Gaza district. With the installation of running water systems, the introduction of food standards regulation and growing access to, and utilization of, preventive and curative health services, the health situation in both areas has improved greatly, indicated by a rise in life expectancy from 48 years in 1967 to 62 years today. Epidemics, once rampant, have been brought under control and, with the immunization of about 90 percent of the areas' children, the incidence of infectious diseases in early childhood has decreased

75

sharply. Great emphasis is being placed on the development of maternal and child health (MCH) services, including pre- and post-natal checkups, health and nutrition education for mothers and monthly examinations for their babies.

In Judea-Samaria the network of MCH and general health clinics has more than doubled, and in the Gaza district new health facilities have been established, providing medical services for every village. Existing hospitals in both areas have been re-organized and upgraded, with emphasis on the development of specialized medicine and diagnostic services. Regular interaction between medical institutions in the areas and those in Israel has served to promote efficient hospital administration and patient care and to provide consultation opportunities for difficult cases.

Today, health services staff numbers almost twice as many as in 1967. Twelve nursing schools, two of which offer BA degree programmes, have been opened in the areas since 1971, with a current enrollment of about 600 students. Voluntary health insurance plans, not available in the areas prior to 1967, are offered to all area residents. The premiums charged per family are ir-respective of family size or pre-existing medical conditions. Today about 40 percent of the residents in Judea-Samaria and 80 per-cent of the population of the Gaza district are covered for hospitalization and other health services.

An Improved Standard of Living

The rapid economic growth that has taken place in Judea-Samaria and the Gaza district since 1967, coupled with the sub-stantial expansion of infrastructure and public services, has brought about a significant rise in the standard of living, result-ing in a greatly improved quality of life for the inhabitants of both areas. While personal consumption has risen with the steady in-crease of real wages, the expanded infrastructure has made modern conveniences such as running water, electricity, indoor toilets and telephones available to more and more residents.

"Israeli policy has worked against any attempt to help create an independent economic base in the West Bank."

Israel Has Harmed Palestinian Living Standards

John P. Richardson

In the following viewpoint, John P. Richardson argues that Israel uses the Palestinian West Bank as a source of cheap labor and as a market for its own products. As a result, the West Bank lacks an independently viable economic system. Richardson is an author who has traveled frequently in the Middle East. From 1966 to 1977 he was the President of American Near East Refugee Aid, an organization that coordinates self-help projects for West Bank Palestinians.

As you read, consider the following questions:

1. How has the Israeli occupation affected education in the West Bank, according to the author?
2. Why does Richardson argue that Israel has restricted the Palestinians' freedom to leave the West Bank?
3. Why does Richardson believe that Israel exploits noncitizen, Palestinian Arabs who work in Israel?

John P. Richardson, *The West Bank: A Portrait*, Special Study 5. Washington: The Middle East Institute © 1984. Used with permission.

In a published summary of the first 13 years of occupation, the Military Government described its goals in the West Bank as "the early achievement of normalization in all walks of life, based on the economic and social well-being of the area's inhabitants" and "the guarantee of personal and civic freedoms." The report described the "heavy stress" placed by the Military Government on "local participation" in "every aspect" of daily life in the West Bank, with personal and civic freedoms "limited only by the necessity to maintain law and order and protect the lives and property of local inhabitants." It characterized Israeli policy as based on "non-intervention and minimal interference" except "in matters that might adversely affect Israel's security."

Government by Fiat

Former Jerusalem Deputy Mayor Meron Benvenisti, an Israeli analyst and critic of the occupation, has argued that the Military Government possesses "unlimited powers" and faces "almost no checks and balances" in its operations. His thesis is that the sum of Israeli legislative enactments, judicial changes, and administrative arrangements in the West Bank has created a system of government that bypasses not only the Geneva Conventions but also the Israeli High Court of Justice, which has consistently ruled that the Military Government is limited to such changes under occupation as are required for the maintenance of law and order, changes which must be "intrinsically temporary." Benvenisti points out that whereas the Military Government describes all the Military Orders as being security-related, most deal with civilian economic, judicial, and administrative matters. "Each [Military Order] is equivalent to a new law," and "the total is . . . an impressive record of legislation which many a Parliament should envy." . . .

The Israeli occupation of the West Bank is an intrusive phenomenon in the lives of the Palestinian Arabs despite the Military Government's officially upbeat view of the situation: "Since 1967, area Arabs [sic] have enjoyed freedom of expression to a degree previously unknown to them or to the citizens of any Arab state to this very day." The Israeli occupation of the West Bank may benefit by comparison with more violent and brutal occupations, but documentation by local and foreign observers since 1967 makes it clear that the Israeli face turned to the outside world and the one turned toward the West Bank are different. Lea Tsemel, an Israeli critic of practices on the West Bank has observed, " . . . an occupation is an occupation, and each and every Palestinian in the occupied territories lives under full occupation," noting that Palestinian rights and status are protected "only insofar as they do not contradict or conflict with the interests of the occupiers." . . .

The entire West Bank has been designated a "closed area," which means that no one can leave without a permit without forfeiting the right to return. For those who need to travel abroad, the ability to obtain exit permits is crucial, and Israeli ability to give, delay giving, or deny a permit provides a means of leverage on the leadership class. Curfews, frequently imposed in the aftermath of a security incident and virtually permanently in effect in certain areas (*e.g.,* Jalazon refugee camp), are a form of collective punishment, and road blocks are a routine form of harassment as well as movement control. House or town arrest is imposed on members of the leadership class whom the Israelis wish to restrict but whom they hesitate to imprison or deport. Bassam Shaka's, former mayor of Nablus, is under town arrest. He reports that while he has no written confirmation of his status, he has driven out of Nablus on numerous occasions, only to be stopped at a point just outside the town limits and forced to return.

At the Bottom

Noncitizen Arabs have not found jobs across the occupational spectrum. Rather, they have concentrated at the bottom of the occupational ladder. Like other ethnic minorities and foreign labor, they tended to fill the low-status, least desirable, menial occupations. They have become the hewers of wood and drawers of water of Israeli society. . . .

The influx of minority workers increases the supply of cheap labor and thereby becomes an immediate target for economic exploitation and discrimination. Indeed, noncitizen Arabs have entered the Israeli labor market at the end of the occupational queue. Their dramatic influx explains, to some extent, why their average occupational position has worsened over time, both in absolute and relative terms.

Moshe Semyonov and Noah Lewin-Epstein, *Hewers of Wood and Drawers of Water: Noncitizen Arabs in the Israeli Labor Market,* 1987.

Confiscation of identity cards is an effective form of control since every West Bank resident must carry an ID card at all times. ID cards are collected from individuals near any security incident, and anyone is liable to arrest if caught without his ID even if he has not been charged with an offense. . . .

All printed matter in the West Bank is subject to censorship, and the sale, distribution, or possession of banned literature makes one liable to punishment. All Arab-owned newspapers are required to obtain annual licenses in order to publish. . . .

The economy of the West Bank has become in effect an extension of the economy of the state of Israel during the 17 years of occupation. The conversion has been continuous and deliberate, and the West Bank population has had no say in the decision-making process. The principal criteria for Israeli decisions regarding the West Bank economy have been to strengthen the Israeli economy and to support Israeli political objectives. In strictly economic terms there has been some short-term benefit to the West Bank in the process, mainly wage employment for the West Bank rural population, with an attendant rise in the standard of living. By contrast with the healthy and diversified economy of the East Bank, however, the West Bank looks distorted and artificial, befitting its role as a supporting actor for Israeli needs. . . .

One of the most significant changes in the West Bank's economic and social structure since the occupation has been the employment of West Bank workers in the Israeli economy, either within the "Green Line" (the prevoius Israel-Jordan armistice line) or in the West Bank for Israeli employers. Starting in 1967 with 5,000 West Bank workers, the number rose to 63,500 in 1982, of whom 43,500 were registered, not including 15,000 from East Jerusalem or 15,000 working in the West Bank in subcontracting work for Israeli employers. The "boom" years in Israel lasted until 1974, but employment patterns were well established by then, and the relative turndown in the economy has not had a major impact on the West Bank worker situation.

The Bottom of the Scale

More than half of the West Bank workers in Israel are in construction, with approximately 20 per cent in industry. They make up several categories, the first of which includes those officially employed, many of whom have been working for the same employer for more than ten years. These workers, who receive some social benefits from the system, are usually landless and often from West Bank refugee camps. The second category is groups of workers that are engaged through a local labor contractor, usually an Arab who handles the negotiations with employers on behalf of the group. These groups often stay together and move from job to job, having little personal contact with Israelis in the process. Some of these workers have farm land which they must tend during growing periods and for which they must be able to take time off from their jobs in Israel. They are unwilling to tie themselves down to a single job in Israel if it means that they can't take care of their crops. The third category is the informal labor market for day workers that has developed as West Bank residents gather at customary locations in the towns, often before dawn, and await the arrival of Israeli van and pickup truck drivers who call out their worker needs and choose from among the many Palestinians available. . . .

West Bank workers in Israel hold the menial jobs that Israelis are ever more reluctant to take. This situation puts the West Bankers at the bottom of the social and economic scale in Israel. Israeli regulations prohibit West Bankers from staying overnight in Israel, but many do so whether because of the distance they must commute or employer preference. In either case their living arrangements are usually rough and lacking in amenities, often filthy and even dangerous since some employers lock them in at night to avoid detection. Fires in rooms locked from the outside have taken the lives of several West Bank workers in Israel in recent years.

A Nonviable Economy

Over the past 20 years, Palestinian and Israeli economists say, the Israeli authorities have worked systematically, and as a matter of policy, to paralyze the local Palestinian economy and make it completely dependent on Israel. The Israeli policy, supported by indirect Jordanian cooperation, and the lack of a national Palestinian authority, has been largely successful. Today, the Palestinian economy of the West Bank and Gaza Strip displays all the symptoms of a nonviable economy. . . .

Palestinians have no illusions about their future. They know very well that their economic well-being is tied to ridding themselves of the occupation.

Sami Aboudi, *Al-Fajr*, May 17, 1987.

Although West Bank workers make up less than five per cent of the Israeli work force, they represent almost 20 per cent of the total in the construction industry. Many Israelis are uneasy about the social and political implications for Israel of becoming dependent on an exploited class of non-Jewish workers, but few are willing to pursue measures that would keep the two societies economically separate. So far the short-term benefits to both employer and employee have been such as to insure continuation of the arrangement. . . .

At the Expense of the Community

The increase in individual standards of living for many rural West Bank workers through jobs in Israel since the occupation has often been at the expense of community well-being because farm hands have not been available to tend the crops. As a result of the shift many villages and individual farmers have abandoned their fields and now have to purchase agricultural commodities previously grown at home. Increases in lower-class spending power on the West Bank look less impressive when compared with post-1967 changes in the East Bank economy, which had to rebuild

81

after the West Bank was occupied and cut off but which has surged ahead in recent years and now requires an estimated 100,000 foreign workers to meet job demand.

While the occupation has proved an economic benefit to the lower social and economic classes in the West Bank, it has been an economic burden to many of the rest, particularly the professional classes and small industrialists who have been swamped by the flood of Israeli imported goods that came with the Israeli occupation and now represent 90 per cent of the West Bank's imports. . . .

Ten per cent of Israel's total exports now go to the West Bank, which has become a "totally closed and protected outlet" for Israeli consumer goods, according to Benvenisti. The West Bank maintains a negative trade balance and depends on external transfers, mainly remittances from West Bankers working outside, to pay for its import surplus. . . .

West Bank agricultural changes under the occupation have been determined by Israeli needs rather than those of the West Bank population; in the case of a potential conflict the needs of the occupier take precedence. West Bank agriculture is not permitted to compete with Israeli agriculture, which is heavily subsidized and whose products have unimpeded access to the West Bank, where they are frequently able to undersell an equivalent Palestinian item. West Bank products, on the other hand, often face tariff or quota barriers to marketing in Israel. Agricultural warfare is frequently waged by the Israelis against the West Bank, including "dumping" of an Israeli product at a critical time in the development cycle of a similar West Bank product or process. As a result of Israeli policy and West Bank agricultural self-defense tactics, West Bank agriculture has evolved into a system that complements Israeli agriculture rather than competing with it, although a certain amount of overlap continues. . . .

Industrial Policy

West Bank industry is no better off than it was before the occupation and probably worse due to uncertainty about the future. It currently contributes less than 10 per cent of the area's GNP and engages less than 15 per cent of the work force. A recent survey showed that workers in two-thirds of the area's 2,587 enterprises are in garages, carpentry workshops, quarries, and small factories; one-third are engaged in textiles, plastics, leather, and food. Only three establishments employ more than 100 workers. Most West Bank industrial establishments are small-scale, low-productivity, labor-intensive operations.

The main reasons for this state of affairs are the lack of invested capital, Israeli obstacles, Jordanian restrictions on manufactured imports from the West Bank, restrictions on West Bank equipment and raw materials imports, and marginal Israeli government investment in infrastructure useful to West Bank industry. Jordanian import curbs intended to protect East Bank industries contribute to the problems facing West Bank industries since only goods from industrial enterprises using raw materials from the West Bank or purchased in Jordan are eligible for import licenses. Representative items purchased from the West Bank include building stone, olive oil, and dairy products. . . .

Few Fruits, Many Burdens

In effect, a "common market" has come into place during the 20 years of occupation, but in this arrangement Palestinians pick few of the fruits and carry most of the burdens. In addition to their direct economic exploitation, they face high taxes, including a value-added—or sales—tax which was imposed illegally in the late 1970s.

With elections in the territories banned by the military authorities since 1976 and Palestinians excluded from decision-making levels in the planning department of the Israeli military administration, Palestinians in the territories have had no control over the budgets for those areas.

Joost R. Hiltermann, *Multinational Monitor*, April 1988.

The most significant characteristic of Israeli-West Bank economic linkage is that the West Bank has become a source of cheap labor for and a major consumer of commodities from Israel. In the short run the occupation has benefitted the lowest rungs on the West Bank socio-economic ladder at the expense of those higher up, creating in the process a "proletarianized" West Bank labor force that does Israel's menial jobs cheaper and more readily than Israelis are willing to do them. Since the onset of the occupation, Israeli policy has worked against any attempt to help create an independent economic base in the West Bank. A microcosm of this problem has been the relationship of the Military Government with foreign voluntary organizations seeking to underwrite small-scale economic self-help projects in West Bank Palestinian communities. Delays and turndowns in this area of program activity are routine, whereas almost any proposal in the field of social welfare or relief is accepted by the authorities.

It is likely that in the absence of major steps to strengthen institutional activities like banking and credit, the West Bank economy will continue its deterioration unchecked. While an unchanged situation would create certain problems for Israel, they would be minor compared with the problems for the West Bank economy, leaving it in a shambles that might take years to repair.

"What is really happening in the West Bank and Gaza today is a full-fledged colonization effort."

Israel Violates Palestinian Civil Rights

Mona Rishmawi

Israel's occupation of the predominantly Palestinian West Bank and Gaza Strip has posed added security problems for Israel. Mona Rishmawi argues in the following viewpoint that Israel exaggerates its security problems to justify its unfair treatment of arrested Palestinians. Rishmawi is a Palestinian lawyer who works for Law in the Service of Man, a legal rights organization located in the West Bank town of Ramallah.

As you read, consider the following questions:

1. What international laws has Israel violated as a result of its policies toward the occupied territories, according to the author?
2. What differences does Rishmawi describe in police behavior toward Israeli Jews compared with their behavior toward Palestinians?
3. What does Rishmawi mean by the "Iron Fist"?

Mona Rishmawi, "From the West Bank: An Arab Voice," reprinted with permission from the Spring 1988 issue of *Dissent*, a quarterly publication of the Foundation for the Study of Independent Social Ideas, Inc., 521 5th Ave., New York, NY 10017.

After twenty-one years of Israeli occupation, the status quo in the West Bank and Gaza lingers on, with dire implications for the future of the entire area. Palestinians and Israelis compete in denying each other's interests and aspirations, or, on a more profound level, each other's reality. The struggle between the two nations is reduced to a mutual refusal to recognize each other's right to exist. But this struggle is unfairly skewed in favor of those who can impose their will. With a deadlock on the diplomatic front, changes are being made on the ground that make a peaceful and just resolution of the conflict increasingly difficult.

On the Palestinian side, demands include the right to self-determination, including the right to choose one's own representatives, and the right to create a state. The Israelis, from their side, affirm the right of their state to exist, based upon their security needs.

The Israelis' right to security is a fundamental issue, taken for granted by most Israelis while generally not acknowledged as legitimate by Palestinians. The main reason for the Palestinian position is perhaps the perception that the Israeli authorities have abused and thereby consistently discredited the security argument during the past twenty years. In our experience in the Occupied Territories, it is evident that the authorities resort to citing security concerns whenever they need to negate a right or principle they cannot easily dismiss by rational argument.

I know from my own professional experience in the West Bank that the official Israeli notion of security is very flexible. The authorities cannot be pinned down on defining exactly what "security" means to them, and they do not indicate what precise criteria fulfill Israeli security requirements in any given case. Even if pushed to clarify this issue, the authorities will not give an answer: neither a definition of the security concept nor precise guidelines in specific cases.

Flouting International Law

In principle there is some legitimacy to the use of the security argument *under certain limited circumstances.* International conventions governing the state of occupation, like the Fourth Geneva Convention of 1949, recognize the security needs of the armed forces in territories they are occupying. But the Israeli government, in defiance of most of world opinion, chooses not to be bound by this convention, claiming that it does not apply to its occupation of the West Bank and Gaza. At the same time, the authorities have indicated that they are willing to abide by the Convention's humanitarian provisions without, however, specifying which these are.

With the criteria remaining undefined, the Israeli authorities have been able to employ the security argument with such flexibility as to justify a number of fundamental features of their occupation, as well as many subsidiary practices. They range from the establishment and expansion of Jewish settlements, contrary to international law and world public opinions, to the introduction of Israeli civilians as heavily armed residents among an unarmed Palestinian population, which is bound to create tension or worse, to drastic changes in the administrative structure of the territories in order to accommodate Jewish settlements, and to actions aimed at controlling the local Palestinian population.

The Israeli concept of security is so far-reaching that not only does it prejudice the rights of the local Palestinians, but also in wider terms it perverts international law and conventions regarding occupied territories.

No Pretense of Justice

I am sitting in the cramped courtroom of the Military Compound in Ramallah, waiting for the opportunity to see my friend scheduled to be brought from his detention in Hebron Prison for a hearing. Neither I, his family nor his lawyer will be able to speak with him, as he is still being held under interrogation. "Legally," according to military law in the occupied territories, he can be held incommunicado for eighteen days, and with the approval of the Prison Authority, an additional 60 days, and more. . . .

There's no democratic separation of powers here, no pretense of judicial neutrality or due process. All the actors know their parts well, although now and then the judge has to prompt the prosecutor to say the right thing for the record. "Security" needs, as defined by the military commanders, replace the scales of justice.

Jan Abu Shakrah, *The Link*, May/June 1986.

A few examples will have to suffice. Both Labor and Likud have vied with each other in advancing Israeli settlement in the Occupied Territories. . . .

Until 1978, the settlements remained legally almost unchallenged. In that year, in what proved to be a precedent-setting case, Palestinian landowners who had lost their land to civilian settlers at Bet El near Ramallah petitioned the Israeli Supreme Court sitting as the High Court of Justice. The military authorities, having requisitioned the land in 1971 for "essential and urgent military need," argued in court that this settlement served the security needs of Israel. The High Court accepted the government's argument by dismissing the contention that settlements are *per se* illegal under international law, specifically under Article 49 of the Fourth Geneva Convention and Article 43 of the Hague Convention. The wording of the Geneva Convention is unambiguous:

86

"The Occupying Power shall not deport or transfer part of its own civilian population into the territory it occupies." The court decided otherwise.

Once the Israeli authorities saw they could override international law to justify settlements, they could override it for other actions to support settlements. So the security argument could then also be used to justify the further introduction of Jewish civilians into the Occupied Territories.

The argument developed in this way. Once there were settlers in the settlements, the authorities claimed they needed protection. The way to do this was to authorize them to carry firearms to defend themselves against any attacks from the occupied population, who quite naturally saw these settlers as hostile and dangerous. A special military order was enacted to enable these Jewish civilians to carry weapons.

Additional steps followed. In order to protect armed Jewish civilians living in the West Bank and Gaza, the Israeli authorities have changed the role of the entire administrative structure in the Occupied Territories—again to maintain "security." One example is the power given the police and, as a result, the attitude of the police toward both Palestinians and Israelis.

The Police and Discrimination

It has become clear that the primary task of the police in the Occupied Territories is to protect Israeli interests and especially those of Jewish settlers. As far as Palestinian residents are concerned, the role of the police is clearly discriminatory.

Let's look at two cases of killings in the Ramallah area. In March 1985, an Israeli settler was shot to death in the vegetable market of al-Bira. Immediately after the shooting, the towns of Ramallah and al-Bira were put under a strict curfew for a week—for "security" reasons. During that week, the deposed Palestinian mayor of Ramallah, Karim Khalaf, died of a heart attack. No Ramallah residents, except the mayor's closest family, were permitted to attend the funeral—apparently for "security" reasons. At the end of the week, however, with the curfew still in force, settlers were allowed to come and pray where their friend had been killed. Apparently, there was no security problem here. Within a few months, the killers of the Israeli settler were arrested, their houses were demolished before trial, and they were convicted and sentenced for the killing.

On December 2, 1985, Aziz Shehadah, a prominent Palestinian lawyer, was murdered in front of his house in Ramallah. That night, and during the following days, police behavior was distinctly different from that following the March killing. Laxness or inefficiency ruled the day. People's movements in the area of the crime remained relatively unrestricted. The information obtained from

Doug Marlette, *The Atlanta Constitution*. Reprinted with permission.

neighbors was not used to prepare an "identikit," and people living in the vicinity were not questioned about the crime. The murderer has not been found.

To summarize: Settlements were established. Settlers were given arms, and a structure was created to protect them. Then the Israeli authorities introduced policies aimed at controlling Palestinians in the territories. "Security" was always the stated reason: the underlying reasons must be sought in nonsecurity concerns, such as the need to appease the settlers, some of whom, at times, have called for the expulsion of the Arab population.

The Iron Fist

The most recent example is the "Iron Fist" policy launched by the Israeli government in August 1985. The rationale for this new policy was, according to the authorities, to clamp down on "terror" in the territories. But no major disturbances had precipitated this new policy. . . .

As a result of the "Iron Fist" policy (and considering the period up to July 1987 only) 41 people have been deported from the territories. In addition, at least 243 Palestinians have been put under administrative detention, that is, imprisoned for renewable periods of six months without charge or trial. In all these cases, the precise nature of the offenses allegedly committed by these people and the evidence bearing on their cases was not revealed—again, for "security" reasons.

By deliberately resorting to measures explicitly prohibited under international law, Israel is asserting an ambiguous concept of security—really a cover for ideological and political objectives. It poses at least a legal and moral dilemma for a country claiming time and again to be committed to democratic values to apply over twenty years provisions and regulations that clearly undercut these very same principles. It is hard to see the moral justification for the actions of successive Israeli governments in carrying out measures, like deportation, that are based on regulations (in this case, British Defence Regulations of 1945) that Israel's own former prime minister, Menachem Begin, once described as "worse than Nazi rules."

"Security" Violates Basic Rights

What is most dangerous about Israel's use of security arguments is the obstinate refusal to disclose the criteria it accepts as essential for a "secure" state of civil society. To be sure, security is a term with military and psychological connotations, but precisely because it is so evocative, it must be strictly defined. In Israeli hands the term has mushroomed to cover virtually all aspects of life, and thus any statement or action deemed unacceptable to the Israeli government becomes a violation of security. . . .

What is really happening in the West Bank and Gaza today is a full-fledged colonization effort. The Israeli authorities are in fact colonizing the whole area through a variety of methods, including land expropriation, settlement, and exploitation of resources at the expense of the Palestinian population. The security argument provides the justification for other nonsecurity-related interests.

"Security" has become a magical word, a catch-all, which speaks to popular fears among Israelis, but which is used time and again by the political leadership to further any or all of its policies in the Occupied Territories. As a result Palestinians cannot challenge the "security" argument in any specific case, because it means everything—and therefore nothing in particular. In their daily lives Palestinians have come to see the security argument as a subterfuge based on fears so exaggerated as to stifle real political debate and (more important) to violate the basic rights of over one and a half million people living under occupation.

"Israel must use as much force as is needed to quash any assault . . . and to punish the assailants and their abettors."

Israel Does Not Violate Palestinian Civil Rights

Peter Schwartz

Peter Schwartz, the author of the following viewpoint, is the editor and publisher of *The Intellectual Activist*, a conservative newsletter that supports capitalism and individual rights. According to Schwartz, the media portrayal of Palestinian victims and Israeli oppressors should be reversed. Israel upholds the Western values of individual liberty and free enterprise, the author argues, while the Palestinians are part of an Arab culture in which despotic governments and collectivist societies are the norm. Schwartz concludes that the Israeli state is threatened by Palestinian rioters, hence it is justified in using the force necessary to quell disputes.

As you read, consider the following questions:

1. Why does Schwartz believe that Israel is the real victim of unrest in the occupied territories?
2. What sort of a state would the Palestinians set up in the West Bank if they were allowed to do so, according to the author?
3. Why does the author believe Israel must continue to use as much force as necessary to subdue Palestinian resistance?

Peter Schwartz, "The Middle East Victim," *The Intellectual Activist*, May 31, 1988. Used with permission of the author.

The news accounts of the Palestinian unrest in the West Bank and Gaza present the story exactly backward. They generally depict the Palestinians as long-suffering victims of oppression, refusing to tolerate their lack of freedom any longer and fighting a desperate battle to gain the rights being unjustly denied them. The accounts suggest that the Palestinians are being deprived of their "homeland," and that Israel has become an aggressive, imperialistic conqueror unwilling to relinquish to the Palestinians what is rightfully theirs. An accurate description of these events, however, requires a transposition of the names: it is Israel that is the innocent victim fighting to maintain its freedom; it is the Palestinians who are the brutal oppressors.

The Real Oppressors

The Arabs who are rioting against Israel do not seek freedom. Theirs is a tribalist, collectivist society which disavows individualism and political liberty. They are in fact far freer even under the so-called occupation by Israel than they would be under any type of Arab government now in existence. A population that actually valued individual rights would *welcome* the opportunity of living under an Israeli government rather than under the various theocracies, feudalist monarchies and socialist dictatorships that make up all the Arab states in the Middle East. But the Palestinians in the occupied territories choose instead to embrace the philosophy and the politics of the Palestine Liberation Organization. They fly the PLO's flag, they eulogize its dead leaders, they acknowledge it—and only it—as their spokesman, they obey its orders regarding what hours to close their shops and what time and place to stage their riots—and they murder any Arab who voices support for genuine peace with Israel. It is the barbarous PLO that the Palestinians wish to enshrine as the dictator of their future "independent" state.

What they desire, in other words, is not freedom, but the primitive, despotic statism of "self-determination." They are hostile to Western values—to liberty, capitalism, individualism, industrialization, reason—of which Israel, in the context of Middle East mysticism, is the embodiment. That is why, although there is constant in-fighting among Arab groups and nations—as there always is among tribalist mentalities—they are quick to unite in attacking Israel. That is also why they are just as quick to prefer living under Arab tyranny rather than Israeli freedom.

How Israel Acquired the Territories

The Palestinians' antagonism toward freedom is the very reason these territories are under occupation in the first place. Prior to 1967, the West Bank and Gaza Strip were under the rule of Jordan and Egypt. Due to their close proximity to Israel, these areas were used effectively in launching wars against Israel. After successfully defending itself in the Six-Day War of 1967, Israel held on to the territories it captured. It sought a means of preventing their being used again in the initiation of physical attacks on its citizens.

This action was similar to the occupation of Germany and Japan undertaken by the U.S. and its allies after World War II, with the aim of establishing a governmental structure in those two nations to ensure that they would no longer become the launching grounds for military aggression. Like Israel today, America then had no interest in retaining control of its enemies' land (although in both cases there is every moral *right* to do so, since dictatorship is being replaced by freedom). The only difference is that then America's foes had been so thoroughly beaten into submission, and the goals of Nazi Germany and Imperial Japan so morally discredited, that a new political system could be imposed and could gradually take hold. In the Middle East, however, the goal of a Palestinian state—which means the goal of entrenching a regime hostile to rational values—is still a widely approved objective.

There is no collective right to a "homeland." There is only the individual right to live in a free society. The proper justification for the establishment of the state of Israel is not "Biblical heritage" or ethnic tradition, but the objective fact that it is Israel alone in that region which upholds the political value of liberty. Were the Palestinians to share that value, there would be no cause for any basic conflict with Israel. There would be no concern over whether the ruling government was run by Arabs or by Jews, but only over

THE STONE AGE

whether the laws recognized individual rights. There would be no concern over whether particular settlements were populated by Arabs or by Jews, but only over whether an individual's property was inviolately his. Arabs and Jews would have the same rights—as they now do in Israel. Arabs and Jews would be equally able to hold political office—as they do now in Israel. It is only because the Palestinians are fundamentally collectivists and statists that clashes with Israel are inevitable.

It is preposterous enough to describe as "refugees" the Palestinians who willingly abandoned their homes in Israel in 1948 (at the behest of the Arab leaders who were initiating the first of their several wars against Israel), and who are now scattered throughout the Middle East, prevented by their leaders from leaving the "refugee camps" and resuming normal lives. But it is the height of absurdity to refer to those who are living in the West Bank and Gaza as "homeless refugees" seeking their rightful home—when the only change in status they desire is to replace Israeli occupation with a PLO state.

Israel Must Not Compromise

Until and unless the Palestinians change their views, Israel cannot make any concessions. Whether stones and gasoline bombs are being thrown by a 12-year-old or an adult, the actions are a genuine danger and must be unhesitatingly terminated. Israel must use as much force as is needed to quash any assault, to deter future ones and to punish the assailants and their abettors. What is definitely *not* a solution is the pernicious "land for peace" compromise, which urges Israel to negotiate a "trade" with the PLO, in which the occupied territories are exchanged for a promise of peace. In saner times, this formula was stated more clearly by highwaymen as: "Your money or your life." The proposal of "Your *land* or your life" represents the same fraudulent attempt to treat the withdrawal of a threat of force as a tradeable commodity. But extortion is not a means of effecting an equal exchange. A promise of peace from the PLO or from any group that lives by force and makes the promise only to be able to assume autocratic powers once Israel moves out, is meaningless. There is one action on the part of the Palestinians that is both the prerequisite for any resolution and the clearest sign of their sincerity when they claim to favor peace. And that is for them to reject the PLO unequivocally. If and when that happens, there will no longer be any reason for Israeli occupation, any more than there is a need now for America to occupy Canada. To put this differently: if Palestinians do not renounce aggression, no compromise is possible; if they do, none is necessary.

The moral perversity here is that Israel is being widely denounced because of its virtues, while the Palestinians are be-

93

ing praised for their vices. One observes the nauseating spectacle of children throwing rocks to tease and provoke Israeli troops, of grandmothers feeling safe in wrestling with armed soldiers, of parents smugly confident that the Air Force will not obliterate their villages in reprisal—while Israel is accused of totalitarian brutality. One observes that the press in Israel is free to interview Palestinians, to cover the rioting and the retaliatory shootings (which are rarely shown in the press as being retaliatory), to print editorials anathematizing the government—while Israel is accused of dictatorial censorship. One observes isolated instances of unwarranted force being used by Israeli soldiers against Palestinians, instances that are reported by the Israeli press, investigated by the Israeli authorities, and concluded by the imposition of prison sentences against the guilty individuals—while Israel is accused of callous indifference to human life. In Israel, as distinct from countries (such as the Arab states) that thoroughly suppress freedom, the opponents of the government readily engage in mass demonstrations because they know that soldiers will not shoot at them except in self-defense. It is only because Israel is cognizant of individual rights—and because its enemies *count on this*—that it has been facing the hit-and-run rioting for so long.

Peace-Loving Palestinian Murderers

The media dwell lovingly on scenes of so-called Israeli brutality: security forces charging Arab crowds, teens in custody being beaten, soldiers kicking in the doors of shops on the West Bank. . . .

For a public accustomed to having complex issues offered up in soothing ethical blacks and whites, it's all quite reassuring. It is also a complete distortion of the political situation in the Israeli-administered territories. . . .

Not a week goes by that an Israeli civilian isn't assaulted (knifed, shot, stoned, or burned to death) by peace-loving Palestinians seeking self-determination. The victims weren't rabble with rocks and iron bars in their hands, but innocents peaceably going about their daily business.

Don Feder, *Human Events*, April 30, 1988.

The Palestinians, on the other hand, have no concern for rights and recognize no moral restrictions upon their use of force. They do not care that they threaten and often injure innocent people with their rock- and bomb-throwing. They have no compunction about embracing the PLO, whose avowed policy it is to blow up schoolbuses, to machine-gun airport lobbies, to hijack planes and ocean liners, to butcher the innocent and the defenseless. Yet the

Palestinians are considered the aggrieved party in the Middle East conflict, and the Israelis the villains. What accounts for this moral inversion, whereby those who endorse authoritarianism and wanton destruction are hailed, while those who support freedom and productivity are excoriated? What explains the view that the rights of the latter must be subordinated to the demands of the former? Only a philosophy that preaches *sacrifice* as a moral virtue.

This philosophy insists that someone's *need* creates a moral claim upon anyone able to satisfy it. Since the Palestinians are "homeless," in need of a homeland that Israel can provide, the doctrine of altruism declares that they are being denied what is morally theirs. They are being oppressed. Their rights are being violated. It does not matter that the Palestinians are to blame for their own misery. In fact, the more at fault the needy are for their own condition—i.e., the less *deserving* they are of help—the more of an altruistic imperative it is that help be given. Israel, by seeking to protect its freedom against the Palestinian threat, is being selfish and immoral, according to this philosophy. It ought instead to sacrifice its values for the sake of those who lack them. For self-sacrifice is not the trading of one value for another, but the surrendering of a value for a *non*-value—the surrendering of Israeli security in return for Palestinian bombs, the surrendering of prosperity for desert wastelands, freedom for tyranny, civilization for terrorism.

Defending Rational Values

This is why the Israelis are under moral attack. It is pointless to argue that justice and reason are on their side. What greater act of altruism could there be than to sacrifice the just to the unjust and the rational to the irrational? In this war of ideas, it is only by upholding the principle that one has the moral right to exist for one's own sake and to live for one's own values that the Israelis can be properly defended.

Distinguishing Between Fact and Opinion

This activity is designed to help develop the basic reading and thinking skill of distinguishing between fact and opinion. Consider the following statement: "A study of Bir Zeit University graduates in the 1970s showed that one-third were still in the West Bank while two-thirds had left." This is a factual statement because it could be proved by checking the study. But the statement, "The Arabs who are rioting against Israel do not seek freedom," is an opinion. What rioting Arabs seek and how they would define freedom is a debatable issue on which many people would disagree.

When investigating controversial issues it is important that one be able to distinguish between statements of fact and statements of opinion. It is also important to recognize that not all statements of fact are true. They may appear to be true, but some are based on inaccurate or false information. For this activity, however, we are concerned with understanding the difference between those statements which appear to be factual and those which appear to be based primarily on opinion.

Most of the following statements are taken from the viewpoints in this chapter. Consider each statement carefully. *Mark O for any statement you believe is an opinion or interpretation of facts. Mark F for any statement you believe is a fact. Mark I for any statement you believe is impossible to judge.*

If you are doing this activity as a member of a class or group, compare your answers with those of other class or group members. Be able to defend your answers. You may discover that others come to different conclusions than you do. Listening to the reasons others present for their answers may give you valuable insights in distinguishing between fact and opinion.

> *O = opinion*
> *F = fact*
> *I = impossible to judge*

1. Arabs desire, not freedom, but the primitive, despotic statism of "self-determination."
2. Upon termination of the British Mandate on May 14, 1948, Israel proclaimed its independence.
3. Prior to 1967, the West Bank and Gaza Strip were under the rule of Jordan and Egypt.
4. Palestinians prefer living under Arab tyranny rather than Israeli freedom.
5. After the Six-Day War of 1967, Israel held on to the territories it captured.
6. The civil administrations in the occupied territories aim to maintain normal life for the population.
7. Agriculture is the chief economic activity in Judea-Samaria.
8. It is absurd to refer to those living on the West Bank as homeless refugees.
9. Israel is being denounced because of its virtues, while the Palestinians are being praised for their vices.
10. The Palestinians have no concern for human rights.
11. In the early 1970s, about half of the adult population of Judea-Samaria and the Gaza district had never attended school.
12. The Jews were never a people without a homeland.
13. The goal of the Arab nations is to wipe Israel off the map.
14. The standard of living for West Bank residents has risen since 1967.
15. Israel's policies toward Palestinians are racist and fascist.
16. Arabs have a nomadic heritage which prevents them from accepting a democratic style of government.
17. The West Bank territory is called Judea and Samaria by the Israelis.

Periodical Bibliography

The following articles have been selected to supplement the diverse views presented in this chapter.

Patrick M. Arnold   "The Palestinians Need a King," *America*, April 16, 1988.

Yedidya Atlas   "The Liberal Media Attack Tough Israel," *Conservative Digest*, April 1988.

Richard Z. Chesnoff and James Wallace   "The Twilight War," *U.S. News & World Report*, May 2, 1988.

Edward Cody   "In Gaza It's Called 'The Uprising,'" *The Washington Post National Weekly Edition*, March 7-13, 1988.

Douglas J. Feith   "Bad Deal for Israel," *The New Republic*, April 25, 1988.

Kathleen Hart   "Israel's Tear-Gas Offensive," *The Progressive*, June 1988.

Joost Hiltermann   "Internal Combustion," *Mother Jones*, July/August 1988.

Walid Khalidi   "Toward Peace in the Holy Land," *Foreign Affairs*, Spring 1988.

Irving Kristol   "There's No 'Peace Process' in Mideast," *The Wall Street Journal*, February 19, 1988.

Tzvi Marx   "The Unilateral Option: Saving Our Soul," *Tikkun*, July/August 1988.

Micah Morrison   "Losing the West Bank War," *The American Spectator*, June 1988.

Daniel Pipes   "Arab vs. Arab over Palestine," *Commentary*, July 1987.

David Pryce-Jones   "Strip Tease," *The New Republic*, February 1, 1988.

A.M. Rosenthal   "The Unholy War," *The New York Times*, May 7, 1988.

Salim Tamari   "What the Uprising Means," *Middle East Report*, May/June 1988.

Russell Watson, Milan J. Kubic, and Theodore Stanger   "Israel's War at Home," *Newsweek*, January 25, 1988.

Ehud Ya'ari   "Runaway Revolution," *The Atlantic Monthly*, June 1988.

Should the US
Support Israel?

Chapter Preface

Is Israel an important US ally, as some believe, or is it an economic and political burden?

Many people believe that Israel is an important US ally because it deters Soviet influence in the Middle East. In addition, Israel's experienced military can aid in US weapons research and development.

Opponents of this position claim that Israel is not only too weak, but at times unwilling, to defend US interests in the Middle East. They contend that Israel acts friendly toward the US in order to continue receiving economic aid. At the same time, it wants to pursue its own objectives which are often antithetical to US policy in the area.

The viewpoints in this chapter debate this and other issues in this complex relationship.

"In terms of defense, what Israel costs us is minuscule, while what it gives us in return is invaluable."

Israel Is an Important US Ally

Steven L. Spiegel

Steven L. Spiegel is a professor of political science at the University of California at Los Angeles and author of numerous articles on the Middle East. In the following viewpoint, he argues that aid to Israel promotes US security by maintaining stability and minimizing Soviet influence in the Mideast. He advocates greater economic and strategic cooperation between the two nations.

As you read, consider the following questions:

1. How is the economy of Israel related to the strategic needs of the US in the Middle East, according to Spiegel?
2. What does the author believe has been the basis for US policy toward Israel?
3. According to Spiegel, how will a greater strategic cooperation between Israel and the US help reduce the amount of US aid needed by Israel?

Steven L. Spiegel, "Israel's Economic Crisis: What the U.S. Can Do." Reprinted from *Commentary*, April 1985, by permission; all rights reserved.

Israel is in serious financial trouble, and the American press is filled with analyses and solutions. Most accounts treat the country as an almost hopeless basket case—at least as an endless sponge off the American taxpayer. Authorities offer differing explanations of the problem: the high rate of government spending (in Israel the national budget is about equal to the country's GNP [gross national product]); the cost of West Bank settlements, or of the Lebanon war; the high rate of private consumption; serious errors in judgment which have impaired the nation's economic performance. While there is disagreement about the cause of the crisis, nearly everyone agrees on the need for a government-imposed austerity program. Even many of Israel's friends in this country believe that budget cuts, not aid, are what Israel requires. Indeed, at the end of 1984 the U.S. refused to increase aid until Israel adopted a much tougher economic policy.

The one element missing from the discussion happens to be the crucial one—the dimension of strategy. Whether and how the United States helps Israel in this period of serious budgetary constraint should depend, in large measure, on the manner in which our interests will be affected by one course of action or another. . . .

Aid to Israel a Bargain for US

In view of the services Israel performs for the U.S., it is possible to argue that the assistance it receives is rather small. Critics often focus on the $2.6-billion [in aid] figure, ignoring the fact that this only approaches 1 percent of the U.S. defense budget. This, for a country that is not a Third World dependency but a major unit in America's network of allies around the world.

In addition, many of the services the United States gets from Israel cost nothing—which is not the case with our other allies. For example, both Israel and West Germany have bases on their soil which might be used by American armed forces in an emergency, but only the bases in Germany are co-financed, i.e., the U.S. pays a portion of the cost but West Germany controls them. This is an element of the NATO [North Atlantic Treaty Organization] infrastructure program to which we contribute about $500 million annually; through the same program, the U.S. pays for a portion of West Germany's radar surveillance and air defense systems. In the case of Israel, there is no comparable burden-sharing mechanism. When Israel's E2C Hawkeyes watch Soviet aricraft activity in the eastern Mediterranean and over Syria, Israel pays the entire bill; when AWACS watch Soviet aircraft in Eastern Europe, the U.S. shares the cost with its NATO allies. The U.S. depends on Israeli control of the eastern Mediterranean, which has key implications for NATO's security, but Israel alone performs the task.

102

The U.S. today has about 330,000 troops stationed in Europe and another 110,000 in East Asia; although the presence of the troops aids these countries in their own defense, it is not called a subsidy. In the critical period after World War II the United States helped Germany and Japan emerge from defeat; the assistance inherent in occupation and alliance was not regarded as largesse. At various points over the last three decades the United States has increased aid to South Korea in response to Seoul's participation in the Vietnam war and to contemplated U.S. withdrawals from other positions in East Asia; the aid, which helped produce the Korean economic advances of the 1970's, was not regarded as charity.

A Worthwhile Asset

Israel's military and political importance in the Middle East and its strategic position stabilize that entire area, including the oil fields of the Persian Gulf. It is a bulwark against the inroads of the Soviet Union. It is a most reliable partner in the promotion of Western strategic interests and in the stabilization of the Middle East. 25% to 30% of its budget goes for defense, compared to 7% in the U.S. and less than 1% in Japan. Israel has one of the best armies in the world. Its navy and air force are the major deterrent forces in the eastern Mediterranean against Soviet intrusion.

Israel effectively secures NATO's southeastern flank, without having a single American soldier stationed in its territory. Still, the superb military installations, the air and sea lift capabilities, the equipment and food storage capacity, and the trained manpower to maintain and repair sophisticated U.S. equipment are instantly at hand in Israel. It is the only country in the area that makes itself available to the United States, in any contingency.

Committee for Accuracy in Middle East Reporting in America, ad in *The New Republic*, December 7, 1987.

The U.S. legitimately subsidizes it allies because they assist in the defense of America's vital interests. But the failure to classify this assistance as foreign aid—or, to put it the other way, the failure to classify aid to Israel as defense assistance—creates a distorted picture, both of our own burdens and of those shouldered by Israel. In 1983, the entire U.S. aid budget worldwide as only $14 billion; the amount allocated to Israel in that budget—17 percent—seems abnormally high. But the *total* aid budget was only 10 percent of what we spent in 1983 on NATO alone. Defense is more expensive than foreign aid. In terms of defense, what Israel costs us is minuscule, while what it gives us in return is invaluable.

Since Israel is obviously important to American interests, why is aid to Israel seen as charity, whereas subsidies to other allies are viewed in terms of security? The answer to this question lies in the history of the overall American approach to the Arab-Israeli dispute.

As Peter Grose has pointed out in his book, *Israel in the Mind of America,* support for the Jewish state was regarded from the beginning as a moral rather than a security commitment by the United States. In the early days of the state, anyone who seriously suggested that Israel could serve as an important asset in the effort to combat Communism in the Middle East was either ignored or derided. To most national-security analysts, indeed, American support for Israel was an act of charity for which the U.S. would suffer, in diminished influence in the Arab world. Only after the Six-Day War of 1967 did Israel begin to be viewed by some officials as having a modicum of strategic utility, but these positive perceptions vanished again in October 1973 with the initially successful attack by Egypt and Syria and the accompanying oil embargo by the Arab members of OPEC. . . .

But if, for a variety of historical reasons, Israel has been widely seen in the United States as either a charity case or a liability, in the late 1970's a series of events occurred which transformed America's relations with most of the states of the Middle East and began to cause some rethinking of the role of Israel.

Changes in Relations

When Egyptian President Sadat traveled to Jerusalem in 1977, he refuted the American view that peace between Israel and the Arab states had to be pursued indirectly and comprehensively. And when, subsequently, Saudi Arabia and Jordan refused to assent first to the Camp David agreements and then to the Reagan plan, it was suddenly *their* turn to incur the displeasure (however qualified) of Washington.

The fall of the Shah of Iran was another factor conducing to a reassessment of the role of Israel in maintaining America's security interests in the Middle East. Successive administrations had seen Iran as a linchpin of the U.S. position. Even Carter, harsh though he was on the Shah's human-rights policies, called him an "island of stability in one of the more troubled areas of the world." If the Shah's regime had proved fragile, how could any non-democratic government in the area be considered stable?

Moreover, the replacement of the Shah's regime by one officially committed to fanatic anti-Americanism triggered a rapid deterioration of U.S. interests. In 1979, panic buying on the stock market led to a tripling of oil prices. Later in the year the hostage crisis drained American energies and influence for months thereafter. The chaos facilitated the Soviet invasion of Afghanistan, bringing the threat of Soviet expansion closer to the Middle East oil fields.

In the fall of 1980 the Iraqi regime—frightened by the Khomeini threat and covetous of territory—attacked Iran. This border war, in seemingly endless stalemate, still continues.

Close Cooperation

Israeli-American strategic cooperation is not a panacea that will blunt all Soviet threats in the Middle East, but without it, the world will be a more dangerous place. Such cooperation deters the aggressive action of Moscow and its regional clients, encourages Arab states to opt for a negotiated settlement rather than military action in the Arab-Israeli conflict, and strengthens NATO's southern flank. Israel has much to offer the U.S. in terms of military intelligence, technical innovation, access to air bases and naval facilities, and a pre-positioning site for fuel, medicine, ammunition, and weapons. Washington should work closely yet discreetly with Israel in order to transcend the zero-sum nature of the Arab-Israeli conflict.

James A. Phillips, Heritage Foundation *Backgrounder*, July 7, 1986.

At the same time, the rise of the Shi'ite threat exacerbated traditional divisions within the Arab world, already sharpened by the growing gap between oil-rich and population-dense countries. When Arab Syria and Libya decided to support Persian Iran against Arab Iraq, the taboo against collaborating with countries at war with a part of the Arab nation was broken no less sharply than when Sadat traveled to Jerusalem. This did not mean that other Arab states were about to follow the example of Sadat (who was assassinated by Muslim fundamentalists in October 1981). But the preoccupation with Iran and with intra-Arab opponents did dissipate energies hitherto directed onto the conflict with Israel and reduced the importance of the Palestinian issue. Israel's smashing of the PLO base in Lebanon in the summer of 1982 further removed the Palestinian issue from the forefront of Arab attention.

Rethinking Policies

All this forced the United States to begin rethinking its policies in the area. Since October 1973, it had been assumed that only a comprehensive settlement of the Arab-Israeli dispute would resolve the energy crisis, improve America's relations with the major Arab states, and enhance regional stability. This ruled out any strategic cooperation with Israel, which, it was thought, would alienate the Arabs and jeopardize the entire structure of American diplomacy in the Middle East. The new crises in the area, for the most part unrelated to Israel yet involving the largest oil-price rises in history, the most violent indigenous Middle East war, the greatest humiliation of the United States, and the most provocative Soviet action ever, thoroughly undermined these assumptions and helped bring about a reconsideration of the role of Israel in American strategy.

To be sure, there were those in Congress and outside government who had already begun to question the treatment of Israel as a problem rather than an asset. These critics argued that the Arab states, whatever objections they might have to close U.S.-Israeli ties, were more interested in their own survival. Were not these Arabs more likely to be alienated by U.S. weakness than by actions—even if taken in concert with Israel—that would strengthen American credibility? And quite apart from the Arab reaction, the fact was that Israel was the premier military power in the area, especially after the Shah's downfall; this alone suggested the need to expand and strengthen our ties with the Jewish state. . . .

Economy and Strategy

Events of the last decade have made Israel more critical than ever to the maintenance of U.S. interests throughout the Middle East; yet Israel stands on the brink of economic collapse. Unless a satisfactory policy is developed for dealing with this situation, the U.S. position in the area will be compromised and America will have to assume a series of new and costly burdens.

Shimon Peres was right when he suggested on his trip to the United States in October 1984 that Israel could have a robust economy or a strong defense, but not both: "Our own problem is either to make Israel weak militarily and strong economically, or to maintain our military posture and try to look for economic assistance." The economic crisis has already forced reductions in defense spending, which will mean cutbacks in procurement, research and development, training, and in the size of the regular army, and is bound to affect morale on the Israel Defense Forces (IDF) as well.

Because the U.S. requires a viable Israeli defense posture, it cannot allow a deteriorating economy to threaten Israeli security policy and ultimately the balance of forces in the area. Yet in recent years, and despite the growing recognition of Israel's strategic importance, American policy has sunk into a vicious circle by which the Israelis are being bankrupted. Billions in arms sales to the Arabs are "balanced" by millions in aid increases to Israel. Israel is then forced to increase spending drastically in order to offset the Arab advances. The Israelis are being swamped by the effects of burgeoning Arab arsenals without the Arabs having to fire a shot. . . .

Out of concern for its own interests the United States cannot permit Israel to suffer a defense breakdown or an economic collapse. The question is therefore not whether to assist Israel, but how. There are four general approaches, and they are not mutually exclusive. The United States can reduce arms sales to Arab countries; accede to Israel's requests for major increases in economic and military assistance; initiate a program of security assistance through the U.S. defense budget; begin to provide the Israeli defense industry with the long-term contracts it requires.

The first two approaches—ameliorating Israel's burdens or offsetting its budgetary pressures—are familiar enough. As to the third, some Congressmen have already suggested placing the increases in assistance requested by Israel within the defense budget. The suggestion has thus far been thwarted by the State Department, which seeks to keep all forms of foreign assistance within its jurisdiction, and by the Pentagon, which is uninterested, but it remains a sensible proposal.

A Solution

The fourth approach is the most intriguing because it is the only one which addresses Israel's key economic problem—the need to increase exports. By providing long-term contracts, some through the defense budget, the U.S. could assist Israel in expanding its high-technology industries, which form the basis of the country's economic future and are central to its continued viable defense. Ironically, defense cooperation with Israel could actually be profitable to the U.S., because the Israelis have developed a host of innovations which could save substantial sums if adopted by the American armed forces. . . .

Mutual Benefits

These are just some of the benefits that might flow from a U.S. policy based forthrightly and not just formally on the notion of strategic cooperation with Israel. Such a policy could serve simultaneously to revive the Israeli economy, insure the Israeli deterrent, save substantial sums in the U.S. defense budget, and safe-guard the American and Western position in the Middle East. Perhaps best of all, in contrast to what happens with foreign aid, such a program would begin to pay its own way immediately. . . .

What is required on the part of American leaders is the wisdom and foresight to initiate a new program with a critical ally. The time to act is now, before Israel's economic crisis becomes so acute, or arms sales to Arab countries so large, that the effectiveness of the Israeli deterrent is compromised and we too begin to suffer the consequences of miscalculation.

"Israel lacks the attributes of
a strategic partner."

Israel's Importance to the US Is Exaggerated

Harry J. Shaw

Harry J. Shaw, a senior associate of the Carnegie Endowment, was chief of the military assistance branch of the Office of Management and Budget during the Johnson, Nixon, Ford, and Carter administrations. In the following viewpoint, he argues that Israel's small size and weak domestic economy prevent it from becoming a valuable strategic ally for the US.

As you read, consider the following questions:

1. Why does Shaw believe that US strategic cooperation with Israel needs to be reevaluated?
2. Why does the author believe the strategic partnership between the US and Israel is a myth?
3. In Shaw's view, how will the perpetuation of this myth make Israel more dependent on US aid?

Harry J. Shaw, "Strategic Dissensus." Reprinted with permission from FOREIGN POLICY 61 (Winter 1985-86). Copyright 1985 by the Carnegie Endowment for International Peace.

Exaggerated claims of Israel's capabilities and willingness to act as a strategic surrogate for America in the Middle East are not merely harmless rhetoric employed to justify U.S. military and economic aid to Israel. These claims confuse and distort the differences in the two countries' interests, responsibilities, and capabilities and hamper America's efforts to protect its interests when Israeli actions threaten them. For if Israel is truly a strategic partner and, as some assert, the only reliable anti-Soviet bastion in the Middle East, it can be argued that Israel's retention of the West Bank and the Golan Heights, its expansionist settlement policies, its aggressive actions against its neighbors, and its use of American-supplied arms, in some cases in violation of U.S. laws, must be ignored to preserve presumed critical strategic benefits. Moreover, in this view, a larger Israel with more secure borders along the Jordan River and on the Golan Heights is all the more valuable as a strategic partner.

The Myth of Strategic Partnership

The strategic partnership myth also exaggerates the military threat to Israel, inflating Israel's military requirements and encouraging Israeli demands for excessive military aid and U.S. acquiescence in these demands. It also encourages mistaken public and congressional impressions that the United States must support extra Israeli military capabilities, beyond those needed for self-defense, and fosters uncritical attitudes toward military aid generally.

Moreover, the myth warps Israel's economic relationship with the United States and deepens an already troubling dependency. It encourages Israel to believe that it is so important to the United States and so influential in American politics as to deserve to be bailed out of an economic crisis rooted primarily in its own disastrous economic policies and inordinate military expenditures. . . .

A Far-Fetched Notion

Like all myths, that of the U.S.-Israeli strategic partnership stems from an underlying reality that reflects believers' aspirations. Limited mutual cooperation between the United States and Israel, especially in the intelligence field, has existed for some years. But the notion that Israel significantly helps defend U.S. interests in the Middle East against the Soviet threat is a more recent phenomenon, born of the sense of crisis engendered by the Iranian revolution, the Soviet invasion of Afghanistan, and the Iran-Iraq war. A partnership in this sense is a creation of the Reagan administration. Presidential candidate Ronald Reagan stated in 1979 that "only by full appreciation of the critical role the State of Israel plays in our strategic calculus can we build the foundation for thwarting Moscow's designs on territories and resources vital to our security and our national well-being."

The strategic partnership was nurtured by former Secretary of State Alexander Haig, Jr., whose attempt to formalize strategic cooperation between the United States and Israel was embodied in a November 1981 Memorandum of Understanding signed jointly with then Israeli Defense Minister Ariel Sharon. But that agreement was scrapped less than 3 weeks later, when the government of then Prime Minister Menachem Begin surprised the administration by in effect annexing the Golan Heights.

Faulty Premises

This belief or perception about Israel's strategic utility is mistaken. It's based on faulty premises and flawed assumptions. . . .

According to conventional wisdom Israel is allegedly preventing the spread of Soviet expansionism in the Middle East; shoring up conservative pro-American Arab regimes; protecting the area's vital oil supplies; and stabilizing the environment for American investment opportunities. These are the premises on which the US-Israel relationship is based. But surely any honest reading of contemporary Middle East history shows that every increment of Soviet expansion in the region has been directly related to a security threat Israel posed to an Arab state or actor, who in turn sought Soviet arms and aid to enhance its own security. . . .

One can point out the fallacies in the idea of Israel as an asset to American power *ad infinitum*. Israel not only does nothing to serve American interests, it repeatedly engages in behavior that is harmful to the United States.

Cheryl Rubenberg, *Al-Fajr*, June 14, 1987.

Strategic cooperation was not resurrected until nearly a year and a half after the invasion of Lebanon. National Security Decision Directive 111 of October 29, 1983, made close "strategic cooperation" a priority of the administration. The directive is classified, and the details of the discussions to implement it have not been made public. The most obvious manifestation of the new policy is the Joint Political Military Group (JPMG), which provides an official forum for periodic U.S.-Israeli discussions. Knowledgeable U.S. officials indicate that although these discussions have been useful, they fall well short of the more grandiose concepts embodied in the literature and in the congressional rhetoric of Israel's supporters.

A review of the so-called partnership should assess the parties' interests and capabilities. Americans need to know what they can reasonably expect from Israel's military forces. Should America support military capabilities beyond those Israel requires for security against actual and potential regional enemies? What can Israel do for the United States with respect to the Soviet threat and to other threats to U.S. and Western interests in the region? What effect would support for Israeli capabilities beyond those needed to meet regional threats have on Arab perceptions, Arab cooperation with U.S. policy, and Arab aspirations for military forces? How would a U.S.-Israeli partnership affect Soviet influence and Soviet military aid in the Middle East?

The Israelis' Claims

There is no better place to start with than what the Israelis themselves do and do not claim for the strategic partnership. Although the official discussions of the JPMG remain classified, and although Israelis differ over what their country's role can and should be, a picture of predominant Israeli views emerged after discussions with a representative sample of Israeli government officials, defense analysts, and knowledgeable journalists.

First, with the reputed exception of Sharon, few Israelis regard it as the task of the Israel Defense Forces (IDF) to engage Soviet forces on land, except if Moscow either is directly involved in an attack on Israel or intervenes in an Israeli engagement with Soviet "proxies" such as Syria. Some Israeli officials explicitly reject Israeli engagement of Soviet ground forces beyond their country's immediate defense, referring to a "division of labor" in which the United States would deter extraregional forces such as the Soviets while Israel would take care of local actors. In short, these Israelis acknowledge as far-fetched the notion that Israeli divisions would advance beyond Israel's borders to meet a Soviet thrust toward the Persian Gulf.

All Israelis are acutely aware of the burden for a country of only 4 million people of lives lost in even short, successful wars. Israel simply lacks the personnel to sacrifice on costly military adventures beyond its immediate neighborhood. Besides, an overt Soviet attack is one of the least likely military contingencies in the Middle East, as most Americans themselves have come to recognize after an initial hysteria over the Iranian revolution and the Soviet invasion of Afghanistan.

Israeli views about the use of its air and naval forces against Soviet forces are more ambivalent than its views about ground forces. Without directly suggesting that the Israeli air force or navy would engage Soviet forces in circumstances other than self-defense, Israelis emphasize the value to America in unspecified Middle East contingencies of the "friendly and reliable" air and naval environment afforded by the IDF. They emphasize that powers hostile to the United States would have to take into account Israeli air and sea power in any planned aggression. Nevertheless, these allusions to possible tangles with the Soviets fall short of

111

suggesting that Israelis would be willing to take on the Soviets strictly in support of U.S. forces rather than in self-defense.

While admitting the limitations and risks of a direct IDF role against Soviet forces, many Israelis stress the value to Washington of "force projection" facilities in Israel. By this they mean that the United States could preposition in Israel equipment for ground forces, operate from Israeli air bases, and use Israeli medical facilities for casualties and the Israeli defense industry for equipment maintenance and repairs, all under the umbrella of Israel's local air superiority. Some Israelis even suggest that the Israeli air force could refuel U.S. aircraft and provide fighter cover for airlift.

Israelis consistently argue that the Soviets would have to factor in Israeli military capabilities in their own assessments of the regional military balance. Nevertheless, Israelis are just as consistently hesitant to spell out the circumstances under which Israel would be willing to risk fighting Soviet forces when it has a choice in the matter. Some believe that the war in Lebanon buried notions of acting as an American strategic surrogate in the Middle East and that Israel must return to its earlier strategy of fighting only "wars of no choice." If so, the United States could not rely on Israeli cooperation in circumstances not directly threatening to Israel. . . .

A Mythical Asset

The notion that the Soviet Union is the source of all of America's problems in the Middle East leads inexorably to the belief that Israel is a strategic asset of the U.S., a vital check on Soviet inroads. Neither of these notions is wholly original with this administration, but Reagan policymakers accept them so much as articles of faith and have developed them to such a point of exaggeration that they have become standard myths of policy.

Kathleen Christison, *Journal of Palestine Studies*, Winter 1988.

The notion of using Israel as a platform for projecting U.S. forces into Arab states that are either under attack from another Arab state or from Iran or threatened by internal anti-American forces is not widely supported outside Israel. Arab analysts argue that an Arab regime that accepted American help funneled through Israel would be discredited with its own people and therefore would be more likely to fall. Moreover, the Egyptians assert that for these reasons their own facilities are much better suited for such missions, although their use cannot be assured in advance.

U.S. officials also are skeptical of the feasibility of using Israeli bases. The Israeli offers may be designed primarily to entice the

United States into closer relations and to enhance the rationale for more U.S. aid without requirements for specific Israeli commitments. Some Israelis, too, express reservations about Israel's willingness to offer use of its bases when the chips are down. Israeli governments have long been chary of becoming a pawn in U.S. Middle East policy when the risks exceed potential benefits.

If Washington could not afford to taint U.S. support for friendly Arab states with indirect help from Israel, it is all the more doubtful that Israeli troops could be used in Persian Gulf contingencies. Indeed, most Israeli analysts admit this. The one exception might be Israeli air operations, which would need to intrude only temporarily into Arab airspace and then could return to Israeli bases after completing missions. . . .

Asset or Obstacle?

Israelis and their American supporters make much of the information America receives from Israel on the combat performance of U.S. weapons and equipment and on the capabilities of the latest Soviet weapons used by Israel's enemies. The benefits of this type of cooperation are obvious, but the Israelis could hardly expect to do otherwise and still receive the latest American arms at no cost. Moreover, intelligence on the combat performance of U.S. and Soviet weapons can only be obtained in the course of wars that may endanger U.S. interests and, possibly, Israel's very survival. Nevertheless, such cooperation is probably the most realistic area of effective partnership.

Beyond these specifics, Israeli analysts argue that a strong Israel is a force for stability in the region while a weak Israel would guarantee instability. The latter claim seems self-evident, but the former claim's validity depends on how that strength is used. If used to hold the West Bank despite reasonable Arab peace offers or to invade Lebanon beyond the border zone, Israel's military power could be an obstacle to peace and stability in the region. The balance sheet on Sharon's Lebanon invasion may be debatable, but it seems clearly to have provoked an upgrading of Syria's Soviet-provided arsenal, which increases the military threat to Israel. . . .

In short, Israel lacks the attributes of a strategic partner in the sense widely used in domestic American public rhetoric. Accordingly, for its own as well as Israel's sake, the United States must base the relationship on a far more realistic appreciation of the two countries' real interests and of their differing responsibilities and capabilities. . . .

Unfortunately, there is no common understanding among the American public about the mutual obligations of the U.S.-Israeli relationship. Moreover, the obligations that are commonly implied are essentially one-sided. For example, the United States seems to have assumed the obligation to protect Israel from external enemies too powerful for Israel to resist alone (essentially, the Soviet Union); to furnish arms to enable Israel to fend off regional enemies and, implicitly, to intervene in the unlikely contingency of threatened defeat by these foes; and to provide economic aid toward undefined objectives.

But if Israel is an ally, what can America reasonably expect Israel to do for the United States beyond defending itself? Strategically, the two countries share an interest in the general stability of the Middle East, for only a stable Middle East is likely to permit Israel to live in peace and prosperity. Middle East stability is also essential to the security of the Persian Gulf and the vital flow of oil to America's European allies and Japan. There are other interests that the so-called partners do not share. For example, the United States does not support Israel's de facto aggrandizement through its West Bank settlements. And officially it does not support Israel's attainment of a nuclear weapons capability.

What should be Israel's role in defending its common interests with the United States? If the United States arms Israel beyond its legitimate needs and orients U.S. military cooperation toward a Soviet threat that the Arab states regard as unreal or remote, Washington will only spur an expensive, futile arms race. The United States would also undercut its reputation as an honest diplomatic broker and strengthen the enemies of Arab leaders who are willing to work toward peace. In the long run, Israel's security is more likely to be assured by political accommodation than by an unending race for overwhelming military superiority. . . .

A More Realistic Relationship

Both Israel and the United States will benefit from quietly discarding the strategic partnership myth and grounding their relationship in greater realism. Others have suggested that the United States clarify its commitment to Israel's survival in treaty form. But in order to do so, the boundaries of the state of Israel would need to be agreed upon—a task sure to be difficult.

By freeing themselves from the strategic partnership myth, the United States and Israel should be able to address more openly and honestly those areas in which their interests conflict. Hiding these conflicts only postpones the inevitable and increases the danger of a major blowup in U.S.-Israeli relations.

"The power of the Israeli lobby over the formation and execution of U.S. Middle East policy has become a virtual stranglehold."

The Pro-Israel Lobby Dictates US Mideast Policy

Cheryl A. Rubenberg

Cheryl A. Rubenberg is associate professor of international relations at Florida International University. She has written numerous articles on Middle Eastern affairs and the American pro-Israel lobby. In the following viewpoint, she argues that the American pro-Israel lobby has such a diverse and pervasive influence in the American government that it virtually dictates US policy toward the Middle East.

As you read, consider the following questions:

1. According to Rubenberg, what constitutes the pro-Israel lobby in America?
2. What are the techniques and methods used by the pro-Israel lobby to influence policymakers, according to the author?
3. What does the author believe matters to the lobby even more than the perception of Israel as a strategic asset to the US?

Cheryl A. Rubenberg, *Israel and the American National Interest*. Urbana and Chicago: University of Illinois Press. © 1986 by the Board of Trustees of the University of Illinois.

The fundamental orientation of pro-Israeli organizations was succinctly expressed by a spokesman for the Conference of Presidents of Major American-Jewish Organizations: "It is our policy to support any democratically-elected government of Israel, and we feel that what is good for Israel is good for the United States." That position was reiterated by Hyman Bookbinder, chairman of the American Jewish Committee: "We bend over backward to help people understand that help for Israel is also in America's strategic interests." That organized pro-Israeli groups have been able to translate their premise into American policy, to have kept the perception of Israel as a strategic asset dominant in American political culture, and to have obtained American support—economic, financial, diplomatic, political, and military—for every one of Israel's policy objectives is, to a great extent, a reflection of their ability to influence the domestic political process.

The term "Israeli lobby" loosely refers to the approximately thirty-eight major Jewish groups that concern themselves with Israel and with influencing U.S. Middle East policy to serve the interests of the Jewish state. (Since the 1982 war in Lebanon there has been a proliferation of new groups, in addition to the thirty-eight, such as AFSI [Americans for a Safe Israel], CAMERA [Committee for Accuracy in Middle East Reporting in America], and others.) Only one of these organizations is registered as a lobby—the American-Israel Public Affairs Committee (AIPAC). It is of interest to note that AIPAC is registered as a domestic, not a foreign, lobby, having been exempted from the Foreign Agents Registration Act. (During the Fulbright hearings of 1963, enough evidence from documents subpoenaed from files of several of the pro-Israeli organizations was found to justify its inclusion in a category described in the title of the published hearings as "Non-Diplomatic Representatives of Foreign Principals"; however, AIPAC's domestic status was maintained.) The issue of "foreign" versus "domestic" lobby is not without importance: pro-Israeli groups are always quick to label supporters of Arab causes as "foreign agents." For example, Thomas Dine, in a speech written for the National Association of Jewish Legislators, said that Arab influence in the United States is directed and financed from "outside." "They," said Dine, "are a foreign lobby . . . their support is not rooted in American soil." Israel, however, is a foreign nation, and those who actively work for its interests could also be considered agents of a foreign government.

Networking

Leaders of the other major Jewish organizations sit on AIPAC's executive committee and this assures that AIPAC's reports on congressional action and its calls for grass-roots pressure go far beyond its own membership, which in 1984 was approximately

44,000. AIPAC is closely associated with the weekly newsletter, *Near East Report,* which all its members receive as part of their $35 annual dues and which it distributes without cost to members of Congress, news media, key government officials, and others influential in the policymaking process.

Most of the organizations represented on AIPAC's board also belong to the New York-based Conference of Presidents of Major American Jewish Organizations. The Presidents Conference is a coordinating body for debate and action on matters relating to Israel and other concerns of American Jewry. Its main functions are to serve as an interpreter of Israel's views and wishes to the American government and to thrash out disagreements among members in private, so others cannot capitalize on them. One of the Israeli lobby's strongest features is the united front it presents to the public, never deviating from the Israeli government line. Traditionally the Presidents Conference has concerned itself primarily with influencing the Executive branch, while AIPAC has focused on Congress, though these distinctions have become somewhat blurred over time.

A Power House

It is not unusual for the president of the US to call on AIPAC for consultations, and to seek their approval for a planned new policy on the Middle East. Recognized as a "Power House," especially with Congress, AIPAC is often called upon to use its influence on Capitol Hill in support of a policy Congress is not likely to approve. Lobbying by AIPAC on behalf of a particular policy guarantees its passage; its opposition to one is almost tantamount to a death sentence.

Ghassan Bishara, *Al-Fajr*, May 29, 1988.

Unlike AIPAC, most of the groups belonging to the Presidents Conference live on tax deductible donations and cannot legally devote a major portion of their resources to direct lobbying. They can, however, disseminate information about particular Representatives and Senators and congressional legislation and alert Jews to undertake pressure campaigns. Moreover, several member organizations of the Presidents conference, such as the American Jewish Committee, the American Jewish Congress, the B'nai B'rith, and the Union of American Hebrew Congregations, have their own Washington representatives who "informally" press Israel's desires on members of Congress and the administration. For example, in 1981 the only issue on which the American Jewish Committee urged a mass mailing to members of Congress was Reagan's proposed AWACs sale to Saudi Arabia. In addition, officials in the Israeli Embassy maintain intimate and continuing ties with mem-

117

bers of Congress and with high-ranking staff in the Executive branch.

Zionist Influence

Important, too, in building support for Israel is a network of Zionist groups, originally organized to work for creation of the state of Israel and now active in supporting it. These include, among others, the Zionist Organization of America, the Zionist Labor Alliance, and Hadassah, the Women's Zionist Organization of America. These groups promote a variety of projects including trips to Israel for politicians and academicians. Indeed, in virtually every metropolis and state throughout the country, pro-Israeli groups facilitate tours to Israel for local civic, religious, and political leaders; state politicians; and Senators, Representatives, and their key aides.

In addition to these various organizations, Israel's interests are advanced by congressional aides with intense pro-Israeli sympathies, who coordinate their efforts with AIPAC. These individuals are not lobbyists as such, but they have considerable influence on the congressmen for whom they work. Morris J. Amitay, former executive director of AIPAC and previously an aide to former Senator Abraham A. Ribicoff (D., Connecticut), explained the contribution of congressional staff members when he was still a Senate aide: "There are now a lot of guys at the working level up here who happen to be Jewish, who are willing to make a little bit extra effort and to look at certain issues in terms of their Jewishness, and this is what has made this thing go very effectively in the last couple of years. These are all guys who are in a position to make the decisions in these areas for these Senators. Besides relying on their own direct efforts, Amitay explained, pro-Israeli congressional aides call, when necessary, for "outside help," which means the application of direct pressure on legislators from influential Jewish constituents and pro-Israeli organizations such as AIPAC. In addition, every president has had a special White House consultant on relations with the Jewish community, who provides a unique channel of direct access for pro-Israeli groups to the president.

Lobbying Techniques

The individuals and organizations comprising the pro-Israeli lobby have a myriad of techniques and methods with which to achieve their objectives. One important method is the careful monitoring of congressional committees that deal with issues of concern to Israel. Former Congressman Paul Findley (R., Illinois) relates an example of the sophistication of the lobby in monitoring committees:

> There was an occasion on which I hadn't even drafted an amendment. I hadn't even spoken to anyone else about it ex-

cept whispering to somebody else on the committee with me that I thought I'd offer an amendment to cut maybe $50 million out of the aid bill to Israel which is just a tiny portion of what was pending. Within half an hour I was visited by two other members of the committee who were in the room during that period. Clearly they'd had calls from their home districts of concern about what this Findley was up to—what amendment he was going to offer. It shows the efficiency of the network. Obviously the word was passed very swiftly and got out to the districts, then calls came back. That was very impressive. Chances are there was an AIPAC representative in the room. They normally are present during all deliberations of the committee. They cover the Hill. They have four or five people full time that deal with Congress. They don't have to cover every committee hearing, just the ones where they need to be present.

Another technique important to the pro-Israeli effort is the ability to exert direct pressure on congressmen from the grass roots. Indeed, AIPAC possesses a computerized listing of supporters of Israel in every state and congressional district. A member of Congress who is undecided or likely to vote against a matter of importance to Israel can routinely expect to receive letters and telegrams, not merely from a scattering of leading citizens in his own constituency, but possibly from past and potential campaign contributors from across the country. AIPAC also has a type of power of attorney from many supporters listed in its computerized files. When a pending matter is urgent, a Representative or Senator may see telegrams from his constituents, billed to their home telephone numbers, even before some of the constituents know the telegrams or mailgrams have been sent.

Control of Mideast Policy

AIPAC is only a part of the Israeli lobby, but in terms of direct effect on public policy it is clearly the most important. The organization has deepened and extended its influence in recent years. It is no overstatement to say that AIPAC has effectively gained control of virtually all of Capitol Hill's action on Middle East policy. Almost without exception, House and Senate members do its bidding, because most of them consider AIPAC to be the direct Capitol Hill representative of a political force that can make or break their chances at election time.

Paul Findley, *They Dare To Speak Out*, 1985.

More important than the specific lobbying techniques that pro-Israeli groups employ is their power to deliver money and votes in elections in quantities far greater than the numerical size of these groups would suggest.

In presidential contests pro-Israeli groups exercise their power through financial contributions, high voter turnout in the primaries, and their demographic distribution in the context of the Electoral College system. . . .

Money provides the complement to the vote in explaining the impact of pro-Israeli groups on the presidential election process. In his study *Jews and American Politics,* Stephen Isaacs documents that "Jews take enormous pride in their prominence in financing campaigns . . . and give like no other group in society." In late 1983 the *Christian Science Monitor* reported that approximately 50 percent of all Democratic party funds come from the Jewish community. . . .

It is important to note, however, that despite the phenomenal success of the pro-Israel lobby on the domestic scene, its interests and efforts are not representative of all Jews in the United States, possibly not even of a majority of Jews. According to one professional on the AIPAC staff: "I would say that at most 2 million Jews are interested politically or in a charity sense. The other 4 million are not. Of the 2 million most will not be involved beyond giving money." Moreover, according to one estimate, all those who provide the political actions for all organizations in United States Jewry probably do not exceed 250,000. It is also interesting to note that five of the thirty-eight "Arab propagandists" listed in *Campaign to Discredit Israel* and six of the thirty-four listed in *Pro-Arab Propaganda in America* are Jewish.

A Stranglehold on Mideast Policy

The power of the Israeli lobby over the formation and execution of U.S. Middle East policy has become a virtual stranglehold. It no longer matters whether elected officials subscribe to the perception of Israel as a strategic asset to American interests or not. What matters is that the Israeli lobby is able to maintain the dominance of that perception as virtually unquestionable political truth and to assure that regardless of how severely American interests in the Middle East are compromised by Israel's policies, the U.S. government will continue to provide Israel with complete support. The lobby's effectiveness in impacting on the electoral process and its ability to shape public opinion and affect political culture are major factors in fostering this perception.

4

"The Jewish lobby is not nearly as strong as its enemies assert, but not nearly as weak as they would like it to be."

The Pro-Israel Lobby Does Not Dictate US Mideast Policy

Hyman Bookbinder

Hyman Bookbinder is special representative of the American Jewish Committee, an organization that works to combat bigotry and protect civil and religious rights. In the following viewpoint, he argues that the pro-Israel lobby does not unduly influence US Mideast policy. He believes that the goals of the pro-Israel lobby and those of the majority of Americans coincide. Therefore, Bookbinder concludes, it is not the influence of one particular group, but rather that of the American people as a whole which dictates US Mideast policy.

As you read, consider the following questions:

1. Why does the author believe that no apologies are needed from the pro-Israel lobby?
2. What or who does Bookbinder say is the cause of the pro-Israel lobby's aggressive reputation?
3. According to the author, why is the pro-Israel lobby so effective?

Hyman Bookbinder and James G. Abourezk, *Through Different Eyes*. Bethesda, MD: Adler and Adler Publishers, 1987. Used with permission.

For about twenty years I was part of the organized Jewish advocacy activities on the Washington scene. While the law did not require that I register formally as a "lobbyist," I happily accepted that designation because I was actively involved in what has come to be known as the "Jewish lobby." For many of those years, I presided over sessions of Washington representatives of all national Jewish organizations. I know how the lobby works; I know its strengths and I know its limitations.

In the narrow sense, the Jewish lobby is a small group of Washington-based professionals performing, within the limits of applicable law, the usual range of duties common to thousands of other representatives of hundreds of American groups or corporations or local political jurisdictions—informing their constituencies of developments important to them, and representing their constituents' interests before the executive branch, the Congress, the courts, and the media.

In the broader and more significant sense, the Jewish lobby is really the whole complex of Jewish organizations, influence, relationships, and community strength across the country. It is the voice—sometimes a single voice around a consensus view, sometimes a range of different voices around an issue—of those Jews who are affiliated with one or more of the many Jewish agencies formed over the years to meet particular needs.

Because of the importance of the Middle East issue, and in order to operate scrupulously within the lobbying and tax laws, the Jewish community has supported the work of AIPAC—the American-Israel Public Affairs Committee. AIPAC is a single-purpose *American* organization, registered under our lobbying law and operating with non-tax-deductible funds, committed to promotion of maximum cooperation between Israel and the United States. It is the heart of what is generally called the "pro-Israel lobby." But most of the other national Jewish organizations proudly consider themselves part of the pro-Israel lobby too, in the sense that they do everything possible, within the law and in the context of their basic mandate, to help Americans understand the historic and emotional ties that American Jews have with Israel. They deal with the entire Jewish agenda—Soviet Jewry, anti-Semitism, church-state relations, human rights at home and abroad, urban problems, women's issues, immigration, and much more—but proclaim without embarrassment or apology that, except for the welfare and security of America, the security of Israel is the highest single priority for them.

No Apologies

Critics of current American Middle East policy have increasingly resorted to attacks on the pro-Israel lobby rather than on the substance of the policy itself. Their tactics remind one of the ancients' killing of the messenger when the message delivered was distressing to them. Unsuccessful in refuting the impressive case that exists for continuation of current policy, some critics have made irresponsible, outrageous accusations about the operation of the lobby.

America Is Pro-Israel

Despite the general antipathy to foreign aid, and despite the great concerns about intolerable federal budget deficits, every recent Congress has approved, with overwhelming bipartisan support, at least the levels of assistance to Israel requested by the respective administrations. There is no other area of foreign policy that commands this kind of consensus.

What explains this? Why is our Congress so pro-Israel?

In the final analysis, it is because the *American people* believe it is right and it is in our American interest to be and act pro-Israel and not, as some would suggest, only because of a particularly powerful Jewish lobby that has somehow fooled or intimidated the Congress.

Hyman Bookbinder, *Through Different Eyes*, 1987.

Their central allegation is that a super-powerful lobby has managed to fool/bribe/blackmail/intimidate public officials and legislators into slavish acceptance of a pro-Israel policy for America. Such an indictment is as ridiculous as it is unfair. My short answer to it has always been: *The Jewish lobby is not nearly as strong as its enemies assert, but not nearly as weak as they would like it to be.*

We make no apology for having developed the strength and skills we possess. There's nothing un-American about being effective or successful. We are not the slightest bit defensive about having learned how to participate in the political process—a participation clearly protected in the constitution and available to every other individual or group of Americans.

We remember with anguish that forty years ago we had not yet developed such skills, that we had failed to arouse sufficient concerns in the general public and in the government about the genocide that was being practiced against our co-religionists in Europe. We are tortured with the thought that had we then been able, for example, to persuade 70 or 80 or 90 senators, or 300 or 350 or 400 representatives to insist that President Roosevelt make even one single plane available to bomb the railroad track to Auschwitz, that the ten thousand killings a day might have stopped, at least temporarily.

Yes, the American Jewish community has made every effort to participate effectively in the political process. But it does not fool itself. It knows its limitations. It knows it cannot impose or dictate public policy on the basis of its own numbers or resources. Jews constitute only 2.6 percent of the U.S. population. In most states and congressional districts, there are too few Jews even to get into the statistics.

If on such issues as Middle East policy or the plight of Soviet Jewry, the "Jewish" view seems to prevail, it must mean and it has in fact meant that a very large number of non-Jews concur with those Jewish views. If it is cynically assumed that officials elected in heavily Jewish areas—there are some such areas—vote and act to please their Jewish constituents, how does one explain the support from states like Montana or Oregon or Tennessee or North Dakota? How does one explain the consistency of national polling data?

What About the Pro-Arab Lobby?

The answer is as simple as it is gratifying. Americans have understood and accepted the basic premises of our policies. If American Jews have worked hard to help Americans understand, should they be criticized for doing so?

The American people have not been deprived of the opportunity to hear the other side. There is much reporting of the Jewish lobby, much less so of the active, well-financed pro-Arab or anti-Israel lobby which has been operating on many fronts.

Relatively few Arab Americans, compared with the proportionate number of Jewish Americans, are known to be affiliated with organizations actively involved in shaping American Middle East policy. But there are a number of active, efficient, energetic Washington-based national Arab-American organizations. They testify frequently before congressional committees, promote advertising and direct-mail campaigns, and engage in a wide range of public relations activities. In addition, some of Washington's best legal and public relations experts are retained by several of the Arab nations.

The pro-Arab lobby's work is enhanced by numerous Arab and pro-Arab scholars at various Middle East institutes on university campuses and at think tanks, often with direct or indirect financing from Arab governments. Less direct, but important, is the help they get from American corporations with Middle East interests, in the form of "public interest" advertising messages or in direct lobbying. Steven Emerson, in his book *The American House of Saud,* documents the major corporate campaign waged in 1981 on behalf of the sale of AWACS planes to Saudi Arabia. The media, both print and broadcast, have been very fair to the pro-Arab side of the debate. Television coverage of hostage situations and other terrorist events usually provides a forum for angry denunciations of Israel and its presumed unfair treatment of Palestinians.

Aware of the deep American commitment to Israel's legitimacy, the Arab-American propaganda campaign does not explicitly challenge that legitimacy. Instead it focuses on four basic themes in an effort to revise American public opinion: (1) Israel's conflict is not with Arab states, but with the Palestinians; (2) Israel is not really a democracy; (3) Israel is not a reliable ally of the United States; and (4) Israel's American supporters are really agents of a foreign power. There is not a single study or poll that suggests significant acceptance of any of these themes by the American people—but each is indeed a serious charge and has required a credible response from the pro-Israel community.

Frustrated, unable to make any real progress based on this propaganda line, pro-Arab forces have made the Jewish lobby the object of much of their efforts. They have zeroed in on the charge that AIPAC and a number of pro-Israel political action committees (PACS) have intimidated Congress into voting the way they do under threat of being defeated for reelection. They point to two or three elections in which, presumably, this is exactly what happened.

An Unclear Relationship

Pro-Israel and pro-Arab interest groups and lobbies are very active in American politics, but the relationship between their activities and subsequent public opinion is unclear. Are special-interest and lobby groups influential because they shape public opinion, reflect public sentiment, or are able to convince politicians and officials to act as opinion makers in defense of a particular approach? Studies of the relationship between pro-Israel and pro-Arab interest groups and American public opinion from 1966 to 1977 did not produce conclusive evidence to this effect.

Eytan Gilboa, *American Public Opinion Toward Israel and the Arab-Israeli Conflict*, 1987.

One of those presumed victims, former Congressman Paul Findley of Illinois, has written a book—and evidently started a new career—to persuade Americans that the White House and the Congress have surrendered to the Jewish lobby. In several face-to-face debates with Findley, I have asked him whether he really means to charge that every one of our presidents—from Wilson to Reagan—and the many secretaries of state and defense and the hundreds of Congressmen from both political parties who served with him—that all of these public officials had shamefully ignored their better instincts about what would best serve America, in their bowing to the pressure of a Jewish lobby. He ignored that question, as he did the observation that he had had the full opportunity, with at least as many resources as his opponent, to make his case before the electorate, but had simply failed to persuade his constituents that he deserved reelection. . . .

It is true, of course, that there are a number of PACS operating across the country that are concerned with the single issue of U.S.-Israel relations. Citizens especially concerned with this issue have the same rights as those who have formed thousands of other PACS on other specific issues—labor, environment, taxes, right-to-life, nuclear freeze, etc. Operating fully within the law, these PACS make contributions to candidates with policies compatible with their own. Supporters of the principle of PACS argue that this makes it possible for small contributors to do more effectively what large contributors in the past have always been able to do: to make candidates aware of the issues that are important to them.

I am as concerned with the proliferation of PACS as I am with the mad escalation of campaign costs. I would not be sad to see the end or the serious curtailment of PACism, and the setting of reasonable limits on total campaign costs. I would urge the Jewish community as such not to resist such campaign reforms. But PACS are part of today's system and their legitimate use by citizens concerned with U.S.-Israel relations should not be singled out for criticism.

An Intramural Debate

Within the Jewish community itself, there is a major debate under way about the most appropriate way in which its agenda—its *entire* agenda—should be pursued. There are those who argue that the issue of Jewish security is so critical—especially the security of the only Jewish state—that Jewish resources should be directed almost entirely to the issue of Israel. They argue that other, more universal interests can be pursued in other organizations or coalitions. But I have joined with others who argue that our concerns about Israel cannot and should not be separated from our general concerns, that while Israeli security is indeed our highest single priority, it is not our *only* priority.

Translated into political action, this debate among Jews comes down to the difference between single-issue pro-Israel PACS and multi-issue PACS. At this time, the former is clearly the dominant, but the latter is growing.

American Jews have every right to know a candidate's Middle East views. If the candidate is deemed to be hostile, or even indifferent, to Israel's security needs, the Jewish voter should and will react accordingly. But Jewish voters also want a candidate's views on national and international issues. Candidates offend Jewish voters when they think they need only display their pro-Israel credentials.

During the 1984 presidential primaries, I was embarrassed and

126

disturbed when two otherwise admirable candidates for the nomi-
nation, both personal friends, competed for the Jewish vote in New
York by overemphasizing the relatively marginal issue of the
location of the American embassy in Israel. In a *New York Times*
piece on March 30, I appealed to both Walter Mondale and Gary
Hart to address themselves to the broader issues of the day. "If
basic sympathy for Israel's security is a necessary condition for
voters' support," I wrote, "it is not a sufficient condition. . . .
Jewish voters will give their votes to the candidate who is most
likely to be an effective president or senator or congressman when
dealing with the *whole* spectrum of national and international issues. . . . They want candidates to discuss with them how best to
use American power in the world; how to assure human rights
progress at home and abroad; how to pursue social justice and
economic growth goals; how to assure further progress for minorities and women in a truly pluralist society. . . . Jews care very
much about the health and strength of America."

The overwhelming, positive reaction to this article was most
reassuring. It supported two firm beliefs I had held for years:

- American Jewish support for Israel and for close U.S.-Israel
  ties is not a narrowly perceived, parochial interest in the Jewish state. It is part of a broader humanist, democratic, pluralist
  commitment that Jews share. We have not abandoned our
  concerns for the best America or best world while engaged
  in efforts on behalf of a secure Israel.
- American Jews can feel free to ask other groups to share our
  concerns about Israel because we have shown we share with
  them a profound concern about the kind of America and the
  kind of world we live in. . . .

Jewish Credibility

If this has made it easier to win friends for Israel, should we feel
guilty or embarrassed? We are an active community. We have
much to be active about. We have organized ourselves to be effective in our work. But, to be frank, when it comes to the Israel
issue, our strongest asset is that we have an easy product to sell.
There is no need for the political intimidation we are charged with.
From time to time, there may be excesses in the language or the
actions of an overzealous advocate. The single-mindedness of
ardent supporters of Israel may disturb some critics, but the record
is clear: no charges of illegal or improper conduct have ever, to
my knowledge, been successfully pressed against AIPAC, any pro-
Israel PAC, or any other Jewish agency. The Jewish community
itself will not be intimidated into silence or inaction by irresponsible allegations of impropriety or implications of divided loyalty.

"America has a national interest in Israel precisely because no other nation invokes at one and the same time so many basic American values."

Americans Should Support Israel

Aaron Wildavsky

Aaron Wildavsky is professor of political science and a member of the Survey Research Center at the University of California at Berkeley. He argues in the following viewpoint that Israel is an island of Western culture in the Middle East and that Americans should therefore value and support Israel as they would America itself. Wildavsky concludes that any moral argument against Israel applies equally to America; to condemn Israel is to condemn America.

As you read, consider the following questions:

1. According to the author, what is included in the concept of national interest?
2. How are cultural and economic interests related, according to Wildavsky?
3. What does the author believe is the ultimate basis of the arguments used by unfriendly nations against Israel?

Aaron Wildavsky, "What's In It for Us?" Published by permission of Transaction Publishers from *The Middle East Reader*, Michael Curtis, ed. Copyright © 1986 by Transaction Publishers.

My argument will be that America's highest national interest is preservation of what gives it its own sense of self-worth—religious liberty, democratic institutions, moral character, and Western culture. If the idea of America became illegitimate to Americans, nothing else would much matter, for our people would have lost both their ability to identify interests and their will to support them. Well and good, one might say, but where does Israel fit in? In the past, our forebears used to refer to America as their Zion, their promised land. In the present, it is hard to find a single objection to Israel (other than its small size) that does not apply equally to America. Israel alone raises questions of the legitimacy of immigration, the value of religion, the desirability of democracy, and the viability of Western culture. To ask if Israel deserves support is to ask the same question about America.

Can there be a concept of national interest that does not include concern for a nation's cultural heritage, its liberties, and its religious and moral character? The answer is "no" because even the narrowest definition—national interest as vital to the physical survival of the country—includes a moral preference for the survival of the nation's way of life. If this were not so, if existence alone were the aim of national policy, then either pure passivity or unlimited aggression would be adequate. On one hand, armies could be abolished and the nation laid open to all comers; alternatively, all efforts could concentrate on national defense even if morality, liberty, and culture fell by the way. But no one, presumably, argues that survival should be America's only interest, or that either pure passivity or all-out aggression is the best way to achieve it. No, the argument is always that the things we care about most are compatible with survival. Like the lady in the lifeboat who refuses to choose which of her children to save, Americans try to make all basic values compatible with surviving to enjoy them. The question here is whether they go along with support for Israel. . . .

A Hospitable Environment

To have interests implies willingness (up to a point), to sacrifice something for them. Unless there are things one is prepared to give up, interests are only unfocused desires. Asked to lay it on the line, how much would Americans be willing to sacrifice for what interests?

My list would include religious liberty, political freedom, economic opportunity, and such other practices as ethnic pluralism, and freedom to travel and choose goods, which define our way of life. Put the matter the other way: Who among us would want to defend an America which lacked these aspects of what is loosely called culture? Indeed, it is this cultural complex that we call the American way of life. If its legitimacy were undermined—if political liberty were a farce, if ethnic pluralism were a delusion, if advancement depended wholly on political favoritism—America would collapse from within long before it was threatened from without. America's first national interest, therefore, is to solidify its own sense of self-worth.

Translated into international terms, America's primary interest is to foster an environment hospitable to its culture. "Fortress America" might be a military goal, but it could never be the cultural one, for that requires a number of nations sharing sites where Western culture is (and historically has been) practiced. Foremost among these, because of the critical part they played in creating our culture, are Jerusalem, home of Judaism and Christianity, and Athens and Rome, originators of our secular civilization.

A Strong Bond

The people of the United States and Israel share common moral and democratic values, and are committed to pursuing just and free societies. For nearly four decades, despite tensions and disagreements, the special U.S.-Israel relationship has continued to reach new heights of cooperation because of the strength of these bonds tying the two allies together.

American Israel Public Affairs Committee, *Journal of Palestine Studies*, Summer 1987.

I presume to remind us of the child's ABC's of Western culture because the cultural importance of these places is not matched in this era by their economic or military significance. Greece and Italy hardly could defend themselves against external attack. They have little to offer economically, and their loans, likely to be succeeded by larger loans, are unlikely to be repaid to the United States and other Western creditors. Much the same, I might add, could be said of Britain, which is not without cultural-historic value among ourselves and other English-speaking states.

Now, in regard to Israel, it is said that sentiment is no substitute for substance. Israel is outnumbered in the Middle East. It is poor while its neighbors grow rich. Israel lacks oil because it is badly located. America would profit materially by being on the good side of the Arabs; it has nothing to gain from Israel. America's interest in Israel, they say, is idealistic—the kind of interest that cannot survive without a material base. Thus, to borrow a phrase from Leon Trotsky, Israel's opponents consign it to the dung-heap of history. And without a material base ("How many divisions does the Pope have?" as Joseph Stalin was reported to have asked) America, according to this logic, can have no national interest in Israel.

Need I say that Americans would be devastated if London,

Rome, Athens, or Jerusalem fell into hostile hands? Deprived of cultural ties and affectionate memories, we could hardly help but wonder if our days were numbered, and whether cultures like ours were doomed to disappear. Let us just say the decline of the West would not be good for American morale.

Presumably it is this cultural interest that is called "ideal" as opposed to "material." Why things worth fighting for should be separated from what it takes to fight for them is beyond me. Would the capacity to use force not be affected by the strength (or lack of it) of the belief in self-worth that underlies the will to defend oneself?

Culture alone, considered as pure preference, is not enough without the means for its realization. As Carl Jung says, "The man who promises everything is sure to fulfill nothing, and everyone who promises too much is in danger of using evil means in order to carry out his promises, and is already on the road to perdition." Interests may become delusions if they're incapable of being realized in actions. America's cultural interest in Israel must be supportable. . . .

Israel As Anomaly

The interests I have discussed are self-interests for America. Having allies or even supporting similar cultures are interests the United States maintains because it believes they are good ones, not because they necessarily represent universal moral principles. That support of Israel is in America's interest does not ipso facto make it right.

Is it arguable that Israel has no moral right to survive? In America, to be sure, the question is always raised the other way around: as ex-Senator J. William Fulbright said, "It is in our interest for Israel to survive because we *wish* Israel to survive," suggesting that Israel's survival is morally right but materially wrong. Yet if the moral justification for Israel is so obvious, why is it so often challenged abroad? Why indeed?

If Israel truly is all that we know it to be—politically free, morally humane, an expression of the best in Western civilization—why does it have so many enemies? This apparent anomaly must be faced. Surface answers suggest themselves. Arabs regard Israelis as intruders and dispossessors, Europeans see them as an inconvenience in making arrangements with Arabs, for the sins of Europe during the holocaust have been transferred to the Middle East. The Soviet Union sees an opportunity to gain a foothold by exploiting enmity against a nation based on a different political system. African and Asian nations see Israel opposed to their "third world" compatriots. At a deeper level, however, we must all recognize that Israel is an anomaly in the world that has taken shape since the Second World War.

This incongruity has been well-expressed by a respected student of Middle Eastern affairs, Professor George Lenczowski, who observes that Israel is the only major exception to the "movement of liberation and anti-colonialism promoted on a world-wide basis by the United Nations and practiced by the major Western powers." Lenczowski says that Israel is a state established

> by immigrant alien colonists in the teeth of native opposition . . . Israel and its supporters in the United States have often argued that opposition to Jewish settlement in Palestine is artificially spurred by self-seeking Arab politicians and that the ordinary Arabs of Palestine stand to gain from Jewish immigration by being exposed to better agricultural techniques, greater employment opportunities, and improved health standards . . . These assertions might have been correct, and yet the world today has repudiated them, recognizing instead the right to independence as a higher value.

Loyal Friends

Israel is our friend. Friendship is often easier to feel, to sense, than it is to define or explain. Israel is a friend because we feel it shares with us the underlying premises of a free, democratic, pluralist society. It is a friend because we know it resists the forces of totalitarianism and autocracy and terrorism—our common enemies. It is a friend because we have felt its pain as it was compelled to fight over and over again for the basic right to exist as a free people. . . .

Even if there were no explicit quid pro quo benefits accruing to the United States from its friendship, it clearly would be in our nation's interest to be seen by the community of nations and by freedom-loving people everywhere as a nation that does indeed stand by this kind of friend, that it is prepared to back its words with appropriate action.

Hyman Bookbinder, *Through Different Eyes*, 1987.

It does no good to say that the United States and the Soviet Union have been far more expansionist in their time, or that Israel has paid for its land whereas others have simply seized what they wanted, or even that Arab Palestinians would have a state if Israel had not been attacked in 1948. True but irrelevant. If self-determination circa 1945 is the standard, Israel wasn't there and the Arabs (though not of course the Palestinians, whose sense of national identity was created by the conflict with Israel) were. The basic argument against Israel is not strategic or material but moral and cultural. Israel is attacked because it represents a different kind of culture—Western culture in a non-Western area of the world.

Whether anyone likes it or not, Israel is of, by and for the West. By deciding for development, Israel feels, smells, and looks like a Western country. Unlike Vietnam or Korea or Angola or Jamaica or wherever you want, Israel is not part of the periphery but contains the core of the West. For better or for worse, Israel is us.

Basic American Values

America's national interest in the security and prosperity of Israel rests on this: any moral argument which condemns Israel applies equally to America itself and any cultural argument against Israel applies to all of Western civilization. In Israel we Americans are brought face to face with our own origins. By acting as if there were no American national interest in Israel, the United States would simultaneously be rejecting its own religious, moral, political, and cultural identity. America has a national interest in Israel precisely because no other nation invokes at one and the same time so many basic American values. What's in it for us?— Our own purposes, values, self-worth, and any other reasons we Americans have for believing in ourselves. When we ask whether we have an interest in Israel we are really asking about ourselves.

This substitution of Israel for America—one promised land for another—may explain a phenomenon I have often observed: Show me someone who believes Israel is not worth defending and I will show you one who thinks America is unworthy.

"Americans are learning to turn their heads away from major crimes committed by Israel in America's name."

Americans Should Not Support Israel

James G. Abourezk

James G. Abourezk is a former US senator and founder and chairman of the American Arab Anti-Discrimination Committee. In the following viewpoint, he argues that Americans ignore Israel's repeated betrayals of American values, like equality, fairness, the democratic process, and human rights. He concludes that for Americans to support Israel uncritically, even when it violates individual human rights, is unwise.

As you read, consider the following questions:

1. According to Abourezk, what is the principal reason Americans ignore Israel's "crimes"?
2. According to the author, why would Zionist Jews align themselves with fundamentalist Christian groups?
3. What are some of the rationales for supporting Israel that the author believes are just rhetorical smokescreens?

Hyman Bookbinder and James G. Abourezk, *Through Different Eyes*. Bethesda, MD: Adler and Adler Publishers, 1987. Used with permission.

Americans are outraged when their own government is caught selling arms to Iran or to dictatorships in Latin America. It is reflected in speeches by members of the House of Representatives and the Senate, in editorials in major newspapers, and in heavy coverage of criticism of such sales by television network news programs. Yet Israel has been selling arms to dictatorships for years, and American arms to Iran, despite an official embargo on such shipments by the United States. Although President Reagan was caught red-handed doing the same in 1986, including sending arms to Iran through Israel, Reagan argued he did so to improve relations with "moderates" in Iran, and to free the American hostages held in Lebanon. We do not know, however, the extent of the monetary profit Israel made on its arms shipments to Iran. Israel's arms customers include Guatemala, Haiti, Honduras, Nicaragua while Somoza was in power, the Philippines under Marcos, and Pinochet's Chile. Arms sales by the United States to these same dictatorships produced loud complaints from some Americans, but those who complained the loudest about America's involvement are silent about Israel.

No Protests Against Israel

Similarly, Moscow received heavy criticism from American politicians when Russia invaded Afghanistan. There seemed no end to the denunciations, the sanctions, speeches, and editorials directed at the Soviet Union for its aggressive actions—and they continue to this day. But when Israel invaded Lebanon in 1982, violating every international standard of morality and legality, American politicians and American entertainers lined up to make speeches of approval in the U.S. and they traveled to Lebanon—behind Israeli lines, of course—singing the praises of the invasion. These were no mere conservatives with long histories of interventionist machismo. They were represented by the likes of Tom Hayden, Jane Fonda, Senator Alan Cranston, Senator Christopher Dodd, and many more such folks who, not long ago were waving a different flag—against wars and aggression and bullies. The power of money flowing from the Israeli lobby to American politicians comes into sharp focus when we learn that they find it easier to criticize a president of the United States than a prime minister of Israel.

And, of course, none of these defenders of human rights would brook a country torturing prisoners. But we hear no speeches on human rights on the Senate floor when Israel is exposed as a major torturer of Palestinians and Lebanese. There are no amendments offered to cut off aid to Israel because of its inhumane practices. . . .

Americans are learning to turn their heads away from major crimes committed by Israel in America's name, principally because

135

very few opinion leaders in the United States have the moral or intellectual courage to protest what is happening. If Americans are in danger of giving up the high moral ground because of permissiveness vis a vis Israel, American Jews who actively support U.S. policies toward the Middle East have even more to lose.

Less than a generation ago, American Jews were in a position of absolute leadership in the struggle for civil rights throughout America, were against the unreasonable build-up of arms, and helped to lead the fight against the strong and powerful taking unfair advantage of the vulnerable and weak.

A Major Question

"How long will the United States government and Congress go on blindly supporting Israel at the heavy expense of the American taxpayer when Israel's policies and actions sometimes ignore and damage America's vital interests and those of its friends and allies?"

Douglas MacArthur II, *The Christian Science Monitor*, March 16, 1987.

Since the creation of Israel on land where the Palestinians once lived, a fiction has been created by Jews to justify the horrendous wrongs committed against Arabs, beginning before 1948 and continuing to this day.

The Arabs left voluntarily, they repeat over and over, as though this lie has made it all right to take over their homes, their crops, and their land.

The Arabs are all terrorists, we are told, again and again, by those who hope that Israel's own terrorism either will be overlooked or rationalized as self-defense.

Israel must sell arms to dictators, and it must do business with South Africa, because, its apologists say, it has very few allies in the world.

American Jews Become Polarized

Occasionally it all becomes too much for some American Jews who grew up with different values, values that demand humanity and concern, and who can no longer close their eyes, or turn their heads while Israel cynically violates every tenet known to the liberal spirit. But each time Jews try to gather in protest of the killing, of torture, of land grabbing, they are cut down—politically and financially—by self-described leaders of the Jewish community—those who brook no dissent from the line laid down by Israel and followed by its professional apologists in America— those whom writer Earl Shorris would define as "Jews without mercy," as Shorris has titled one of his books. A group called Breira once existed as an alternative to the increasing militancy of or-

136

ganized Jewry, but faded into obscurity when its contributors learned of its mild opposition to some of Israel's more egregious crimes. The New Jewish Agenda has since attempted to offer the same kind of alternatives, as has a new Jewish journal called *Tikkun*. The efforts to exert peer pressure on these dissenters are enormous, the result of which is to ensure that other dissenters think long and hard before breaking ranks.

Most rank and file Jews in America have a strong feeling for the concept of a Jewish state, often offering blind unquestioning support. A class of American Jews has come into view who have learned that the route to political and financial power in America lies in using broad Jewish support for Israel as a club to enhance their own power. It includes Jews who have made a profession of championing the arms build-up by the United States, who provide needed public support for the incursions of a warlike Ronald Reagan in Grenada, Nicaragua, and Angola. . . .

Ignoring Racism

As an idea to create a haven for Jews trying to escape historic racism directed against them by host countries, establishing a Jewish state seemed to offer the answer. The problems arose when the Zionist movement chose a land already inhabited by people who desired their own independent state. Because of this, the effort to find justice for Jews has created great injustice for Palestinians, as well as others around them. The concept of Israel—a settler state forcibly implanted in the midst of a group of Third World nations—has created many more problems than it has solved.

In their zeal to do Israel's bidding, American Jewish leaders, instead of standing firm against it, have chosen to look the other way even in cases of racism against Jews in the United States. Clearly, caving in on such an important principle has more to do with protecting Israel than with protecting Jews, as several examples have shown. Jesse Jackson, always suspect in the eyes of Zionist leaders, was hammered unmercifully for labeling New York "Hymietown." But it was different when Republican Congressman Robert Dornan took to the floor of the U.S. House of Representatives to attack a Soviet spokesman, Vladimir Posner, as a "disloyal, betraying little Jew who sits there on television claiming that he is somehow or other a newsman. It's an affront to decency and dignity and to Jewish people all around the world." Jews who saw Dornan's outburst on television told me his tone and manner were "frighteningly anti-Semitic." Labeled by the *Washington Post* as a long-time critic of the Soviet Union and an ardent supporter of Israel, Dornan told a reporter that a pro-Israeli group had called him and said he had no reason to apologize for his remarks. Because of his support for Israel, he was publicly forgiven by two of his pro-Israeli, Jewish House colleagues, Representative Steven Solarz of New York and Representative Tom Lantos of California. Lantos joined Dornan at a press conference called to soften the anger of American Jews around the United States who had seen him making the statement on television. Lantos said Dornan had "made a slip of the tongue. We all do." Solarz sent a statement to the press conference in which he said, "A misspoken phrase in a moment of heated debate should not be allowed to overshadow Bob's long history of support and involvement with Israel, Soviet Jewry and other Jewish causes."

The view of some who were concerned with anti-Jewish racism was not as forgiving as Lantos, Solarz, and the unnamed pro-Israeli group. One letter writer in the March 5, 1986 *Washington Post* called Dornan's remarks a racial slur worthy of Joseph Stalin, and went on to say, "Hypocritical apologetics aside, Representative Dornan's behavior was itself an 'affront to the decency and dignity of Jewish people around the world.' We will not be used to advance the political agenda of anyone, including congressmen." . . .

A Distinctly Disturbing Pattern

A catalogue of alliances built up by Zionist leaders has created a distinct pattern, extremely disturbing in its result. Zionist leaders will befriend anti-Jewish racists so long as they support Israel.

Bob Englehart. Reprinted with permission.

Israel will support South Africa because South Africa supports Israel, despite South Africa's crimes against humanity. Israel will sell arms to Iran to prolong its bloody war with Iraq because Iraq is an Arab enemy. Where are the human values in this policy? Where is the symbiosis with the liberality of American Jews, or non-Jews for that matter? Why are Israel's objectives (rather than Israel's survival) more important than the safety of individual Jews? Again, where is the United States' interest?

American politicians, because of the enormous amount of money poured into their campaigns by Jewish contributors, long ago decided to give Israel its free ride, not only in terms of excessive American aid money, but in terms of political and diplomatic protection when Israel's victims seek formal censure of Israel for its violations of international law.

I know U.S. senators who, just prior to attending fund raisers for their campaigns in New York or Los Angeles, have made either anti-Arab, or pro-Zionist speeches on the Senate floor, making certain to have them reproduced from the *Congressional Record* for distribution to Jewish contributors. . . .

In 1985, the campaign manager of a congressman who was preparing to run for the Senate called to ask if I thought American Arabs could raise more money for his candidate's senate campaign than American Jews. My answer was no, that Jews obviously could raise much more. Not more than two weeks later I saw in the *Congressional Record* a speech inserted by the congressman that clearly marked the beginning of his fund-raising effort. For the first time in his career he made a speech on the House floor calling for increased emigration for Jews from the Soviet Union.

Smokescreen Rhetoric

All that seems harmless, except when it comes to the divergence of American and Israeli interests, a condition that occurs more frequently than anyone likes to admit. Senators and congressmen cannot, of course, admit publicly that the U.S. credit card that they've handed Israel is a direct result of the money Israel's supporters pour into their campaigns. A credible, public reason is necessary to explain such blind, unquestioning support. As a consequence, their rationale comes in a great many other forms, many of them most ingenious.

"Israel is the only democracy in the Middle East." The Palestinians in the West Bank should be asked about this.

"Israel is the only bastion of support against Soviet aggression in the Middle East." However, in the unlikely event that the Soviets moved troops beyond the buffer states on their borders, and into an Arab oil country, it is even more unlikely that Israel would sacrifice even one soldier to challenge it, or that it would be able to make a difference if it did.

"Israel is America's strategic ally." After years of using this excuse, of taking money, of keeping America in hot water with allies in the Arab world, Israel finally had a chance to prove its value as a strategic ally during the hijacking of TWA Flight 847 in the summer of 1985. Those holding the American passengers hostage were demanding the release of the Lebanese hostages held by Israel in Israeli prisons. Defense Minister Yitzhak Rabin, when asked by a journalist if Israel intended to do so, flatly stated that the hijacking was America's problem, and not Israel's. Israel eventually agreed to release the Lebanese hostages they were holding, but not until the American hostages and their families, and, in fact, the entire country was held in anguish. So much for Israel's value as a strategic ally.

American Naiveté

After years of stumbling around trying to find some credible public reason why we continue to pour billions of taxpayers' dollars into Israel, their apologists have finally settled on citing Israel's intelligence value to the United States. It is a good choice, since one can neither document nor disprove the claim. It's classified, you see.

Several books have been written about the Mossad, most of them creating a mystique of infallibility, raising the suspicion that they must have been written by Mossad publicists, particularly after the assessment delivered by former C.I.A. Director, Admiral Stansfield Turner, who said, unequivocally, that the Mossad's best work was in promoting its own image. (One wonders, however, if Israel's intelligence is so good, why was it necessary to turn Jonathan Pollard into a traitor to his own country, paying him to steal information which Israel boasts about giving to us in the first place.)

When Abba Eban was foreign minister of Israel, his song to American audiences was give Israel weapons and money and it will hold off the Soviet Union for you. It is an amazing claim, but one that found an audience in American politicians eager to please the Israeli lobby.

But after all the lame excuses are given, one fact remains unchanged: Israel pursues its own interests whether or not they are damaging to the United States. It is naive in the extreme to think otherwise.

Distinguishing Bias from Reason

When dealing with controversial subjects, many people allow their feelings to dominate their powers of reason. Thus, one of the most important critical thinking skills is the ability to distinguish between statements based upon emotion and those based upon a rational consideration of the facts.

The following statements are taken from the viewpoints in this chapter. Consider each statement carefully. *Mark R for any statement you believe is based on reason or a rational consideration of the facts. Mark B for any statement you believe is based on bias, prejudice, or emotion. Mark I for any statement you think is impossible to judge.*

If you are doing this activity as a member of a class or group, compare your answers with those of other class or group members. Be able to explain your answers. You may discover that others come to different conclusions than you do. Listening to the rationale others present for their answers may give you valuable insights in distinguishing between bias and reason.

> R = *a statement based upon reason*
> B = *a statement based upon bias*
> I = *a statement impossible to judge*

1. AIPAC, a super-powerful lobby, has managed to fool, bribe, blackmail, and intimidate public officials and legislators into slavish acceptance of a pro-Israel policy for America.

2. The US should subsidize its allies because they help defend America's vital interests.

3. Having allies or even supporting similar cultures are interests the United States maintains because it believes they are good ones, not because they necessarily represent universal moral principles.

4. Jews constitute only 2.6 percent of the US population. The American Jewish community knows it cannot impose or dictate public policy on the basis of its own numbers.

5. The power of the pro-Israel lobby over Congress has become a stranglehold.

6. The effort to find justice for Jews has created great injustice for Palestinians, and almost everyone else too.

7. The Arab threat to Israel is real. Arab states attacked Israel when it was created in 1948, and again in 1967 and 1973.

8. In presidential elections, pro-Israeli groups exercise their power through financial contributions and high voter turnout in the primaries.

9. Israel is a hopeless basket case—an endless sponge off the American taxpayer.

10. The Democratic Party is strongly influenced by the Jewish vote. In late 1983, the *Christian Science Monitor* reported that approximately 50 percent of all Democratic funds come from the Jewish community.

11. Very few leaders of public opinion in America have the moral or intellectual courage to protest Israel's atrocities.

12. Zionist leaders will defend anti-Jewish racists as long as they support Israel.

13. America and Israel are based on the same cultural values. For that reason, any argument condemning Israel also condemns the US.

Periodical Bibliography

The following articles have been selected to supplement the diverse views presented in this chapter.

George T. Abed	"Israel in the Orbit of America," *Journal of Palestine Studies*, Autumn 1986.
Moshe Arens	"Israel Deserves Better Advice from Its Friends," *The New York Times*, March 9, 1988.
Kathleen Christison	"Blind Spots: Official US Myths About the Middle East," *Journal of Palestine Studies*, Winter 1988.
Commentary	"Symposium: American Jews and Israel," February 1988.
Robert I. Friedman	"Selling Israel to America," *Mother Jones*, February/March 1987.
Robert W. Gibson	"Israel: An Economic Ward of the US," *Los Angeles Times*, July 20, 1987.
Jeane Kirkpatrick	"Denouncement of Israeli Policies Perplexing," *Conservative Chronicle*, January 20, 1988. Available from Box 29, Hampton, IA 50441.
Lewis H. Lapham	"Notebook: The Road to Shaaraim," *Harper's Magazine*, June 1988.
The Nation	"Time to Dissociate from Israel," February 13, 1988.
William Safire	"Israel in Trouble," *The New York Times*, September 9, 1987.
Ariel Sharon	"To America from an Israeli Friend," *The Wall Street Journal*, February 24, 1988.
Milton Viorst	"Ending the 20-Year War," *Newsweek*, June 15, 1987.
James M. Wall	"Israel Is Losing the Living Room War," *The Christian Century*, January 27, 1988.
J. Weisberg	"The Lobby with a Lock on Congress," *Newsweek*, October 19, 1987.
Moshe Zak	"Israel and the US: Forty Years of Manna in the Wilderness," *The World & I*, May 1988.

4 CHAPTER

What Is Israel's International Role?

Chapter Preface

Israel has an ambiguous role in the global community. Some nations perceive Israel as a constructive member of this community. It has given technical and advisory assistance to developing nations of the Third World and is seen by some to be the embodiment of democratic and egalitarian ideals.

Other nations, however, regard Israel as a disruptive force. They see it as a nation that supports racist and colonialist regimes in order to sell arms and foster political support for itself. They also argue that Israel disregards the directives and principles of the United Nations.

The viewpoints in this chapter debate the accuracy of these perspectives.

"Israel's cooperation with the Third World still continues and is perhaps greater than before."

Israel Aids the Third World

Dan V. Segre

Dan V. Segre is an author and professor of political science at Haifa University in Israel. In the following viewpoint, he argues that it is Israel's policy to cooperate with the developing nations of the Third World. Segre contends that Israeli technical training and assistance is freely given to any developing nation that requests it.

As you read, consider the following questions:

1. In Segre's view, what events in the history of Israel's relationship with other developing nations demonstrate the spirit of cooperation between them?
2. What reasons does the author give for the cooperation between Israel and the Third World?
3. In the author's opinion, what Israeli resource is most responsible for building Israel's friendly relations with Third World countries?

Dan V. Segre, "Israel and the Third World." Published by permission of Transaction Publishers from *The Middle East Reader*, edited by Michael Curtis. Copyright © 1986 by Transaction Publishers.

Israel's relations with the Third World are today the subject of controversy. To some they constitute a very successful example of international cooperation. To many others they serve as an example of neo-colonialism and imperialism. The distinction between these two approaches is obviously a personal one, and it would be very difficult to reach any sort of agreement on them if one took the short-term view of the problem. It is a fact that Israel does not operate in the Third World for charitable reasons; it operates for political reasons, like any other state. It is also a fact that Israel tries to foster, in these countries, its own national interests. Since these interests are linked with the profound, deep-seated and prolonged crisis with which the Afro-Asian countries are involved, it is inevitable that, if we take the short-term view of the problem, the Middle East conflict will reverberate on the whole effort of Israeli-Third World cooperation.

To extract the substance, however, of this cooperation, one must take a long-range view, and ask what will remain, what will be said of this effort of international cooperation of a small, developing state with other small—and not so small—developing states, twenty, thirty or forty years hence.

I think that what will remain will be an acknowledgement by Israel of the evolution of a number of comprehensive techniques of development, which I would define under the general term of micro-cooperation, as opposed to other techniques of development practiced mainly by the great powers, which are usually termed *macro-cooperation*.

Two Kinds of Cooperation

The distinction between micro-cooperation and macro-cooperation is not only in size—although that is, of course, very important—but also in strategy of development. Macro-cooperation tends to change the environment, in the hope that people will eventually adapt to a new environmental condition and therefore modernize their habits. Micro-cooperation, on the other hand, concentrates its efforts on the attempt to change people's habits, in the hope that eventually, because of this change, they will be more open to accept innovation. There is also another difference. In practice macro-cooperation is an activity which tends to groom "Generals" of development. Micro-cooperation—the type of cooperation which Israel has been developing over the last ten or fifteen years—is, on the contrary, mainly concerned with the training of the "Non-Commissioned Officer" of development.

It is in this perspective that I would like to retrace the history of Israeli cooperation with the Third World, the reasons which have brought it about, the conceptual structures behind it, and some of its major—as I view them—failures and successes.

This history begins with the Bandung Conference of 1955 to

which Israel was initially invited, only to have the invitation revoked. The Conference decided (on behalf of two and a quarter billion people belonging to the Afro-Asian family) that the people of Israel (at that time numbering 2.2 million) not only did not belong to the Afro-Asian nations but were, in fact, the spearhead of all the evils besetting the Afro-Asian countries—racialism, colonialism, imperialism, etc.

The shock of this resolution was deeply felt in Israel and was, in all probability, the beginning of the new Israeli appraisal. Then came the Suez war of 1956, which opened the Gulf of Aqaba to Israeli navigation and thereby created new opportunities for contact and trade in the Red Sea, East Africa and the Indian Ocean. Starting from 1959, new states in Africa obtained their independence and consequently Israel became interested in establishing immediate relations with them. The period from 1961 to 1966 marked the peak of this cooperation between Israel and mainly African, but also several Asian, states—relations which developed in the field of agriculture, military cooperation, in much diplomatic contact and in joint deliberations (mainly at the U.N.). There was even, for a moment, some talk of an "Israeli-African Bloc for Peace" at the U.N. General Assembly of 1961 and 1962. The proposals which this bloc put forward with a view to fostering direct talks between Arabs and Israelis, were not accepted, but they indicated the closeness of the cooperation. And of course there was recognition of Jerusalem as the capital of Israel by the majority of those African states which had sent their presidents to visit Jerusalem.

Sharing Development Experience

Israel is one of the many states that have become independent in our time, in the historic process of decolonization. With most of the other developing states, Israel has had not only friendly diplomatic ties but close cooperation in every field of progress. They have seen in Israel a pilot plant for themselves: a new state that was too small to arouse any fear of domination, yet possessed the skills, training and experience in nation-building that they lacked; Israel, for its part, felt a sense of Zionist mission in helping other developing countries.

Michael Comay, *Zionism, Israel, and the Palestinian Arabs*, 1983.

Then came the war of 1967, which registered as a great traumatic experience in the relations between Israel and the Afro-Asian states as a whole, but mainly with Africa. This was because Israel found herself victorious over an Arab-African state—Egypt, and because this war seemed, to the Africans, to have encroached on one of the fundamental principles of the Charter of African Unity—that no border should be changed by force.

It is probably one of the proofs of the solidity of the relations between Israel and the Afro-Asian countries that only one African country (Guinea) broke off relations with Israel at the time, and that it took 5 years of direct Arab pressure and large Libyan financial grants to persuade two others—Uganda and Chad—to follow suit. In fact, Israel's cooperation with the Third World still continues and is perhaps greater than before, although with a change in focus developing today toward the Latin American states.

In 1971 there was intense political activity on the part of the African states, who sent a delegation of four presidents to Cairo and Jerusalem that December to try to find a compromise formula that would, somehow, reactivate the Gunnar Jarring U.N. mission. It was not very successful. Then came the crisis of 1972, between Israel and Uganda, which has had a traumatic effect and will, I think, still have much influence and impact on the future of Israeli-African relations.

Reasons for Cooperation

What are the reasons for the intense activity of cooperation reflected by some 17,000 Afro-Asian trainees in Israel, and some 2,500 Israeli experts in these countries? On the Israeli side, as we have mentioned, there are diplomatic reasons—the necessity of being present on the spot; collaboration with African countries at the U.N.; there are economic interests—promoting the import of some very important raw materials, promoting exports and investment. (The whole of the Israeli diamond industry, for example, which is Israel's major export, depended at a certain moment upon supplies of diamonds from Africa.) There was certainly also a deep psychological urge to break out of that claustrophobia, that feeling of being besieged, that Israelis had been suffering from, and to go to a world which was free of prejudices about the Israeli-Arab conflict. To all these reasons I would add one minor, but at the time relevant, fact: some of Israel's new immigrants, mainly those coming from French-speaking North African states, were young intellectuals, available for service, who found themselves during 1964-65 in difficulties with regard to their own internal assimilation in Israel. The fact that they could go out as experts to the French-speaking, former colonies of France in Africa was a kind of creation of a new Negev for them in Africa, beyond the frontiers of Israel. All these things were important.

From the point of view of the recipients, I would point out, firstly, that most of these states viewed Israel as a small state which provided aid based on its own experience of development, which was very congenial for geographical and historical, as well as ideological reasons; Israel was not an impressive power—there were no strings attached to its aid; there was also a strong religious attraction for a country which has Jerusalem as its capital. The major political reason for this interest, however, was that Israel could, it was felt, be used as a lever by those Afro-Asian states who could not turn to the communist bloc in order to pressure the western bloc. These states could use Israel as a lever, that is, to obtain concessions from the old metropolitan countries.

The Conceptual Structure of Cooperation

Israel's aid to the developing countries has undergone many changes. There was, at first, the intense and sentimental need to help others; there was a sense of mission which has not died out even today; there was the idea that Africans and Jews had something in common (slavery and Auschwitz); there was the idea that Israel could, perhaps, produce a new type of technique that would suit developing countries.

Israel and International Cooperation

Israel's technical assistance programmes in Africa, Asia, Latin America and the non-Arab Near East have written a remarkable chapter in the annals of international cooperation. Starting with Burma in 1953, and Ghana in 1957, a network of projects and courses spread to over eighty countries. About 600 Israel experts a year were working abroad, mostly in direct bilateral programmes, but also through United Nations agencies. Some 1,300 students and trainees from these countries attended courses in Israel each year, and another thousand or more graduated from courses run in the developing states by teams of Israel instructors.

There is no inherent or genuine conflict of ideology or interest between Israel and the developing world.

Michael Comay, *Zionism, Israel, and the Palestinian Arabs*, 1983.

All the factors were important to begin with, but they did not cut very deep into the problems of cooperation. In this field, one of the ideas which Israel really brought forward—and this, I think, is still operative—is that poverty is not only a matter of economics: it is above all a matter of social structures, of adequate bureaucracies, of dedicated elites. Efforts, therefore, must be made on a comprehensive scale to combat poverty, and not in single packages, only in one direction or the other.

The second idea on which Israeli cooperation founded its strategy was that development—the process of catching up—must create hope. Hope can be instilled through ideology and through example. Israel could export some ideological jargon of a socialist

150

type, but not a revolutionary ideology. It did, however, have a large reserve of people who could set an example in the field of cooperation, a real "army" of trained carriers of know-how, of innovation, who could help to stimulate imitations and activate the potential skills of the local traditional elites, who would, in turn, influence their own societies. This idea, that one can find ways and means of "manipulating" the traditional elites through an appropriate carrier of an innovation, had been tested in Israel over a long period. It was embodied in the person of the *madrich* (lit. "guide"). The *madrich* is a young (or sometimes not so young) man (or woman) who takes charge mainly of young people. These may be immigrants from Aliyat HaNoar (Youth Immigration) who have come to Israel in the main as orphans and who were helped, prior to the creation of the State of Israel and immediately thereafter, to become integrated into Israeli society. The *madrich*, thus, has had to be a leader, teacher, father and—what is more important— he has had to adapt himself to the changing condition both of his charges and of their environment.

At a later stage, the *madrich* turned into the technical instructor of the new immigrant. In the development towns and villages he became, of necessity, much more than an instructor: he had to set a personal example if he wanted his instruction to be followed in, for example, the fields of agriculture, cooperative work or artisanship.

Practical Development Schemes

The *madrich* as a "commodity" was produced in Israel in considerable quantities. But just because he seemed to be so linked with the very special social and historical situation of the Jewish return to their homeland, no one dreamt that he could be used beyond the borders of the Israeli environment. It was only when Israel began going out to the new countries of Africa and looking for the right men to send there, that it realized the value of *madrichim* for technical cooperation and made them one of its resources in the field of assistance to development.

Furthermore, it was through the work of the *madrichim* that Israel was able to work out practical development schemes which tended to activate the traditional elites for the purpose of legitimating the acceptance of an innovation. Let me give an example drawn from personal experience. In Madagascar, the social structure of the indigenous society is based on the belief that dead ancestors take an active part in the existence of the living. If, therefore, one wants to introduce some change into village life—for instance, to start a weaving cooperative—one must have the agreement not only of the inhabitants, but also of their dead ancestors, through the latter's appointed "speakers" in the village. Otherwise one will achieve no practical results, or—as in my own case—see the new income realized from cooperative work being spent on improving the tombs of the dead rather than the conditions of the living.

So much for the main conceptual structures behind Israel's international cooperation. Let us now turn very briefly to some of the results.

Evaluating Israel's Activities

Israel's major success, and the reason for her outstanding position in Africa and Latin America (where she is indeed considered a major factor in the field of aid) is that she has never had the financial resources to spend on large projects. Whenever she did have funds for large projects, the results were usually poor—as is generally the case elsewhere. Israel's greatest opportunity, therefore, and major source of success, was the poverty of her material resources and the richness of her human resources. Yet this was also sometimes a source of failure.

Just because some of these carriers of innovation were so successful on occasion, they engaged their government in activities which went beyond the original goals. This was the case in Uganda, where the success of the Israeli military experts on the spot drew Israel into political involvements quite beyond the limits of her original political objectives. After years of intense cooperation, when General Idi Amin's extravagant requests for military aid had to be rejected, the African disappointment was as great as its hopes had been. Helped by Arab money and propaganda, and aware of a very delicate local political situation, the Ugandan government found it convenient to turn its irritation into violent hostility which forced all Israelis out of the country. For the Israelis this was a deep, but to some extent a salutary shock.

What will remain of the Israeli effort? Some people think it will all boil down to a few diplomatic gimmicks. I think that eventually there will be something more. This experience has lasted almost 15 years already, it continues to grow and is unlikely to stop for some time to come. I cannot forsee whether this effort will eventually be seen as an original breakthrough in the field of cooperation, but it will certainly be remembered as one of the most successful efforts so far made in this field. More than any other country Israel has proved the validity of the old Chinese proverb which says that if you give a man a fish to eat, you will satisfy his appetite for one day. If you teach him how to fish, you will satisfy his appetite for much longer.

"Slowly but surely, the Israeli . . . becomes as diabolical a symbol as the Yankee in the eyes of the oppressed and tortured populaces of the teeming Third World."

Israel Harms the Third World

Benjamin Beit-Hallahmi

Benjamin Beit-Hallahmi is an Israeli clinical psychologist, author, and professor at Haifa University in Israel. In the following viewpoint, he argues that Israel has aligned itself with reactionary governments in the Third World. He concludes that Israel is attempting to halt decolonization and liberation of Third World peoples to protect its own colonialist position.

As you read, consider the following questions:

1. According to Beit-Hallahmi, why did Israel lose its originally favorable position with Third World countries?
2. What does the author see as Israel's basic stance toward the world?
3. What is unique about Israel's enterprise in the Third World, according to Beit-Hallahmi?

From *The Israeli Connection: Who Israel Arms and Why* by Benjamin Beit-Hallahmi. Copyright © 1987 by Benjamin Beit-Hallahmi. Reprinted by permission of Pantheon Books, a division of Random House Inc.

The aim of Israel's foreign policy since its founding has been to achieve legitimacy as a "normal" state, despite its abnormal history, through diplomatic contacts and recognition, and to deprive the Palestinians of similar legitimacy. For the first few years, this policy was a success. On the day of Israel's founding in 1948, the two superpowers vied for the privilege of being the first to accord it diplomatic recognition, and in its first year it won recognition from fifty-three states. In 1959, Israel was represented in fifty-five countries, and in early 1967, seventy-eight. But this base of legitimacy has been eroding with the progress of decolonization and the rise of the Third World, largely in reaction to the 1967 and 1973 wars.

The Third World is a world of struggle, misery, and suffering, the part not included in the First World (the industrialized West and Japan) or the Second World (the Soviet bloc). [According to R.J. Barnet,] "It is roughly equivalent to what used to be called the underdeveloped world, or in official U.S. parlance 'LDC' (Less Developed Countries)." [C. Clapham notes,] "The 'third world' is one result of the process by which, since the late fifteenth century, the previously scattered peoples of the globe have been brought together into what is in many respects a single society, economy and political system. By far the major part of this process has taken place over the last century, while its political aspects . . . are the product of the emergence of third world states which, except in Latin America, have mostly become independent since the Second World War." The Third World is separate from, and subordinate to, "the dominant industrial economies which have developed especially in Europe and North America. . . . They have entered the world economy especially through the supply of primary products such as minerals and cash crops to the industrial economies, and for the most part continue to be primary export producers."

The Third World today consists of about 120 countries. Most of its nations export raw materials at low prices, and pay for processed and manufactured goods, made of the same raw materials. Attempts to change this economic reality are the source of conflicts with the First World. . . .

Israel and the Rise of the Third World

The Asian-African Conference at Bandung, Indonesia, in April 1955 was the first step in the emergence of the Third World coalition. The participants represented twenty-nine countries, divided into four regions: the Arab world, Southeast Asia, South Asia, and black Africa. The nine Arab countries were the largest group. There were only three African countries: Liberia, Ethiopia, and not-yet-independent Ghana. The participants were deeply divided in their ideologies and alliances, from Japan to North Vietnam and

154

China, from Ethiopia and the Philippines to Egypt. Israel, South Africa, South Korea, and Taiwan were not invited. Israeli leaders expressed disappointment and surprise at their exclusion. These professions of surprise might have reflected ignorance or naiveté, but the Bandung Conference made it clear that the emerging coalition was likly to be less than friendly toward Israel.

For many of the Third World nations gaining their independence in the 1950s and the 1960s, the history of the Arab-Israeli conflict was almost unknown, and the setting quite distant. When the details of the conflict did become known, not too surprisingly, attitudes tended to favor the Arab bloc, as a Third World partner in the same struggle against the West. In the various meetings of the Third World coalition after 1955, the Arab-Israeli conflict was often mentioned, but it was only after 1967 that the rights of the Palestinians became a permanent part of the agenda.

Palestine has become a symbolic issue for the whole Third World, matched only by the issue of apartheid in the intensity and frequency with which it has been raised. [According to B. Rivlin and J. Fomerand,] "The anticolonialist/antiimperialist ideological lens directed the Third World toward a pro-Palestinian Arab and anti-Israel position. This was reinforced by the largely Western bourgeois style of life that developed in Israel, by the treatment of the Arab minority, and by the collusion with Great Britain and France, the arch-imperialists, in the 1956 Suez operation. Since 1967, Israel's heavy reliance upon the United States for military and economic aid eventually sharpened the negative image of Israel among Third World states."

Birds of a Feather

What is Israel's role in Central America, and why have the nations there sought arms and military advisors from Israel? . . .

A factor is the self-perception of some Central American regimes as internationally isolated and politically undervalued, trapped in a political state of siege, usually on the basis of their atrocious records of human rights abuses. They presume, in other words, a political affinity with Israel as a fellow "pariah state."

Milton Jamail & Margo Guttierrez, *Middle East Report*, May-June 1986.

Indeed, the Third World's view of Palestine is diametrically opposed to Zionism. It sees the Palestinians as the victims of colonialism, and the Israelis as guilty of colonialist dispossession. Palestine has become a symbol of one more colonialist account to be settled with the West. The Third World coalition is divided on many political issues, and it is far from the automatic, anti-Western voting bloc mentioned so often in the U.S. media. Thus, for example, the Third World is evenly divided on Kampuchea and East Timor, and it overwhelmingly opposes the Soviet Union on the Afghanistan issue. Nevertheless, there is a complete unity on the two remaining colonial issues, namely South Africa and Israel-Palestine. South Africa and Israel have come to play a special symbolic role for the whole Third World. They are regarded as the two last bastions of colonialism. Even right-wing countries that have close relations with Israel, such as Zaire and Honduras, are pro-Palestinian; their leaders do not hesitate to voice support for the Palestinian cause and for the idea of a Palestinian state during official visits to Israel. When Edgardo Paz Bárnica, the Honduran Minister of Foreign Affairs, visited Israel in August 1985, he openly expressed his support for an independent Palestinian state.

A Bad Reputation Develops

A worldwide consensus against Zionism has been developing since the late 1960s, reaching its clearest expressions in repeated condemnations of Zionism by the United Nations in the next decade. Israel's growing isolation has reflected the Arab countries' growing diplomatic power. In the 1950s, the Arabs were militarily weak, but gathered both Soviet and Third World support. After 1967, the diplomatic front changed quickly, with the Arab camp winning more sympathy in the Organization of African Unity (OAU), at the United Nations, and in the nonaligned movement. In the late 1960s, the Palestinians penetrated Third World consciousness, and started forming relations with Third World radical movements.

The military shock of the 1973 war was accompanied by political setbacks. It was during the war and immediately afterwards that many African countries broke off diplomatic relations. In November 1973, the OAU Ministerial Council denounced Israel for its "expansionist designs." During the war, all European countries except Portugal refused to allow the use of their airports and airspace for the U.S. resupply shipments to Israel. On November 6, 1973, the European Economic Community issued a communiqué that called on Israel to end the occupation of 1967, and to recognize the legitimate rights of the Palestinians. The years 1973-1975 saw growing isolation and repeated failures, and the experience of those years has become a nightmare that Israeli leaders vowed not to relive.

The process of decolonization also created a Third World majority at the United Nations, which until the 1960s was very much a European club. The U.N. General Assembly voted in the fall of 1974 to suspend South Africa's participation in the General Assembly (the vote was 98-23-14) and to allow the PLO to present its views before the same body (the vote was 105-4-20). Before 1967 the Palestinians were largely absent from world consciousness, and just after 1967 references to them were mostly negative (terrorists, spoilers of Western designs), but after 1973 positive references started to appear even in the West. By the mid-1980s, the Palestinian people and the PLO have gained such wide recognition that Israeli leaders have increasingly felt the panic of growing desertion and isolation.

UN Censure

The historical change in United Nations membership, from 51 states, mostly European, at the first General Assembly, to 159 nations forty years later, was accompanied by a decline in Israel's fortunes. The voting tallies over the past thirty years clearly demonstrate that decolonization is a threat to Israel—it means more and more opponents and less and less diplomatic support. The Partition Resolution of November 29, 1947, which called for dividing Palestine between an Arab state and a Jewish state, could not have passed in the General Assembly in 1985—or any time after the late 1960s, for that matter. The Third World victory at the United Nations was symbolized by the recognition of the Palestine Liberation Organization in 1974, and in the condemnation of Zionism in 1975.

Profit Over Principle

While Jewish prisoners held without charge in Argentine jails were being forced to kneel before pictures of Hitler and tortured to accompanying chants of "Jew! Jew!", Argentina was receiving a series of high-ranking Israeli military officers on "friendly visits" to sell arms. Considering that the Argentine junta's anti-Semitic activities were well-known, having been documented by the U.S. Congress, the Catholic Church, and especially by the local branch of the American Jewish Committee, it is impossible that Israel was "not aware of the situation."

It couldn't have been unaware either, of the repressive records of other governments in the market for military electronics and on up to fighter planes. Israel's selling of arms to South Africa and Nicaragua in the 1970s was from the same passion for profit over principle that led to sales to China and Khomeini's Iran in the 1980s.

Colman McCarthy, *Manchester Guardian Weekly*, May 29, 1988.

The General Assembly resolution of 1975 equating Zionism with racism was the result of the emerging Third World consensus. While the First World steadfastly considers Zionism a legitimate political ideology, the Third World regards it as a form of colonialism to be relegated to the same class as apartheid. . . .

157

Currently, only 75 countries have diplomatic relations with Israel, as compared to 115 that recognize the PLO. In 1966, the number of countries recognizing Israel was about 110. In an attempt to overcome this isolation, which is clearly in evidence at the United Nations and other international organizations, Israel is always on the lookout for allies, and cannot afford to be choosy. Every nation tries to broaden its base of political support and is ready to enter alliances without regard to seeming ideological and historical constraints. This is true of the Soviet Union, which had close relations with the right-wing generals of Argentina between 1976 and 1983, and of the United States, which has supported Pol Pot of Kampuchea after denouncing him as a mass murderer. Israel's effort to overcome growing isolation by forming as many contacts as possible is not unique. . . .

A Conservative Stance

Since Israel has been unable, [as Aaron Klieman writes] "to reverse [its] decline internationally through statecraft," its leaders have become ready to ask for very little overt recognition in return for their aid to foreign governments, especially military aid. Beggars can't be choosers, and in the arena of international relations, Israel—together with Taiwan, South Africa, and Paraguay—is indeed a beggar.

To understand the Israeli leadership and its perplexing decisions, we have to enter its world, share its perceptions and fears. We need not only sympathy, but empathy. The basic Israeli stance toward the world is a conservative one. After 1948, Israel was interested in conserving its achievements, as it was after 1967. After 1973, Israel was interested in conserving the world order, to prevent her precarious position from becoming untenable. A red thread leads from the 1954 Cairo affair, an attempt to stop decolonization in Egypt, to current events in Central America. Stopping decolonization is the only way Israel sees to ensure survival, and in the 1980s it has to be stopped on a global scale: every national liberation movement is a danger and an enemy.

Israel's survival strategy has achieved survival, but not acceptance by either the Arab world or the rest of the Third World. The Israeli involvement in the war with the Third World can only lead to more antagonism. The more Israel acts to stop radicalization in the Third World, the more hostility will result, justifying the Israeli claim that "the whole world is against us."

Such an ardent supporter of Zionism and Israel as M. Brecher notes that Israel's leaders never used the term "liberation movement" to refer to Zionism. His interpretation is that "it symbolizes the unwillingness of Israel's decision makers to identify their struggle with the anti-colonialist revolt." And indeed, the term "national liberation movement" has taken on positively frightening attributes for most Israelis, and with good reason. "Self-determination," "liberation," "revolution"—these words sound ominous to Israeli leaders, and they should. The expression "self-determination" has been banished from Israeli political discourse because it obviously brings to mind the Palestinians. The connection between Palestinian rights and the rights of other oppressed groups in the Third World is never far from anybody's mind. And so the feeling is that Israel has to commit itself to stemming the tide of radicalism, to trying to reverse the current of decolonization. . . .

Direct Involvement

What seems unique about the Israeli enterprise in the Third World is the readiness of the Israelis—government and individuals—to get involved "on the ground" in the armed struggle, on the side of a government as military or counterinsurgency advisers. Israel makes its mark in the Third World "trouble spots" through direct involvement, by getting Israeli hands dirty, and sometimes bloody. This is what we have observed in South Africa, Sri Lanka, Zaire, and Nicaragua. This readiness is unique because, unlike other cases, it is not officially acknowledged. When the United States, the Soviet Union, or Cuba have military advisers in the Third World, it is usually officially admitted. With Israel it is always denied. The nature of some of the governments Israelis work with so directly makes them singular. Several are regimes that no one would want to have anything to do with, regimes abhorrent to most of the world.

The result of all these activities is that the popular perception of Israel in many Third World countries is negative. While right-wingers all over the world have become Israel's ardent admirers, those who fight them and suffer under them have begun to see Israel and Israelis as diabolical, omnipotent forces.

3

VIEWPOINT

"Israel . . . has chosen to support the South African Government—thereby sanctioning the brutal suppression of [black] people."

Israel's Foreign Policy Supports Racism

Jane Hunter

Jane Hunter is an author and publisher of *Israeli Foreign Affairs,* an independent monthly research report. In the following viewpoint, she argues that Israel's continued close relationship with the racist South African government proves that Israel's foreign policy supports racism. Despite international criticism and sanctions, she argues, Israel continues to provide South Africa with the means to oppress its non-white citizens and neighbors.

As you read, consider the following questions:

1. What benefits does the author believe Israel gets from association with South Africa?
2. According to Hunter, why does South Africa look to Israel for aid?
3. What are some of the similarities between the Israeli government and the South African government, according to Hunter?

Reprinted from *Israeli Foreign Policy: South Africa and Central America* by Jane Hunter with permission from the author and South End Press, 1987.

Israel's ties with South Africa seem to be especially disturbing to many who follow Israel's international activities. Perhaps it is natural that Israel has been castigated more harshly for its arms sales to South Africa than for its sales to other countries: first, because there has been for a decade an arms embargo against South Africa; and second, because of the unsurpassed criminality of the white regime and the uses to which it puts the Israeli-supplied weapons.

It has also been said that those arms sales are understandable, given the striking similarities between the two countries in their day-to-day abuse and repression of their subject populations, South African blacks and Palestinians under Israeli rule; in their operating philosophies of apartheid and Zionism; and in their similar objective situations: "the only two Western nations to have established themselves in a predominantly non-white part of the world," as a South African Broadcasting Corporation editorial put it. That understanding, however, is somewhat superficial, and the focus on similarities of *political* behavior has somewhat obscured the view of the breadth and depth of the totality of Israeli-South African relations and their implications.

Israel's relations with South Africa are different than its interactions with any of its other arms clients. That Israel gave South Africa its nuclear weapons capability underscores the special nature of Tel Aviv's relations with the white minority government and begins to describe it—a full-fledged, if covert, partnership based on the determination of both countries to continue as unrepentant pariahs and to help each other avoid the consequences of their behavior.

The Illusion of a Progressive Israel

For South Africa's sake the partnership is designed to thwart international efforts against apartheid. What South Africa is expected to do for Israel is not as easily delineated; some Israeli critics, in fact, have argued that nothing South Africa can do for Israel is worth the price Israel has paid in international opprobrium.

> Israel has become embroiled in an unequal relationship with ambiguous returns. The scope of exchange, though diverse, is meager. The benefit Israel derives from these interchanges is unclear; in any event it is in no way commensurate to that reaped by the other partner in the equation.

Beyond the guessing game (due to the strict secrecy maintained by Israel and to a lesser extent by South Africa) into which discussions of Israeli-South African links frequently deteriorate, it is certain that something of value is being received in Israel. To Naomi Chazan, the Israeli critic whose words appear above, that value received might be worthless, even negative, as she is holding it up to a standard she describes as "the nature and de-

161

PEOPLE ARE ALWAYS GETTING ON MY CASE...

...ABOUT ISRAEL'S DEALINGS WITH SOUTH AFRICA.

DON'T BE CONCERNED. IT'S A PURELY ECONOMIC RELATION-SHIP!

COMMODITIES, MOSTLY.

WE TRADE ISRAELI ORANGES, LEMONS AND GRAPE-FRUITS FOR...

...SOUTH AFRICAN LUMBER!

(C)J.D. PHILLIPS - ROTHCO

velopment of an Israeli ethos" out of what she views as Israel's contradictions.

Chazan's image of a liberal, beneficent state of Israel is also the dominant one in the minds of many North Americans. However, during its 40 years, the liberal, or socially progressive state of Israel has existed mostly in the blandishments of fundraisers and the flatterings of the U.S. media, where it has existed at all. The Israeli leadership, from the start, were hardened people, who took a hard lesson from the Holocaust and the centuries of Jewish travail that preceded it. The current leadership, where it differs from the founders, almost all of whom have come through the higher ranks of the Israeli military, have not softened.

> Their understanding of modern Jewish history, with its themes of the Holocaust and powerlessness, reinforced by long professional military training, causes these elites to be impressed by visible manifestations of power and strength at the same time as they are inclined to be cynical toward false standards of international conduct.

Whatever the large and small incentives to be found in links with South Africa, Israel's leaders have pursued them avidly. . . .

A number of circumstances propelled the bonding process. The lessons of Israel's [1973] war took on new significance for South Africa as Portugal was forced to give up its African colonies and South Africa worried about a military threat from the newly independent Mozambique and Angola. Moreover, the Nonaligned Movement, then coming into its own as a force of the developing world, was bringing increasing pressure to bear on South Africa.

Because of its intransigent refusal to negotiate a withdrawal from the territories it had occupied since 1967 and the brutality of its occupation of them, Israel was also the object of intense international criticism. In November 1975, the United Nations General Assembly passed Resolution 3379 declaring Zionism a form of "racism and racial discrimination." The resolution also condemned "the unholy alliance between South African racism and Zionism." Also in 1974, the UN began steps that would result in the conferral of observer status on the Palestine Liberation Organization.

In late 1974, Israel's resistance to the U.S. peacemaking efforts led the Ford Administration to declare an aid moratorium to all countries in the Middle East while Washington "reassessed" its policy in the region. The anxiety this caused Tel Aviv was considerable. . . . A scandal breaking in 1975 over CIA "dirty tricks" in Angola led Secretary of State Henry Kissinger to suggest to Israel that it help South Africa with its invasion of Angola. Israel complied with Kissinger's request by sending counterinsurgency weapons and instructors. In July 1975, a former Israeli intelligence chief said that senior Israeli military officers were giving South African troops counterinsurgency training. *The Economist* said Israel had stopped short of sending the troops which Kissinger had wanted, but that the Israelis took his suggestion as a green light for developing a closer relationship with South Africa. . . .

A Strategic Meshing

In March 1976, then Defense Minister Shimon Peres made a secret visit to South Africa and invited the South African prime minister to visit Israel. John Vorster arrived in Israel the following month, eager for his first official visit to a democratic state.

The visit by John Vorster was certain to be provocative, but the isolated Israelis must have felt they had very little to lose, and, in South Africa, with its gold and minerals and its complement of transnational corporations, they must have seen a possible substitute for the U.S. . . .

There was more to receiving Vorster than a provocative and defiant political statement. It is generally accepted that among the comprehensive set of bilateral agreements announced as having been concluded during Vorster's trip to Israel—covering comercial, trade, fiscal, and "cooperative" arrangements—were secret pacts covering arms sales and nuclear cooperation. All of the agreements, the departing Vorster told reporters, would be overseen by a joint cabinet-level committee which would meet annually to review and promote Israeli-South African economic relations.

163

Vorster also spoke of a "steering group" to coordinate the exchange of information and encourage the "development of trade, scientific and industrial cooperation and joint projects using South African raw material and Israeli manpower."

What Israel and South Africa had accomplished was a strategic meshing of strengths and weaknesses: South African capital and raw materials to Israel, counterpoised against the transfer of Israeli weapons and advanced technology to South Africa. The 1976 agreements have been periodically renewed. As the years progressed the strength generated by Israeli-South African cooperation would be turned outward to sanctions-busting, allowing South Africa to fend off internal and external pressure for reform.

In Deep

Although Israel is uneasy at times at the prospect of arousing bad international publicity, it is now so deeply implicated in the running of apartheid that South Africa can hold it to blackmail. In any case, Israel's active part in reinforcing the Bantustan system and in sanctions-busting (in sports and art as well) offers additional proof of its real outlook.

Yezid Sayigh, *Middle East International*, 1988.

Israel has also reaped benefits from the relationship—in the tangible sense for the development of its arms industry, and in a not altogether ephemeral sense, politically: as long as South Africa remains the focal point of international outrage, Israel escapes the brunt of that attention; moreover, as long as it can be shown that sanctions are ineffective against South Africa, there is less chance they will be imposed on Israel. . . .

Israel as Model

As it came snarling and hissing into the 1980s in its own region, South Africa has also looked to Israel for help and inspiration.

Many parallels in the tactics and strategies employed by Israel and South Africa have been noted. Partly this is a result of collegiality: the military attaches of Israel and South Africa "consult frequently on counterinsurgency tactics." Yet there is an unmistakable teacher-student pattern in the communication of the very techniques which have brought down international criticism on both. As in the direction of the technology flow between the two nations, the imparting of repressive techniques usually casts Israel in the mentor's role.

The South Africans greatly admired the Israeli raid on Entebbe airport. "South African generals now consciously emulate the flamboyance of the Israeli generals," wrote [Paul Moorcraft] a

164

specialist on the South African military. Even before 1976 South Africans had looked to Israel for techniques they might adapt. Describing the lecture given by Air Force General Mordechai Hod during his 1967 visit to South Africa, a member of the select military audience said, "It was an intensely interesting lecture, which made it apparent that the tactics employed by the Israeli Air Force were brilliant. The Israelis seem to have been as clever as a cartload of monkeys."

The South Africans began teaching the lessons of Israel's 1967 war at their maneuver school, and Israeli advisers began teaching the Boers the arts of suppressing a captive population and keeping hostile neighbors off balance. In the Vorster agreements discussed earlier, Israeli advisory services for South Africa were institutionalized. [As James Adams observes,]

> Senior army officers in Israel have confirmed that IDF [Israeli Defense Forces] personnel have been seconded to all branches of the South African armed forces, and according to senior sources in the Israeli defense establishment, there are currently some 300 active Israeli servicemen and women on secondment in South Africa. These include army, navy and air force personnel who help train the South Africans, border security experts . . . counter intelligence experts . . . and defense scientists who cooperate on the development of new weapons systems. In addition, there are several hundred South Africans in Israel at any one time, being trained in weapons systems, battle strategy and counterinsurgency warfare.

The white government's practice of domestic counterinsurgency combines outright military brutality with the extensive use of informers and collaborators. It is impossible to know how many refinements of these age-old techniques have been borrowed from the Israelis' occupation of the West Bank, Gaza, and the Golan Heights. The Israeli system of village leagues is obviously comparable to the hated town councils imposed on segregated townships by the apartheid government. The collective punishment employed by the Israelis, such as the destruction of a whole family's home when one of its members is arrested as a *suspect* in an act of resistance, has lately been matched by the recent South African practices of sealing off townships, and assaulting entire funeral processions. What is perhaps more salient is the South African victims' perceptions of Israel's involvement in their oppression and how readily that perception is communicated.

The Oppressed's Perception of Israel

At a party in Santa Cruz, California, a South African student passes around a photograph of a street scene in Soweto, the large black township outside Johannesburg. Somewhat reproachfully he calls attention to the white policeman in the picture and the [Israeli-made] Uzi he's holding.

Nobel laureate Archbishop Desmond Tutu, was more direct when he told guests at a San Francisco breakfast sponsored by the American Jewish Congress that he was troubled by reports of Israeli collaboration with South Africa, "with a government whose policies are so reminiscent of Nazis." (While quick to point out the contributions of individual Jews to the struggle against apartheid, Tutu has in the past lambasted Israel for its "monopoly on the Holocaust."

Even those South African blacks willing to cooperate with Israel have publicly called on Tel Aviv to stop selling arms to South Africa. Chief Gatsha Buthelezi, a great favorite of Israel, told reporters there that he favored an international arms embargo against South Africa. One member of a group of black South African "activists" brought to Israel for a training program told the press that Israel was "among the countries that sell weapons to South Africa, which kill [sic] blacks with them, including three-year-old children."

"Israel," wrote a reader to the *City Press,* a black South African paper, "has chosen to support the South African Government—thereby sanctioning the brutal suppression of our people."

"Designating Israel . . . as 'racist' or equating it with South Africa rests on inappropriate analysis at best and on deliberate obfuscation at worst."

Israel's Foreign Policy Opposes Racism

Michael Curtis

Author and professor of political science at Rutgers University, Michael Curtis argues in the following viewpoint that Israel's reputation as a racist state is undeserved. He believes that Israel is the victim of Arab and Communist propaganda. In truth, Curtis argues, Israel supports the struggle of the black African nations for independence and opposes racism, including the *apartheid* system of South Africa.

As you read, consider the following questions:

1. According to Curtis, what means has the "Arab-Communist coalition" used to link Israel with South Africa?
2. In the author's opinion, what are the reasons the black African nations withdrew support from Israel?
3. What issues does the author believe need to be separated to recognize the fallacy of charging Israel with racist policies?

Michael Curtis, "Africa, Israel and the Middle East." Published by permission of Transaction Publishers from *The Middle East Reader*, edited by Michael Curtis. Copyright © 1986 by Transaction Publishers.

International politics frequently demonstrates the validity of Walter Lippmann's observation that people respond as powerfully to fictions as they do to realities. Nowhere is this as demonstrable as in the changing international perceptions of the policies of Israel and its relations with Black African countries and with South Africa.

Black African countries have been interested primarily in the right of national self-determination, development as independent nations, and the elimination of discrimination on the African continent. Israel has been concerned with survival in the midst of hostile neighbors who have tried to undermine its legitimacy by a variety of means, including a policy of deliberate distortion of its actions. This distortion has aimed at changing the perception of Israel held by Black Africans and the rest of the international community by equating Zionism with racism and by depicting Israel as a close associate of South Africa.

Few political issues today strike such strong emotional chords or enjoy such universal consensus as the condemnation of the South African political regime. Though this regime has recently made certain minimal changes and promises to make others, it still denies political rights to 21 million black citizens and consigns them to an inferior status in law and therefore deserves to be criticized for its policies of *apartheid*. Everyone sincerely concerned with the issue of human rights in South Africa must therefore be troubled about the misuse of the opposition to *apartheid* for partisan, irrelevant, and self-interested motives.

Arab and Communist Distortions

Representatives of Arab countries and the Communist bloc, in which human rights are sadly lacking, indulge in the luxury of anti-Zionist rhetoric and even occasional antisemitic incitement. They also make it their duty to denounce Israel not only as a racist state but even as the fount of racism. In their eagerness to misrepresent, exaggerate, and distort the actions and policies of Israel, these countries are apparently not troubled by the fact that their actions are weakening, indeed betraying the valid anti-*apartheid* cause.

The Arab-Communist coalition, in a mixture of cynicism and opportunism, has skillfully used international forums, especially the United Nations and its specialized agencies, to pass resolutions linking Israel and South Africa. In true Orwellian fashion it has attempted to expunge the memory of the historic Jewish opposition to racism in all its forms and the record of Jewish willingness to fight and suffer for the civil rights of blacks. These resolutions obfuscate the reality that the state of Israel is founded, as its Declaration of Independence says, on the principle of complete equality of social and political rights. The anti-*apartheid*

cause, in which South African Jews were prominent in dispropor-
tion to the total white population, and which Israel supported in
the United Nations until 1972, when the cause became linked with
the opposition to Zionism, has been misused by the Arab-
Communist coalition rather than honestly employed against its
proper target. Consensus exists that the Arab countries support
African-sponsored resolutions, at the U.N. only if they are linked
to the Palestinian question. Even Ali Mazrui argues that the Organization of African Unity (OAU) has become "a mechanism by
which the Arabs can politically influence black Africans." As a
result of this Communist-Arab effort, Israel's previously cordial
relations with Black Africa have been undermined.

Israel and Africa

One of the most impressive features of the early decades of
Israeli policy was its concern for and interest in humanitarian
action in Third World countries, especially in Black Africa. To
some extent this was a policy of enlightened self-interest whereby Israel sought to win friends and gain political support in the
international community. But more significantly, its actions were
an illustration of the concept of social justice that underlay the
regime and a demonstration of genuine sympathy for other new
developing nations engaged in nation-building. These new nations,
seeking non-obligating guidance and support, were able to benefit
from Israel's own unique development experience, especially in
agriculture, regional planning, zone development, water management, cooperatives, community development, education, health
and youth programs. Because of Israel's limited capital funds, most
of the early aid was in the form of technical assistance.

Abhorrence for Apartheid

I am encouraged and inspired by the complete abhorrence
which . . . the Israeli people have for apartheid, and the commitment of the Israeli people to its destruction.

Mangosuthu Buthelezi, *Near East Report*, August 19, 1985.

Israeli policy was based on certain guidelines. Diplomatic relationships and mutual recognition were essential. Israel would
assist in administration and development if formally requested
and if action could be taken quickly, without long-term study. The
host country would cover expenses if there was local participation. And the Israeli presence would be phased out at the completion of the project.

On this basis, relations between Israel and Black Africa took
a number of forms: expert help, trainee programs, cooperative ef-

forts, military aid, and diplomatic relations. . . .

For Israel this set of relationships meant enlarging its circle of international contacts with the hope that African countries would support—or at least not oppose—Israel's struggle for existence. Israel recognized the strategic value of the African countries along the Red Sea for its own security, and the importance of protecting shipping in the Gulf of Aqaba passing through Bab-el Mandeb to the Indian Ocean. Trade between the Black African countries and Israel, largely an exchange of raw materials and finished products, was important not only in itself, but also in that it constituted a significant check on the Arab boycott of Israeli products. The Labor Zionist ideology of many of the Israeli leaders led them to a genuine concern to aid new, developing nations in the Third World, some of which seemed to rest on political aspirations similar to those of Israel. Golda Meir herself saw Israel's African policy as "a continuation of our own most valued traditions and as an expression of our own deepest historic instincts."

Israel As Leader and Ally

For their part, African countries saw Israel as an example of a newly independent nation pointing a way to economic modernization and political development that they could follow. From Israel they could obtain technical assistance without danger of a neo-colonialist presence or fear of being drawn into a military alliance or being pressed for military bases. They recognized a new nation with which they shared some common features: a history of past persecution, a mixed economy that was neither capitalist nor socialist, a country facing danger of intervention by external forces, and a certain political balance in international East-West relations in the early years.

Israel frequently voted in the United Nations against the system of *apartheid* and in 1961 supported the call for sanctions against South Africa. Parenthetically, Israel also voted in favor of the decolonization of Portuguese territories in Africa. In 1963 Israel reduced its diplomatic representation in South Africa to consular level, and in 1966 voted against South Africa's mandate over Namibia. Black African countries did not vote alike on Middle East questions. Some, especially the Francophone countries, tended to vote in support of Israel until the 1970s. Significantly, countries which received aid from Israel did not automatically vote in its favor. But most Black African countries did not accept the Arab argument that Israel had cooperated with South Africa and Portugal, the two main enemies of Africa. . . .

The African countries have also understood that economic realities, of which the Arab boycott is a major element, oblige Israel to trade where it can just as they themselves do. Such trade implies neither close cooperation nor commitment to similar social and political values. Indeed, they can recognize that the sincerity of the Israeli rejection of *apartheid* is the result of Jewish historic suffering from racist policies to which Jews were subject.

A Fading Fantasy

Only the Communist and Arab countries engage in the vitriolic attacks on Israel or the invidious comparisons of it with South Africa. . . . The non-Arab and non-Muslim African countries, with rare exceptions, refrained from similar condemnation.

This change in attitude suggests that the fantasy created by Arab and Soviet political legerdemain is starting to fade. Rational analysis of the real relationship between the two countries may dispel the phantasmagoria of "close cooperation" or "infamous alliance" in trade, military, nuclear, diplomatic and cultural matters.

Michael Curtis, *The Middle East Reader*, 1986.

Designating Israel in the international organizations as "racist" or equating it with South Africa rests on inappropriate analysis at best and on deliberate obfuscation at worst. Legitimate differences may exist regarding the treatment of Arabs inside Israel and the condition and destiny of the Palestinian population in the territories administered by Israel. But rational criticism of Israeli actions and policies ought to fall far short of attacking it as a "racist" state. To say that Israel was founded as a *Jewish* state is not to say that it has a separatist ideology; the crucial determining fact is that the 18 percent non-Jewish part of its current population possesses full legal, religious, civil and political rights. From an ideological point of view, Zionism, a national liberation movement calling for the ingathering of Jews, is totally different from *apartheid*, which is based on racial distinctiveness and the superiority of some races to others. Zionism is a philosophy related to the Jewish people; it is not related to race in any way. The people is composed of individuals from widely different backgrounds and races. Ethnic demands have been made in Israel, and inequality exists—as it does in all countries—in the distribution of economic resources and political power. But Israel is a democratic society with a population of all different colors, and its political system is open to a variety of pressures: between different ethnic Jewish groups, between the Arab minority and the Jewish majority, between the religious orthodox and the non-religious, and within all of these groups.

If no rational argument is sufficient for those who have labelled Israel as a "racist" state or who refuse to see the Law of Return as religious and moral, not exclusive, in character, the example

171

of Operation Moses, the extraordinary and successful transporting of over 10,000 Ethiopian Jews to Israel in late 1984 and early 1985 ought to show unmistakably the falsity of accusations of colonialism, racism or color prejudice. Immediately on arrival in Israel these black Jews, self-styled members of *Beta Israel* (the House of Israel) were given citizenship as part of a common people. . . .

Discerning Rhetoric from Reality

African countries have become aware that the issue of racism, on which they rightly feel so strongly, has been exploited for the political advantage of others. They understand that the Arab-Israeli conflict is a political problem having no connection with the elimination of racial discrimination in Africa. They can perceive the irony of Syrian President Assad, who slaughtered 20,000 of his own people in Hama in 1982, writing of "the racist-Zionist regime's inexplicable crimes, atrocities and acts of aggression" to the *1983 Second World Conference to Combat Racism and Racial Discrimination."* Everyone genuinely concerned with that combat must help ensure that political hatred and vituperative rhetoric will not destroy the ability of international bodies to correct injustice.

"Israel has defied all U.N. resolutions, and has shown no respect for the sanctity of international agreements."

International Criticism of Israel Is Legitimate

Muhammad El-Farra

Muhammad El-Farra spent eleven years at the United Nations as the ambassador from Jordan. In the following viewpoint, he argues that Israel disregards the authority of the United Nations concerning the partitioning of Palestine. El-Farra concludes that Israel has betrayed its original promise to the international community to be a peaceloving nation.

As you read, consider the following questions:

1. Why does El-Farra believe Israel has little respect for the international community and world opinion?
2. According to El-Farra, why is Israel an illegitimate nation?
3. What are the author's reasons for criticizing Zionism?

Muhammad El-Farra, *Years of No Decision*, published by KPI Ltd., London, 1987.

When the United Nations General Assembly recommended the establishment of a Jewish state, it was the conviction of those who supported the resolution that Israel would be peace-loving; that its people would benefit from their past tragic experience and champion human rights, and help in putting an end to lawlessness in world affairs. They could never expect that a new and aggressive Israel would itself defy the United Nations. Indeed, Israel was only admitted to membership of the United Nations after Abba Eban came before the United Nations and declared that his government unreservedly accepted the obligations of the United Nations Charter and undertook to honour them from the day when it became a member of the United Nations. He expressly undertook, on behalf of his government, to implement the U.N. partition plan and the protocol of Lausanne, and thus undertook to ensure the repatriation of over two million refugees expelled by Israeli forces from their homes and homelands, and to pay adequate compensation to those who chose not to return.

In practice, however, Israel has defied all U.N. resolutions, and has shown no respect for the sanctity of international agreements. The flouting of U.N. resolutions for over thirty-seven years indicates how much respect the Israelis have for the family of nations and world public opinion. The whole policy of piecemeal expansion and annexation was part of the original plan. Theodor Herzl, the founder of Zionism, declared openly that when the Zionists occupied the land they would spirit the population across the frontiers. A later affirmation of this same view can be found in the Report of the King-Crane Commission in 1919 that "all the Zionists who testified before us spoke of the eventual dispossession of non-Jewish communities in Palestine who then constituted more than 90 per cent of the population."

The Real Story

The facts, of course, tell the real story. In 1947 the Zionists accepted the United Nations partition boundary; in 1948 the Israelis advanced further into Palestine land, then claimed the new Armistice Agreement and its demarcation line as the border. As a result of the 1967 invasion and occupation of all Palestine, they called the whole occupied area *Eretz Israel,* and claimed that the Jordan River was the border. Now they are occupying more Arab lands still in line with their *"fait accompli"* policy.

It is since the occupation by Israel of yet more Arab territory in 1967 that the United States has made it a condition that the PLO should first recognise the legitimacy of Israel before it could itself be granted recognition. Israel was established by the same U.N. partition resolution which also recommended the establishment of an Arab State of Palestine. Following the 1948 War, however, Israel enacted legislation by virtue of which much of

174

the territory set aside for the Arab State of Palestine was incorporated into Israel. By virtue of that legislation 94.4 per cent of Arab territory is now considered by virtue of this legislation Israeli property.

On the other hand would not Palestinian recognition of the legitimacy of Israel amount to acceptance of its illegal legislation and admission of the impossibility of achieving the Palestine state, prescribed by the United Nations? Does it not mean waiving all Palestinian rights, property and statehood? Would it not, indeed, violate the partition resolution itself, which has been regularly re-affirmed ever since it was first passed?

Growing Isolation

Several U.N. bodies have been set up to deal with the Palestine question and with Israeli-occupied territories. Israel has refused to cooperate with these U.N. bodies, which have initiated many conferences and prompted many U.N. resolutions, again emphasizing Israel's growing isolation. . . .

The U.N. Security Council has voted on about two hundred anti-Israel resolutions since 1967, which either were adopted or were defeated only by American veto (about 30 times). Most U.N. resolutions condemning Israeli policies are not binding, since they are passed in the General Assembly, and even Security Council resolutions do not lead to action. But for Israel they are writings on the wall, symptoms of a progressive isolation and a growing hostility within the world.

Benjamin Beit-Hallahmi, *The Israeli Connection*, 1987.

Does it make sense, moreover, that the victim of aggression should be the first to recognise the other side? How can the Palestinians give Israel documents that would ensure its right to live, the right to peace and the right to security, before Israel has even recognised the existence of the legitimate rights of the people of Palestine, which have been recognised by the United Nations and which Israel itself accepted as a basis for settlement when it signed the Protocol of Lausanne on 12th May 1949? To do this is for the Palestinians to surrender to Israel before it withdraws from Palestinian and other Arab territories, and before it recognises that the people of Palestine have more legitimate rights in Palestine.

Israel's Defiance

I once had occasion to remind the Special Representative of the Secretary-General of the United Nations, Gunnar Jarring, that the United Nations Palestine Conciliation Commission consisting of France, the United States and Turkey, had reached in Lausanne on 12th May 1949, an agreement called the Protocol of Lausanne, which was signed by Israel and all parties concerned. The agreement stated clearly that the partition line, as fixed by the partition resolution of 29th November 1947, would be the basis for any settlement and reiterated the international commitment to establish a Palestinian Arab State. The Protocol was later unilaterally revoked by Israel in defiance of the Commission. No action was taken either by the United States or by any other permanent member of the Security Council to remedy the situation, although the Charter gave them a special responsibility for world peace and security. This encouraged Israel to continue its defiance. Prior to the 1967 war, Israel used to claim that the Armistice lines were her borders, while we used to answer that the Armistice Agreement did not fix boundaries but simply fixed Armistice demarcation lines pending a final settlement of the problem on the basis of the partition resolution.

I explained to Ambassador Jarring that the Arabs had always sought peace but that it had not been achieved because Israel's leaders lived in the colonial era of the last century. They feel at home not with the spirit of today, but with a vicious ideology of domination and expansion—an ideology of the past. Their behaviour revealed their hidden intentions. It showed that their acceptance of the United Nations resolution and the partition line as the boundary was meaningless and that their undertaking to abide by the terms of the partition resolution was also meaningless, although they owe their very existence as a state to this partition resolution.

Israeli Trickery at the UN

The obdurate Israelis today should also consider the last words of Chaim Weizmann, the first President of Israel, words which I cited time and again in the Security Council. The last occasion was while dealing with the Jerusalem Question on 2nd July 1969:

> "We are a small people but a great people, an ugly and yet a beautiful people; a creative and a destructive people—a people in whom genius and folly are equally co-mingled. We are an impetuous people who have time and again repudiated and wrecked what our ancestors built. For God's sake let us not allow the breach in the wall to swallow us."

Israel's representatives at the United Nations have resorted to all kinds of tricks to defend their expansionism, showing the impetuosity and folly to which President Weizmann referred. . . .

A Fait Accompli Policy

The United Nations passed the partition resolution in November 1947. Another resolution six months later, on 17th April 1948, called on, *inter alia,* all persons and organisations in Palestine to "refrain, pending further consideration of the future government of Palestine by the General Assembly from any political activity which might prejudice the rights, claims or positions of either community."

When, therefore, the Zionists proclaimed their state, they did so in complete disregard of this resolution which, in effect, froze the situation "pending further consideration of the future *government* of Palestine by the General Assembly." What is more, the letter requesting recognition sent to the American President at his suggestion also violated this resolution of which neither the Jewish Agency in Washington nor the President himself could claim ignorance since the United States had voted for it. American recognition accorded to Israel is therefore an illegitimate recognition without legal basis, of a state which is itself without legal foundation. Its proclamation was a unilateral act, an act which has set the tone of every subsequent Israeli action and the first demonstration of the *fait accompli* policy.

Subsequently those same people wanted all Palestine, despite the United Nations Partition Resolution, on the grounds that since the Arab side had not accepted the partition resolution earlier they had no right to seek the implementation of that resolution later. This argument does not hold water. It is true that the Arab States objected to the competence of the United Nations to adopt a resolution which violated a basic principle embodied in its Charter

Steve Sack. Reprinted with permission of StarTribune.

namely the principle of self-determination. This was a constitutional question which the Arabs, as a last resort, wanted the International Court of Justice to adjudicate upon. Unfortunately because of the pressure of the United States, and that of President Truman in particular, the Arab request did not get the necessary votes in the General Assembly. It is clear, however, that this legal process did not deprive the people of Palestine (who were not even parties to the vote) of their right to a sovereign state prescribed by the United Nations in the very resolution which created the Jewish State. No argument can enable the Israelis to go beyond the specific terms of that same resolution nor can they exceed or infringe the rights of others laid down in the resolution, the more so since the United Nations reaffirms this same resolution every year thus reminding the Israelis of its continuing validity.

Another Israeli Trick

After this unilateral proclamation the Israelis proceeded to flout every act in the book. It may be recalled that Israel's admission to the United Nations was conditional on its observance of the partition resolution and was granted in the belief "that Israel is a peace-loving country." It was also conditional on the right of Palestinians to return home. Furthermore, it was conditional on observance of the Protocol of Lausanne, signed by Walter Eitan one day before Israel's admission to the United Nations. Almost immediately after Israel's admission Mr. David Ben Gurion revoked his country's adherence to the Protocol on the grounds that Eitan had never been invested with the authority to sign such a commitment. It became clear later that signing the protocol was nothing but one of the Israeli tricks to secure admission to the United Nations. . . .

Israel today seeks nothing less than the total disappearance of the Palestinians—apparently by whatever means, however crude. This attitude bears a remarkable resemblance to Hitler's "Master Race" theories, against which the world united in World War II, their triumph. Nevertheless, these same theories, emanating from another part of the world, are today radiating outwards with appalling speed—not least because Israel enjoys the support of the United States—moral, economic and military.

But it seems that it is with impunity that the emerging new master race pursues its murderous policies. Israel is the embodiment of Zionism and Zionism was condemned on 10th November 1975 by the United Nations General Assembly "as a form of racism and racial discrimination." Furthermore, Israel is in flagrant breach of every promise it made before admission to the United Nations and is patently not a "peace-loving" nation "able and willing to uphold the principles of the Charter."

"The campaign of anti-Semitic and anti-Israel slander has reached levels never before experienced in the United Nations."

International Criticism of Israel Is Not Legitimate

Ralph Cwerman

Ralph Cwerman is a political analyst on Middle Eastern and United Nations affairs. He argues in the following viewpoint that Arab propaganda has prejudiced the international community against Israel. He criticizes the UN for not responding to Arab terrorism and concludes that the UN is no longer capable of promoting Arab-Israeli peace.

As you read, consider the following questions:

1. In Cwerman's opinion, what initially disillusioned Israel with the UN?
2. To what does Cwerman attribute the UN's lack of response to Arab terrorism against Israel?
3. According to the author, how has the UN's anti-Zionism resolution hurt the UN more than Israel?

Ralph Cwerman, "Israel and the United Nations," *Issue Analysis*, No. 23, August 1986. Reprinted with permission of the American Zionist Federation.

In 1985 the largest gathering of world leaders in history met in New York to celebrate the 40th anniversary of the United Nations. When the time came for Israel's Prime Minister to address the General Assembly, Arab, Moslem and Communist delegates, repeating their annual exercise, demonstratively exited the great hall. On a symbolic level, after nearly 40 years, the refusal by some UN delegates to even sit in the same room as an Israeli leader perhaps best illustrates the UN's dismal record in the Middle East.

On the political level, the UN's notorious anti-Israel campaign continues to dominate its agenda. Over the years, the UN's collective wisdom has equated Zionism with racism, and singled out Israel as a "non-peace loving country" and as an "affront to humanity." It has accused Israel of "war crimes," of being the source of South Africa's apartheid policy and, of course, of administering the most oppressive and violent occupation policies since Hitler. Likewise, since 1982, the General Assembly implements its annual ritual of attempting to expel Israel from the United Nations.

The strategy behind the annual repetition of anti-Israel resolutions at the UN has been largely successful. The double standards and unfair practices employed by the United Nations against Israel have become commonplace. The UN's anti-Israel bias, its distortions of the facts and its misrepresentations of the truth have been passively accepted by most people. Under the cover of UN "legitimacy," Arab propagandists have achieved remarkable international success in their defamatory campaign against Israel.

A Good Start Gone Bad

The relationship between Israel and the United Nations has not always been characterized by such troubling developments. On November 29, 1947, the General Assembly adopted Resolution 181 (II) endorsing and recommending the establishment of a Jewish homeland in Palestine. Six months later Israel renewed its statehood with much goodwill toward the United Nations. The founders of the State solemnly proclaimed that Israel would dedicate itself to the message of hope embodied in the newly-founded international organization's charter.

As a result of the UN's handling of the 1948 War of Independence, however, the expectations Israel had placed in the United Nations were quickly tempered. While the war raged, the Security Council issued several cease-fire orders and called for a truce. But countless Arab infractions of these arrangements made them ineffective. Although the Security Council warned it would send forces to the area to enforce its call for a truce, no such deployment ever took place. Instead UN observers stood idly by while Israel incurred over 6,000 casualties, 2,000 of them civilians. This was one per cent of Israel's Jewish population at the time.

The only measure taken by the UN was its appointment of a mediator, Count Folke Bernadotte, whose mediation effort itself was to sow the seeds of profound disillusionment with the UN among Israeli leaders. This feeling would never dissipate and still exists today. The objectivity and fairness of UN machinery for resolving the major political problems between Israel and the Arab world was, from that time forward, questioned by Israeli leaders. . . .

The Issue of Terrorism

Since the late 1960's, the issue of terrorism has been a particularly troublesome aspect of UN-Israeli relations. The United Nations has been depressingly and consistently silent over terrorist attacks against Israeli targets, not seeing fit to issue even a word, much less a condemnatory resolution over such horrendous attacks as the 1972 Munich Olympic massacre. Likewise, it was only with difficulty that a Security Council condemnation of Israel for the Entebbe rescue was averted in 1976. In sharp contrast, repetitive and shrill condemnations of Israeli retaliatory actions against Palestinian and other terrorist bases is a matter of course. This pattern of failure to censure Arab countries providing bases and support for terrorist activities against Israel while condemning Israeli retaliation can be attributed to the anti-Israel majority coalescing in the UN.

Déjà Vu

Arab aggression against Israel scored its first decisive strike when it discredited the right of the Jews to a national homeland within the walls of the very institution that had confirmed that right in 1947. United Nations Resolution 3379, declaring Zionism a form of racism, proclaimed the Jews to be a pariah people, as the Germans had done several decades earlier—this time, in full view of the world. The passage of that resolution affirmed not only the enduring strength of Arab hostility to the Jews, but the inability or unwillingness of the international community to counteract the Arab threat.

Ruth Wisse, *Commentary*, May 1988.

This has become a consistent pattern in the General Assembly. Any movement to draft a convention aimed at combatting international terrorism is quickly "neutralized" by excluding from its scope persons who "perpetrated such acts in the struggle against colonialism, foreign occupation, racial discrimination and apartheid." During the 40th General Assembly session a resolution condemning terrorism was adopted with great difficulty, but again, it was neutralized and the resolution implied that in certain "situations, including colonialism, racism . . . and those involving foreign occupation" violence, construed by some parties as international terrorism, was justified. . . .

The New Majority

During the critical UN debates in the summer of 1967 the Arabs failed to muster the necessary support in the General Assembly for the adoption of their proposals. Likewise, Resolution 242, not to the Arab group's liking, attempted to present a reasonably neutral text to permit diplomatic processes to restart. The lesson of this was not lost on the Arab diplomats, and a change soon came. The efforts to consolidate the non-aligned states behind the Arab position went hand in hand with a sustained campaign to portray Israel in the bleakest possible terms.

This campaign began in the Commission on Human Rights in March 1968 and at the International Conference on Human Rights held in Iran later that same year. The pretext became what was labelled the "oppressive situation of the Arabs in the occupied territories." That issue became firmly established in the General Assembly where it remains to this day. Among other new issues drawn into the scope of this process has been the question of Jerusalem and the matter of the "inalienable rights of the Palestinian people."

To all these specific issues must be added the unremitting Arab attempt to inject anti-Israel or anti-Zionist elements into virtually every item of the UN agenda. The annual Arab refugee debate assumed new importance in the general onslaught on Israel in the UN and the specialized agencies. As a result, the sessions have become a forum from which hatred is spewed and restraints rarely imposed. The main objective, apart from the obvious propaganda motives, is to ensure the complete isolation of Israel in the UN—its reduction to a pariah status. This would undo the major implication of Israel's admission into the UN—the normalization of the international status of the Jewish people through the Jewish state.

This ongoing process has no end in sight and has virtually violated all the accepted canons of UN parliamentary diplomatic procedures. The tightly consolidated group of Arab, Communist, and hostile Third World forces easily commands a simple majority in the General Assembly. Since 1971 it has become numerically sufficient to overpower any opposing third of the voting members, making the necessary two-thirds majority an automatic feature. . . .

Israel's relations with the UN reached a crisis point on November 10, 1975, when the General Assembly adopted the infamous resolution equating Zionism with racism. Although not the first attack on Zionism in the UN, this was the turning point that sapped what little moral authority the UN still commanded. Voting against Israel, using all the resources of George Orwell's massive doublespeak, the General Assembly stigmatized Zionism as a racist ideology and established the foundation upon which future similar resolutions would be based.

Anti-Zionism Is Not Legitimate

In certain ways contemporary anti-Zionism is very close, very similar to the anti-Semitic ideologies of the past: There is the same tendency to generalize, to lump all Jews together in the same category, to judge them and condemn them through the same schemes and stereotypes. Nevertheless it differs in the specific type of rationalization and the new slogans and code words it conveys. This time the indictment of the Jews, the Jewish People and Judaism is done by condemning the Jewish State and the nationalism which is its *raison d'être*, namely Zionism. . . .

Anti-Zionism seeks to overwhelm the Jewish State with all the sins of the world, to demonize it, to qualify it as nazi, and thus to make it lose all legitimacy including of course whatever could have been bestowed on it by the Holocaust in the eyes of some.

Yohanon Manor, *The Threat of Anti-Zionism*, 1984.

In many ways this resolution harmed the UN more than Israel or any other country. It demonstrated in precise terms how far the world organization had strayed from its original ideals. It also showed the world the extent to which the General Assembly was able to distort the truth. Resolution 3379's powerful language and sentiment was met with unconcealed disapproval and even the hostility in many quarters throughout the world. The sponsors of the resolution, realizing that they had perhaps gone too far, found more circumspect formulations to attack Zionism in later years such as the General Assembly's systematic campaign linking Zionism with apartheid.

From Resolution 181 (II) in 1947 endorsing a Jewish homeland in Palestine to Resolution 3379 equating Zionism with racism— this is the measure of the UN's downfall in the eyes of Israel and other democracies around the world.

Anti-Semitism at the UN

Abraham Joshua Heschel, the great Jewish theologian once said, "Of all organs with which the body is endowed, none is as dangerous as the tongue. The Holocaust did not begin with building crematoria; it began with uttering evil words . . . it began with defamation."

183

Although Heschel was writing of Nazi Germany, his words accurately portray one of the most troubling trends at the UN today. Undoubtedly, the UN's single most indecent act was the adoption of Resolution 3379. In recent years, however, the campaign of anti-Semitic and anti-Israel slander has reached levels never before experienced in the United Nations.

These slanders range from simple name-calling to racial and religious incitement. Examples of the former are the designation of Israel as a "cancerous Zionist entity" (Iran), or as the "Zionist Israeli monster" (PLO). A more ominous aspect of this campaign is the willful attempt to deny, minimize and distort the reality and significance of the Holocaust, thus echoing themes and slogans currently spread by neo-Nazi organizations. To this category belong expressions such as "the so-called Holocaust" (Syria), "so-called anti-semitism" (Kuwait), and the assertion that the "Jews in Europe were sent into concentration camps by the Zionists" (Iran). A particularly shocking instance of this abusive language was the statement calling the Prime Minister of Israel a "neo-Nazi whose hands are still dripping with the blood of innocent Palestinian and other children" (PLO), and also one of the "collaborators with the Nazis [who] should be summoned to appear before a resumed Nuremburg trial" (PLO).

Classical anti-semitism, the fomenting of hostility and hatred against Jews throughout the world, was also very much alive during the 40th anniversary session of the General Assembly. The best illustration of this incitement came from the representative of Bahrain who said in a debate on—of all things—the elimination of religious intolerance that "the Jews had killed Jesus Christ."

This rhetoric has, more or less, become standard fare during UN deliberations. Ignoring Israeli protests over the use of such abusive language, chairmen of the various committees where such utterances are heard sit passively and watch the absurdities unfold.

No Useful Role

The United Nations, as it exists today, provides no useful role in helping Israel normalize its relation with the Arab world. Indeed, if the United Nations continues to renounce all initial disposition to seek out reasonable compromises, it could potentially generate and perpetuate hostility and even open warfare in the region.

Locating Scapegoats

During World War II, the Nazis in Germany systematically killed millions of Jews. The Nazis continually propagandized the outrageous lie that Jews were responsible for many of Germany's social problems. Jews became the victims of irrational leaders who glorified force, violence, and the doctrine of racial supremacy. One of the principal propaganda weapons used against the Jews by Germany's leaders was the tactic of scapegoating.

On an individual level, scapegoating involves the process of transferring personal blame or anger to another individual or object. Most people, for example, have kicked their table or chair as an outlet for anger and frustration over a mistake or failure. *On a group level, scapegoating involves the placement of blame on entire groups of people or objects for social problems that they have not caused.* Scapegoats may be totally or only partially innocent, but they always receive more blame than can be rationally justified.

The cartoon on the next page uses Palestine Liberation Organization (PLO) leader Yassir Arafat as a scapegoat. While Arafat undoubtedly has been a controversial figure in Middle Eastern politics who arouses animosity in some people, it is clearly unfair to say that he is entirely responsible for all the problems facing Israel. Israel's difficulties are too complex for such a simple answer.

Because human societies are so complex, problems are often not completely understood by any single citizen. Yet people always demand answers and there exists a human tendency to create imaginary and simplistic explanations for complex racial, social, economic, and political problems that defy easy understanding and solution. The conflict between Israelis and Arabs falls into this category. The complexity of their relationship has so far defied any equitable and peaceful solution. In such a frustrating and emotionally charged situation, scapegoating can occur.

185

In Israel, We Believe Yassir Arafat is a responsible leader...

WHEN THERE'S TROUBLE, Arafat's responsible!

©1988 DW

Dick Wright. Reprinted by permission of United Feature Syndicate, Inc.

Examine the following statements. *Mark an S by any statement that you believe is an example of scapegoating. Mark NS by any statement you believe is not an example of scapegoating. Mark a U by any statement which you are unsure is an example of scapegoating.*

S = *an example of scapegoating*
NS = *not an example of scapegoating*
U = *unsure or undecided*

1. Palestinian terrorists are to blame for the Arab-Israeli conflict.

2. There would be peace in the Mideast if it weren't for communist meddling there.

3. The United Nations should renegotiate a peace plan for the Arab-Israeli conflict.

4. There will never be peace between Arabs and Jews.

5. Arabs would live together in peace if only the Israelis weren't around.

6. The United Nations is responsible for the mounting tension in Palestine.

7. The Arabs and Israelis are both partly to blame for the Palestinian conflict.

8. Israel's unholy alliance with the racist South African government is the cause of all Israel's problems.

Periodical Bibliography

The following articles have been selected to supplement the diverse views presented in this chapter.

Jonathan Alter
"A Maze of Double Standards: When It Comes to Israel, Everyone Applies Them," *Newsweek*, January 11, 1988.

Henry Fairlie
"Among the Anti-Semites: Memoirs of a British Zionist," *The New Republic*, June 8, 1987.

Don Feder
"What a Friend Israel Has in United Nations," *Conservative Chronicle*, January 7, 1988. Available from Box 29, Hampton, IA 50441.

Hirsh Goodman
"Pretoria Connection," *The New Republic*, April 20, 1987.

Jane Hunter
"The Israeli Connection," *Middle East International*, May 14, 1988. Available from PO Box 53365, Temple Heights Station, Washington, DC 20009.

Journal of Palestine Studies
"Report of the Secretary-General of the United Nations to the Security Council Regarding the Situation in the Occupied Territories," Spring 1988.

Jeane Kirkpatrick
"Branding of Israel as Racist Halted Dream of UN as Forum for Peace," *Los Angeles Times*, September 10, 1985.

John J. McTague Jr.
"Israel and South Africa: A Comparison of Policies," *Journal of Palestine Studies*, Spring 1985.

Rafael Medoff and Mordechai Haller
"South Africa in the Mind of Israel," *National Review*, April 15, 1988.

Norman Podhoretz
"The Jackals Are Ganging Up on Israel," *Conservative Chronicle*, April 6, 1988.

Michah L. Sifry
"Israel and South Africa," *The Nation*, February 13, 1988.

Jennifer Trainer
"The United Nations: A Life-Draining Virus," *The Intellectual Activist*, April 17, 1987. Available from PO Box 582, Murray Hill Station, New York, NY 10156.

What Is the Future of Israel?

Chapter Preface

In 1968 Rabbi Moshe Levinger got permission from Israeli military officials to lead a small band of followers to Hebron, a holy site in the West Bank territory which Israel had captured in the 1967 Six-Day War. Levinger told the authorities he wanted to celebrate Passover there. Once in Hebron, however, Levinger and his followers announced they were settling and they refused to leave. Levinger's action served as a precedent for further religious settlements. Twenty years later, over 60,000 Jews are living in over one hundred settlements on the West Bank—land that still technically belongs to Jordan. Some live there for religious reasons, but for others, it is because the West Bank is a convenient commute from Tel Aviv. These settlements are a central factor in the debate over Israel's future.

Levinger's actions were based on his belief that the West Bank, which contained many of Judaism's most holy sites, was an important part of the Jewish state that had existed in the Old Testament. By capturing it in 1967, Israel was fulfilling a divine plan that Levinger believes makes compromise impossible. As Levinger himself has said, "You can compromise about unimportant things, but . . . to compromise on our own home, a home that belongs not only to us but also to God, is abnormal."

The settlements have become a factor no Israeli leader can ignore when considering how to achieve peace in the Middle East. If Israel were to cede the West Bank as a Palestinian homeland, it would need to evict thousands of Israeli settlers or leave them to live in a Palestinian-dominated state. Either option could lead to civil war. Hence Israel is caught in an impasse: Keeping the territory fuels Palestinian unrest; relinquishing it would threaten national unity.

The authors in the following chapter present their views on what the future holds for Israel, with the controversial Jewish settlements remaining an important factor in this complex debate.

"The PLO cannot be a participant in any political process."

Negotiating with the PLO Would Endanger Israel

Yitzhak Shamir

Yitzhak Shamir became Israel's prime minister in October 1986. He previously served as foreign minister in Menachem Begin's and Shimon Peres's administrations. In the following viewpoint, Shamir discusses Israel's goals for the future. He believes that direct negotiations with other Arab countries, particularly Jordan, can promote peace. He concludes that Israel will not negotiate with the Palestine Liberation Organization (PLO) because it rejects Israel's right to exist.

As you read, consider the following questions:

1. What steps has Israel already taken to achieve peace, according to the author?
2. What reasons does Shamir give for the creation of the PLO?
3. Why does Shamir believe Israel's invasion of Lebanon was necessary?

Yitzhak Shamir "Israel at 40: Looking Back, Looking Ahead." Reprinted by permission of *Foreign Affairs*, Vol. 66, No. 3. Copyright © 1988 by the Council on Foreign Relations, Inc.

One of Israel's leading poets wrote that the State of Israel is the realization of the greatest collective effort of the Jewish people since Moses led the Hebrews out of Egypt. In the forty years since the leadership of a small community of 600,000 souls proclaimed the establishment of the state, this effort has shown dramatic results indeed.

On the very first day of Israel's existence, we were invaded by the armies of seven countries, whose combined populations outnumbered ours by more than a hundred to one. A full one percent of Israel's population was killed in our war of independence —in American terms today that would mean the loss of two-and-a-half million people. . . .

Israel's citizens—Jews, Muslims, Druze and Christian—are equal before the law. Its judiciary is totally independent and beyond reproach; its elections, in which 70 to 80 percent of the electorate vote, are exemplary; its parties, from the extreme left to the extreme right, are all represented in parliament; and its numerous newspapers, in Hebrew, Arabic, English and other languages, reflect an incredible diversity of opinions. The Arab citizens of Israel are the only Arabs in the Middle East who can vote freely for a representative democratic government and who enjoy freedom of speech, assembly and movement.

Israel's Objectives

Israel's declaration of independence, which proclaimed the rebirth of the Jewish state in its historical home, set down three main objectives. The first was to provide a haven for every Jew who needed and wanted it. The second was to make Israel a spiritual fountainhead and emotional magnet for the Jews of the world, so that those among them who wished to fulfill their lives as Jews would settle in it.

The third objective deemed important enough to be included in the declaration was peace with our neighbors. We wanted the state to be the fulfillment not only of our prayer "Next Year in Jerusalem," but of the prayer "He who makes peace in His high places, may He make peace for us."

There was no Palestinian problem as such at that time. The only people who called themselves Palestinians then were the Jews of Palestine. Our English-language newspaper was the *Palestine Post,* our orchestra, the Palestine Symphony, and our fundraising organization, the United Palestine Appeal. The Arabs living in Palestine insisted that they were part of the Arab nation and shunned the appellation "Palestinians." It is a common misconception today that Israel replaced some kind of Palestinian entity. In fact, in the 3,000-year history of the country, which we know as the Land of Israel and the world calls Palestine, the only independent national sovereignty ever to exist there has been Jewish.

191

There was little we were not ready to do to achieve peace. Attesting to that was the very fact that we accepted the General Assembly resolution on the establishment of a Jewish state in ten percent of the area originally allotted to a national Jewish homeland by the mandate of the League of Nations. But the Arabs around us found unacceptable the existence of an independent non-Arab state in any area, however small, of what had once been part of the Arab empire, and they continued to war against us. In 1967, as a consequence of one of these wars, we brought Judea, Samaria and Gaza, as much parts of the Land of Israel as any other, under Israel's control. Today, a little less than one-quarter of the area of the original Palestine mandate is in our hands. The other three-quarters, now called the Hashemite Kingdom of Jordan, is in Arab hands. Jordan, whose population consists of people from both sides of the Jordan river is, therefore, a Palestinian Arab state in every respect except in name.

The Arab Response

When Israel accepted the United Nations partition plan, it was the only nation ever to recognize a Palestinian state. Arab armies responded with war. Had Israel's peace offer been accepted in 1948, Jaffa and Lydda would be Palestinian today. . . .

As long as the P.L.O. remains a terrorist organization, as long as it has not given up on its goal of destroying Israel, why should Israel negotiate with its leaders? But then, if the P.L.O. is not an interlocutor, who could be? There must be, and are, moderate Palestinians. But many have been assassinated—not by Israelis.

Elie Wiesel, *The New York Times*, June 23, 1988.

When King Hussein's grandfather proclaimed his independence from Britain, he wanted to call his country Palestine. The British Foreign Office dissuaded him. King Hussein himself, and all other Palestinian leaders, have stated that the Arabs on both sides of the river are one nation. And indeed, two-thirds of Jordan's population is from western Palestine, as are most of the members of its parliament and the best-known prime ministers and members of the government. Stating these facts does not, of course, imply opposition on our part to King Hussein's rule in Jordan. But, clearly, another Palestinian state between Jordan and Israel, in the 2,000 square miles of Judea and Samaria—an area the size of a large county in the western United States—makes no sense politically, cannot be viable economically and can only serve as a terrorist, irredentist base from which both Israel and Jordan will be threatened.

What does make sense is continuing the peace process via the one and only route with a proven track record: direct negotiations between the parties to the conflict. I believe peace with Jordan is a realistic, eminently attainable goal. A de facto peace between our countries has existed for quite some time. Movement of Arabs from both sides of the Jordan river is free. Trade between Jordan and Judea and Samaria flourishes, and Palestinian Arabs in Judea and Samaria carry Jordanian passports and can vote in elections for Jordan's parliament. From the present conditions to a close cooperation with Jordan in a large variety of spheres is but a relatively small step, one which could lay the foundation for a formal peace treaty.

I have declared time and again that I am ready to meet King Hussein anywhere, anytime, without preconditions, to discuss peace. Direct negotiations with Jordan can start tomorrow, in Amman, in Jerusalem or on "neutral" ground such as Camp David, with the full blessing and unreserved backing of every member of the Israeli government.

Seeking a Political Solution

A formula for negotiations was worked out at Camp David between Egyptian President Anwar al-Sadat and Prime Minister Menachem Begin. The centerpiece of the Camp David accords is the autonomy plan for the Palestinian Arabs, which includes a five-year transition period—a vital test of coexistence between Jews and Arabs. It leaves open for later deliberation the sensitive issue of sovereignty. And although it falls far short of our demands, it embodies a realistic attempt to move forward a political solution. . . .

The complex and sensitive nature of the issues between Israel and Jordan are such that only direct, independent, open-ended, face-to-face negotiations can provide the unpressured atmosphere that is absolutely vital for reaching an agreement. In these negotiations, representatives of the Arab residents of Judea and Samaria—not members of the Palestinian Liberation Organization and not terrorists—should of course participate. It is, after all, *their* autonomy that will be discussed. And while the exact nature of the autonomy should be left to the negotiating table, Israel's record of response to genuine peaceful intent speaks for itself.

Unfortunately, Palestinian Arabs in the past have too often entrusted their fate to other Arab governments and extreme elements such as the PLO. Terrorist organizations have used threats and assassination against those Arabs who showed an inclination to negotiate with us. That is why victory over terrorism is an essential prerequisite for the achievement of peace, and not, as some would have it, the other way around.

It is also necessary for Egypt and Jordan to join in the process

John Trever for the *Albuquerque Journal*.

and give the necessary backing to those Palestinian Arabs who will opt for negotiations and coexistence with Israel.

I am often asked why we do not simply ignore PLO terrorism and negotiate with this organization, recognized by the Arab League as the sole representative of the Palestinian people. It is an astonishing question. No country has ever been asked to negotiate with an organization that denies its right to exist. The PLO is not a Palestinian creation, nor has its existence anything to do with the so-called occupation of Judea and Samaria (the "West Bank"). It was organized by Egypt and Syria three years before the 1967 war to conduct terrorist warfare against Israel, and it is dedicated not to liberating this or that territory, but to the annihilation of Israel. That a terrorist organization, established less than 20 years after the holocaust and committed by its constitution to the destruction of Israel, enjoys observer status at the United Nations and diplomatic standing in many capitals is a sad commentary on the state of international morality. . . .

The tensions during the Lebanon war were caused, I believe, by the chasm between the Israeli and American perceptions of the PLO. Despite its record of heinous crimes almost exclusively against civilians, the PLO was seen by some Americans at the time as a product of injustice and refugee camps, a guerrilla army fighting against the "occupation of the West Bank and Gaza."

Israel knew it to be a terrorist arm of Arab governments, an instrument of state-sponsored terrorism, which used victims of frustration and misery in the Arab world—by no means only in refugee camps—as its recruits for murder. Formed in 1964 it operated mostly from Jordan until chased out by King Hussein in the "Black September" clampdown of 1970, in which thousands of PLO members were killed. The PLO then settled in Lebanon, again on the initiative of the Arab governments, and developed an infrastructure of a despotic ministate and a center of world terrorism.

There was almost no terrorist group in the world that did not receive training, logistical assistance, financial support and weapons from the PLO. It succeeded in assembling over 20,000 trained men who, unlike regular armies of sovereign states, could hide behind the shield of civilians no one wanted to hurt. It threatened to become a serious destabilizing force not only against Israel and Jewish targets in Europe but against the whole free world.

Beyond that, Israel saw in the PLO the embodiment of Arab rejection of Israel's right to exist. The greatest obstacle to peace in the Middle East still is the insistence of Arab governments that the organization whose charter stipulates the destruction of Israel is the sole representative of the Palestinian people.

The US Viewpoint

Washington did not always see it our way. While conceding our right to security on our northern border, it opposed the destruction of the PLO and intervened to rescue Yasir Arafat and his organization twice during the Lebanon war: once from the Israeli siege of Beirut, and then from the Syrian-sponsored attack by his rival, Abu Musa, in Tripoli. . . .

Israeli forces withdrew from Lebanon in 1985. Only a six-mile-wide security belt on our northern border is under Israeli control. Without it, the Galilee would be exposed to the same intolerable harassment—shelling and terrorist infiltration—to which it was subjected in the eight years preceding the Peace for the Galilee operation of 1982. But the partial reorganization of PLO elements in Lebanon and the introduction of hundreds of Iranian-sponsored Hezbollah terrorists into the area threatened to turn it again into a dangerous terrorist base. Until an independent, sovereign government is established in Lebanon and the Syrian occupation is removed, Israel will have to maintain a security belt and take the necessary measures to defend its northern region against terrorist incursions and shellings. . . .

Our goals, not in any particular order, are as follows:
- *Solidifying Israel's friendship and cooperation with the United States.* This entails further deepening and institutionalizing

of trade, strategic and political collaboration, and greater efforts in achieving economic independence and explaining our position to the American public.

- *Strengthening the peace with Egypt.* Our partner in peace should shoulder with us the responsibility for normalizing relations between our countries and for bringing our other neighbors to the negotiating table.
- *Attaining peace and coexistence with all our neighbors.* This entails projecting the message that violence will not bring a solution to the conflict; that terrorism must end; that the PLO cannot be a participant in any political process; that Arab refugees must be resettled; and that direct negotiations without preconditions is the only viable option for reaching peace.
- *Fulfilling the ideal* of making Israel the home of the Jewish people and an Israeli society that is founded on the moral principles of the biblical prophets.

The Real Threat to Peace

In February 1969, Yasser Arafat, at the head of the PLO's largest constituent faction, Fatah, took control of the entire organization. Since then, the PLO has perpetrated some 8,000 acts of terror, mostly against Israeli civilian targets, causing the deaths of over 650 Israelis and the wounding of thousands more. Other victims have included Jews abroad, innocent bystanders of many nationalities and Arab political opponents. . . .

The threat to the prospect of peace in the Middle East, therefore, comes not from Israel's anti-terrorist campaign, but from the PLO murderers themselves. Thus, the fight against terror is a fight for peace. It is those who support the PLO, with Arafat at its head, those who seek ways to have a dialogue with it, those who see the PLO as having moderated its views and those who are under the illusion that the terror will not strike them—who constitute the greatest obstacle to the peace process.

Israel's Ministry of Foreign Affairs, *The Threat of PLO Terrorism,* 1985.

The roots of Jewish and Arab heritage—in language, history, culture and religion—have much in common. Together the two peoples can usher in a renaissance chapter in the region. Our vision of peace is not limited to ending hostilities, or even to eliminating the threat of war. What we strive for is the fulfillment of the dream of the founder of Zionism, Theodor Herzl, who envisioned ninety years ago that a Jewish state would be a partner in bringing about an economic renaissance and unprecedented growth in the region, the realization of its unlimited potential, the flourishing of its culture, and a life of coexistence, amity and goodwill for all its people.

"Any solution that does not take the PLO into account will be no solution at all."

Negotiating with the PLO Would Bring Peace to Israel

Kathleen M. Christison

In the following viewpoint, writer Kathleen M. Christison criticizes Israel's leaders for refusing to negotiate with the Palestine Liberation Organization (PLO). Christison, a former political analyst in the Central Intelligence Agency, believes that Israel's policy is unrealistic. No matter what Israel thinks of the tactics the PLO uses, she argues, it ignores at its own peril the popular support the PLO has among Palestinians. Christison predicts that Israel's obstinance will lead to further unrest on the West Bank.

As you read, consider the following questions:

1. According to Christison, how do some Israelis support their argument that the Palestinians do not exist?
2. Why does the author believe it is unrealistic for Israel to refuse to negotiate with the PLO?
3. What reasons does Christison give for rejecting the idea that nations should never negotiate with terrorists?

Kathleen M. Christison, "Myths About Palestinians." Reprinted with permission from FOREIGN POLICY 66 (Spring 1987). Copyright 1987 by the Carnegie Endowment for International Peace.

A certain mythology has come to surround the Israeli-Palestinian dispute—shibboleths concerning the existence and legitimacy of Palestinian nationalism that have become accepted as fact by most Americans and that have shaped their views and the policy of most U.S. administrations toward the Arab-Israeli conflict. Then Israeli Prime Minister Golda Meir gave blunt expression to this mythology's core in an interview published on June 15, 1969, in the *Sunday Times* of London. There was "no such thing as Palestinians," she declared. "It was not as though there was a Palestinian people in Palestine considering itself as a Palestinian people."

If some Israelis were embarrassed by Meir's statement, it was not because they viewed it as false, but simply because it too baldly asserted a sentiment that most Israelis deep down wish were true. Many Israelis, of course, have no such compunctions—for instance, right-wing settlers on the West Bank, who see Jewish settlement there as a God-given right. A settler spokeswoman, Schifra Blass, told a group of American visitors in October 1985 that Palestinians have no rights whatsoever and that if they exist at all, they should go to Jordan. But the majority prefers to justify its beliefs with a kind of mythology that attempts to deny the legitimacy of Palestinian nationalism.

Subtle Arguments

Some of the arguments for this mythology are subtle, using genuine, though selective, historical data to support their theses. They note, for example, that "Palestine" historically has never been an independent entity. Other arguments are crude and heavy-handed, such as the novelist Leon Uris's depiction of the Palestinians as "people who don't have the dignity to get up and better their own living conditions." And still others appeal to logic or to the emotions with statements only tangentially relevant to the realities of Middle East politics or to U.S. or Israeli national interests. Israel's occupation of the West Bank, many observe, is more benevolent than any Arab rule would be; the Palestinians, they frequently say, are simply terrorists who murder innocent women and children. All of these arguments lead to the conclusion either that Palestinians do not deserve independence or that the Israelis should not negotiate with those who put themselves forward as Palestinian representatives.

The few who challenge these sacred cows are usually scorned as radicals or anti-Semites. But determined challenges are urgently needed. It is time that the United States and Israel accepted the realities of the Middle East. It may be comforting to deny that Palestinian nationalism has any legitimacy today because it never existed until the Zionists came along, or because Palestine Liberation Organization (PLO) chairman Yasir Arafat is a terrorist, or because Israelis are better than Palestinians at making the desert bloom, but it is not realistic.

Nationalism does not exist mainly in the eye of the beholder. The fundamental mistake made by those who would explain away the Palestinians is forgetting that nationalistic feeling is sustained by the people who profess it. Nationalism is in large measure a matter of emotions or a state of mind, and it cannot be denied by those outsiders who find it inconvenient. The only true test of a nationalism's legitimacy is its power to galvanize people to its cause. As David Ben-Gurion, later Israel's first prime minister, told a Zionist meeting in 1929: "The obvious characteristic of a political movement is that it knows how to mobilize the masses. From this perspective there is no doubt that we are facing a political movement, and we should not underestimate it."

By this criterion, Israel and the United States are still facing a national movement today. No matter how unappealing Arafat may be to Americans or Israelis, and no matter when or why Palestinian nationalism arose, that nationalism is staring the world in the face now, and Israel and the United States argue against its existence only at their own—especially Israel's—peril. The histories of South Africa, Northern Ireland, and Lebanon show that suppressed nationalisms can be a powerful revolutionary force and are dangerous to ignore.

A Rallying Point

I don't think anybody in the world has stopped recognizing the PLO as the body that speaks for the Palestinians. . . .

Most important is the Palestinians' perception of the PLO. The PLO is their flag—a framework, a rallying point. It is the only Palestinian body with a parliament and an executive with offices all around the world, that speaks and simulates a government.

Mordechai Bar-on, *New Perspectives Quarterly*, Spring 1988.

But the delegitimating mythology also includes specific arguments that must be confronted. The main problem with these arguments is not that they are wholly false—indeed, some isolated facts they use are true, even though the mythology as a whole rests largely on pseudohistory. Rather, they are so utterly beside the point. None has the slightest connection with any of the policy alternatives realistically available to the United States or Israel today. And all have bogged down policymakers and citizens alike in the fruitless tasks of debating might-have-beens and proving the unprovable.

Israelis and their supporters often contend, for example, that the nationalistic feelings of the Arabs in Palestine were weak or nonexistent before Israel's birth in 1948. Because this nationalism was allegedly created after the fact, they say, it can be ignored and will eventually fade away. . . .

The mythology's conclusion—that because Palestinian nationalism is artificial it will eventually disappear—seems to have been fatally undermined by the aftermath of Israel's 1982 invasion of Lebanon. Some observers contend that the PLO's "political, ideological, and military survival" depended on the freedom and geographic proximity to Israel provided by its presence in Beirut and that exile in distant Tunisia has been a near fatal blow. Militarily this is certainly true. Politically as well, the 1982 Lebanon war once again showed that as far as the Arab states are concerned, the Palestinians are basically on their own in their struggle with Israel.

But the spirit of Palestinian nationalism lives on, and those who have written it off or predicted a radical change in the character of its revolution are ignoring intangibles—will, morale, and, perhaps most important, the desires of the PLO's constituency, the residents of the West Bank and the Gaza Strip.

By Ben-Gurion's criterion, the Palestinian movement still thrives because it is still able—perhaps better able after the Lebanon war—to rally the masses. National movements have disappeared frequently throughout history, but never has a state the size of Israel permanently snuffed out the nationalistic impulses of a people as numerous as its own population.

Is Jordan Palestine?

The "Jordan is Palestine" argument is another irrelevancy that has gained popularity. The gist is that Jordan is merely an artificially created fragment of the whole of Palestine and that, if Palestinians want a homeland in Palestine, they should look for it in Jordan. But Palestine itself, no less than Jordan, was an artificial creation of the old colonial powers who carved up the Ottoman Empire after World War I and arbitrarily split off the area that came to be called Palestine from the Syria-Lebanon area. The former came under British control, the latter under French control. Indeed, those who contend that Palestinians should be happy in Jordan because for 4 years before Jordan's creation both banks of the Jordan River were part of the same colonial entity tend to be the same people who ridicule Syria's claims to any rights in Lebanon, even though Syria and Lebanon, too, were once part of the same entity.

Nevertheless, the overriding point today is that 4 million Palestinians around the world trace their roots not to Jordan but to the area west of the Jordan River that now constitutes Israel and the occupied West Bank. They—to say nothing of King Hussein—do not want a Palestinian state in Jordan or anywhere else outside their homeland. And it makes no more sense to expect them to accept such a solution than it did for Great Britain to expect that the early Zionists would settle for making the Jewish "national home" in British East Africa. The area that the Palestinians can reclaim must be limited by Israel's presence, but their desire for self-rule in a part of western Palestine cannot be ignored.

An Obvious Point

The first thing, surely, is to figure out some formula for recognizing the Palestine Liberation Organization. The arguments against doing so are perfectly plausible, perfectly honorable, perfectly persuasive. But they are serving to subsidize a situation that grows progressively intolerable. . . .

The Israeli government cannot live with itself over a protracted period if it finds that every day, more and more people are mutilated and killed in order to document Israel's right to prevail over 1.5 million Palestinians with a resident force on the order of 75,000. That there should be negotiations is obvious unless it is equally obvious that neither side is prepared to yield a single inch.

William F. Buckley Jr., *Conservative Chronicle*, March 16, 1988.

It is reasonable to ask why, if Palestinians are to be given rights in a part of Palestine, they will not attempt to assert those rights in all of Palestine. What is to stop them and their supporters, if they are given the West Bank and Gaza, from demanding all of Israel proper? The answer is that Israel is there; its right to exist within a prescribed set of borders is recognized by most of the world; and, far more important, it is too strong to be destroyed and all but the most radical Palestinians now accept that fact. . . .

Negotiating with Terrorists

The only position concerning the Palestinians on which both the Israeli left and right wings can agree is that Israel cannot negotiate with the PLO because it is a terrorist organization and is not representative of the Palestinians. This position is also official U.S. policy.

No one can deny that the PLO conducts terrorist operations, and no one can defend the killing and maiming perpetrated by terrorists—or dismiss the moral degradation that befalls terrorism's perpetrators. But moral outrage will not make terrorism go away, and force alone will not end it. How many governments in the last 40 years have ultimately had to negotiate with their terrorist and guerrilla foes? After all, during the Vietnam War the United States did not balk long at the prospect of negotiating with the National Liberation Front, a guerrilla and terrorist organization

201

that used tactics and strategy similar to the PLO's.

Further, many modern states have been led, and led quite effectively, by figures who used terrorism in their countries' struggles for independence: Algeria's Houari Boumediene, China's Mao Zedong, Cuba's Fidel Castro, Egypt's Anwar el-Sadat, Israel's Menachem Begin and Yitzhak Shamir, Kenya's Jomo Kenyatta, Vietnam's Ho Chi Minh, and Zimbabwe's Robert Mugabe. Although not everyone has agreed with all of their policies, most people today consider these men to be, or to have become, respectable citizens—leaders now, if terrorists before. Who can say who is righteous and who is immoral—the former Jewish terrorist who has given up his old calling because he happens to have succeeded, or the present-day Palestinian terrorist who still struggles for similar goals?

Moreover, a distinction must be made between the kind of automatic hatred that drives a Muammar el-Qaddafi or an Abu Nidal and the tactical considerations of Arafat and the PLO mainstream. Arafat and the PLO are fighting for something. Libya's Qaddafi and Palestinians like Abu Nidal, who have been so envenomed by their years of terrorism that hatred is their only motivation, are only fighting against something, or, more likely, against everything—Israel, the United States, imperialism, capitalism, and the West in general. Nothing will satisfy this kind of terrorist, certainly not negotiations. But the kind of terrorist who is striving to achieve a constructive goal is more likely to respond to arrangements with an adversary that are relevant to that goal.

Courting the PLO Mainstream

Were the PLO mainstream satisfied with achieving a West Bank state, clearly the movement's radical fringes, who demand Israel's destruction, would feel even more aggrieved. International terrorism would not cease and might even increase. Terrorists would strike against the new West Bank state and its leaders, and radicals would attempt to infiltrate the new state and attack Israel from bases there.

With adequate security arrangements and its massive military strength, however, Israel could deter or, if the worst happened, defend itself against any such aggression. Israel can be attacked today from across the Jordan River as easily as it could at some future date from a West Bank in Palestinian hands. Theoretically, terrorist attacks could also be launched quite easily into and across the Golan Heights from Syria. The fact that Israel has not been attacked for years from either Jordanian or Syrian territory attests not to Hussein's or Hafez al-Assad's moderation but to Israel's own overwhelming strength—a strength the United States should and would continue to guarantee after a West Bank peace settlement. . . .

Despite the PLO's profound difficulties in recent years, the organization and Arafat have grown in popularity on the West Bank. Polls and spontaneous demonstrations—such as occurred at the funeral of Zafer el-Masri, the Israeli-appointed mayor of the West Bank town of Nablus who was assassinated in March 1986—have consistently shown overwhelming support for Arafat and the PLO in the occupied territories. And their ratings have risen as Israel has cracked down in the West Bank and as Arafat and his wing of the PLO have drawn away from the radical wing.

Two surveys conducted soon after Arafat's expulsion from Lebanon in December 1983 showed that nearly all West Bank Arabs preferred Arafat to the more radical PLO leaders who were fighting him. And in a poll released in September 1986, in which traditionally politically active professional and white-collar workers on the West Bank were heavily represented, 70 per cent supported Arafat as the preferred leader of the PLO and 93.5 per cent supported the PLO as the "sole legitimate representative" of the Palestinian people.

The PLO cannot be ignored, no matter how distasteful some of its policies and tactics may be, no matter how undemocratic it may be, and no matter how repugnant most Americans may find Arafat. Any solution that does not take the PLO into account will be no solution at all, for in the absence of any better organization, it is the voice of the Palestinian people, and it is quite capable of disrupting any peace in which it does not take part. . . .

Time Is Running Out

The likelihood that Palestinian nationalism will explode in Israel's face can be diminished only if the movement is recognized for what it is—a vibrant, growing force that cannot be wished away or suppressed forever. Only if Israel and the United States face the realities of the situation and stop promoting and blindly following the mythology that denies Palestinian nationalism will there be any hope of a solution. Time is running out.

"A state can defend poor borders, of the kind we will have after withdrawing from the West Bank and Gaza, but it cannot defend itself if half its population is loyal to the enemy."

Keeping the Occupied Territories Threatens Israel's Future

Yehoshafat Harkabi

In December 1987, Palestinians living in the occupied territories rioted against Israeli control. After several weeks of riots, a controversy arose among Israeli Jews concerning the future of the territories. The following viewpoint by Yehoshafat Harkabi represents one view of the debate. Harkabi argues that Israel must pursue immediate negotiations with the Palestinians. He believes that Israel cannot keep a hostile, growing population within its borders and be secure. A former head of Israeli Defense Forces intelligence, Harkabi teaches international relations at Hebrew University in Jerusalem.

As you read, consider the following questions:

1. What events could lead to war, according to the author?
2. Why does the author believe it is essential that Israel reach an agreement with the Palestinians as soon as possible?
3. What examples does Harkabi cite to support his argument that Israel's negotiating positions are unrealistic and foolish?

Yehoshafat Harkabi, "A Policy for the Moment of Truth," *Jerusalem Post International Edition*, February 13, 1988. Used with the author's permission.

For many years, the Arabs were absolutely opposed to the existence of Israel. But the dispute has been a learning process in which some important Arab circles began to moderate their political position, even if they clung to the dream of Israel's disappearance. This development is what led former Egyptian President Anwar Sadat to agree to peace with us. What is important to us is that the goal of eliminating Israel ceases to be "policy," as distinguished from "grand design." There is no way of extinguishing a people's vicious dreams, which are liable to persist even after political accommodation. A political settlement eventually uproots the vicious dreams and cancels them out, while lack of political accommodation establishes and reinforces them.

The distinction between the "grand design" that Israel disappear and agreement to a "policy" of political accommodation with her spread from Egypt to Jordan and the PLO. This change occurred not because we endeared ourselves to them, but because they realized that Israel's elimination is impossible, or would exact too high a price from the Arabs, and that lack of a settlement would lead to a hell in which all would suffer, and first among them, the Israelis and the Palestinians.

As a result of this change, the PLO and Jordan offered Israel a political accommodation in the Hussein-Arafat agreement of 1985, which was based on a principle that is revolutionary in the history of this dispute: "land for peace," which is to say a willingness to make peace in return for a withdrawal from the territories occupied in 1967. The emphasis on the *1967* occupation recurs in other Arab documents, including the decisions of the Fez summit (September 1982) and Amman (November 1987).

Moderation Should Be Rewarded

The Arab formulations are by no means sufficient, and they are ambivalent, but they are a beginning that must be seized. Moderation will not come from the Arab side unless it is certain to be rewarded, as Sadat was certain. The Hussein-Arafat proposal met total rejection from the Israeli side.

The choice before Israel is not between good and bad, but between bad and worse. In the absence of an accommodation, the following developments can be expected: Demographically, the Arabs will become a majority, or near-majority, and we cannot take for granted the long-term existence of a Jewish state in which half the population is Arab.

The hell that develops here will boil over into the further hell of war with the Arab states. The Palestinians are not orphans, and they will have the violent support of Arab states, which, at the summit in Amman, opted for military preparedness by adopting the Syrian principle of "strategic parity" as a Pan-Arab principle.

The peace with Egypt will collapse overnight and we will again

have to divide our army between two fronts. As in 1973 and 1982, an Israeli victory is liable not to be translated into political results (let us remember that the Americans were infinitely stronger than the Vietnamese and were nevertheless defeated). Iraq will finally be released from its war with Iran which, like all wars, will end. The Arab armies are growing stronger, in quantity and quality.

Any future wars will be disastrous because of the destructiveness and precision of weapons, and our ability to absorb losses is limited. The greater our losses, the greater the shock to our very existence. The possibility of wars in the absence of an accommodation is today only a trend, but trends must be discerned before they turn into facts.

The longer an accommodation is postponed, the more inferior the terms we will be able to secure. Even now, they are worse than what we might have achieved in 1985. Once we might have reached an agreement with Hussein alone, but we refused. Hussein was forced to include the PLO to make any progress; then he had to include the Syrians.

Once the Americans would have sufficed; now we can go nowhere without the Soviets. An accommodation at our initiative, with heads high, would have yielded much better results than one we are forced into, arriving on all fours.

With difficulty, a state can defend poor borders, of the kind we will have after withdrawing from the West Bank and Gaza, but it cannot defend itself if half its population is loyal to the enemy. With all its nuclear arsenal, the U.S. would not be able to defend itself if it had 120 million Russians within its borders. The inability to understand this problem is evidence of skewed national thinking that is cause for concern.

We will have to negotiate with the Palestinians, the majority of whom, in any referendum, would vote for the PLO as their representative, not out of love, but as the unparalleled symbol of the idea that the Palestinians are a human public worthy of political expression. The U.S. does not determine the composition of the Soviet delegation to negotiations, and Israel's presumption in trying to determine the composition of the Arab delegation is an absurdity bound to fail. The wish for a local Palestinian representation detached from the PLO and more moderate than that body is merely delusion. The complaints about the PLO voiced in the territories (for instance, by the Islamic Jihad) concern its excessive moderation. . . .

The riots in the territories perhaps evoke a "hawkish" stance among our soldiers, at the personal level, accompanied by a political dovishness—"We have to get rid of the terrorities." In part of the nation, the riots awakened doubts about our ability to maintain control in the long run. But in the other part, not overly eager to acknowledge its error, the riots merely strengthened the belief that no accommodation is possible, that there is no one to talk to, that this is an "us or them" struggle.

"Absolutizing" the Dispute

This group has a vested interest in Arab extremism as a justification for Israeli extremism, and thus, unwittingly acts in such a way as to encourage it. It is not true that there is no one to talk to, but we do our best to make sure there will not be. This practice of "absolutizing" the dispute (after "relativization" has started) occurs also among the Arabs (the Salvation Front, which is outside the PLO, as well as some PLO elements, and the Islamic Jihad). This is going for broke. . . .

Arab moderation cannot maintain itself without moderation on our side, and for that reason is not autonomous, whereas Arab extremism can persist as is. There is no chance that the Arabs in the West Bank and Gaza will agree to remain under our control, and, in the long term, not even under full autonomy which, as it becomes established, will evoke the demand that it be extended into independence. Arabs in an autonomous entity will be in a better position than they are now to wring concessions from us. . . .

The central norm of the international system and international law is self-determination.

An Iron Fist of Hate

In another thirteen years there will be two million Arabs under Israeli rule in the West Bank and Gaza Strip. In 2010 their numbers will equal ours.

There are those who say it is possible to continue on in this way for years. That over the years the "fabric of life" (mutual acquaintance, economic links, and so on) will overcome enmity. That is idiocy, and reality proves it even now. As long as the present "fabric of life" continues, it is wrapped around an iron fist of hate and revenge. . . .

I have a bad feeling: I am afraid that the current situation will continue exactly as it is for another ten or twenty years. . . . I am also sure that the moment will come when we will be forced to do something, and it may well be that our position then will be much less favorable than it is now.

David Grossman, *The Yellow Wind*, 1988.

The great changes of our times, and the freeing of the colonies, occurred in its name. A country that insists that it can exist only if this principle is violated is destined to endanger the legitimacy of its own existence.

Reality will force Israel to retreat from her political stance, to withdraw from the territories and to negotiate with the PLO. She will undergo a tremendous crisis when she realizes her political stupidity. The blow will be as severe as the hopes were high.

It's a dangerous situation, since the nature of men is to refuse to recognize their errors, particularly if they prove them to be fools. Thus they are liable to refuse to learn the lesson, and in fact increase their devotion to the old, mistaken policy. . . .

Faulty reasoning has been fostered by demagoguery. The leadership praises itself for its desire for peace and for a political accommodation when its intention is a political solution that will recognize Israeli control of the territories whose practical implication is annexation. This is a delusion. The leadership is extending the Arabs an invitation to negotiate on an agreement and at the same time the prime minister declares repeatedly that even after autonomy Israel will not give up any part of Eretz Yisra'el. The leadership is expecting the miraculous appearance of some kind of magic formula to which the Palestinians, Arabs, and the world will agree. In so doing, it bases its policy on unrealistic hopes and a gamble—a "Toto policy" at the national level. Anyone who does not believe in this national "Toto" is depicted as a person of little faith.

Our leaders are portraying conflict as though it were simply a fight against terror; the PLO is a terrorist organization and could only emerge from a terrorist people, and the UN which recognizes it and the 100 countries which allow them diplomatic representation are merely encouraging terror.

I am not claiming that the PLO is a pleasant organization; it is ugly both in theory and practice. But we negotiate not because we have awarded our adversary a certificate of good behavior—but because he is an adversary.

There is also demogoguery in the perpetual refrain of our leaders following every mishap that "we have to explain," as though the rest of the world were waiting to be enlightened by our words of wisdom. Any opinion different from ours is termed lack of understanding. Perhaps it is we and our leaders who don't understand.

Any scrutiny of our problems is lambasted as defeatism, pessimism, and undermining of the peoples' faith in itself—as though the ship of fools were not actually the cause of the erosion of our faith in ourselves. Everything is topsy-turvy. The attempt to prevent Israel's downfall and defeat is itself stigmatized as defeatism. Witlessness can no longer be distinguished from the laudable virtue of optimism.

The Need for Criticism

The claim that any criticism gives comfort to the enemy is no less demogogic. It only reveals a profound misunderstanding of how little the Arabs are in need of our advice or encouragement. They comprehend the situation and its potential perfectly well, and their leadership is in no way inferior to ours. The Arabs have learned a great deal from us, however, in the past few years. They have ceased to esteem our sagacity, and this gives them hope that they will indeed overcome us.

There is self-righteous blindness in the proposition that the problem is enhancing the quality of life for the Palestinians—as though that, and not the national problem, were their complaint.

Bribery never succeeded in endearing colonialism to the colonized people. No improvement in the quality of life will persuade the residents of the territories to agree to remain under our control. Neither will they accept an interim arrangement like autonomy without some statement of where it will lead. An Arab leader cannot start negotiating without some guarantee of ultimate success. . . .

An Extraordinary Fantasy

The idea that we can rule over all the area between the Jordan and the sea, with all its population, seems to me the most extraordinary fantasy to which any large number of Jews has been attached since the false messiah Shabbetai Zevi in the 17th century.

The United States is very strong. But nothing could save it from disintegration and collapse if it were to try to exercise dominion over 95 million Russians. In other words, what really defines the survival of the state is the inner harmony, the common allegiance that makes the people want to live together as a state.

The question is how to start negotiations. And the crux of it is Palestinian representation. It's no use wanting your adversary to be represented by people so pliable that they're not representative. You make peace with those who were at war with you.

Abba Eban, *The New York Times*, January 24, 1988.

In discussing the solution of the dispute, we should distinguish what the sides are likely to accept, and what they will reject, because it is important for us to understand what are the limits of concessions we can expect from the Palestinians. Those limits certainly will be influenced by negotiations and the pressure activated on them, but they have minimum demands that they will not give up.

Recognizing the Palestinians

Their most basic demand is the recognition that the Palestinian people constitutes a political entity whose collective existence deserves political expression as a state. Afterward, that state could establish confederative connections with Jordan and accept limits, but nevertheless at first it must be recognized as an independent state. In the past the Palestinians claimed that only they and not the Jews deserved a state. Meantime, some of their leaders have moved away from that position. We can't expect them to agree that only the Jews should have a state while the Palestinian Arabs are eligible only for autonomy as a political body under the auspices of Israel.

They proclaim steadfastness (*sumud*) in the demand for a Palestinian state and the battle for it shows their readiness for many losses. We are proud of the self-sacrifice we displayed in the battle for our country. We must recognize that we are not unique in that. . . .

Certainly after an agreement there will be Arab elements interested in violating it. But there will be others with no desire to return to the hell of the past. The negotiators will have to create facts and guarantees which make a return to hostilities difficult. Our control of the passage between the West Bank and Gaza will give us leverage for exerting pressure. And the international community will support the strengthening of the agreement.

A Moment of Truth

Israel faces a moment of truth, in the full sense of the word. My only message is this: Let us begin to think about our situation seriously. I am still optimistic about the possibility of an agreement. Our sages said that no one leaves the world with even half his desires achieved; the same applies to the nations of the world, and to us. I have not come to preach morality. My only concern is how Israel can achieve the best possible results. In the past, Zionism accomplished so much with so little, and developed a sophisticated diplomacy. But we have undergone a process of stupidification. We must divest ourselves of the ideology and the ethos which were at the base of this process. We must develop a vision of "the Zionism of quality"—and we have the prerequisites for that in the vast talent in this country—instead of a "Zionism of acreage" and populism. We must develop an attitude of mature, healthy self-criticism, which will protect us from illusion and adventurism. Only in this way can we broaden the general pursuit of excellence: "Would that all the Lord's people were prophets." (Numbers 11:29).

4

"If Israel forfeits its right to enter the towns and villages, they will be transformed . . . [into] little Beiruts from which violence will radiate unhampered."

Relinquishing the Occupied Territories Threatens Israel's Future

David Bar-Illan

Many Israelis oppose the idea of a Palestinian state because they fear that it would be used to launch terrorist attacks against Israel. In the following viewpoint, David Bar-Illan argues that although unstable and often violent relations with Palestinians in the occupied territories are far from ideal, Israel's alternative of conceding territory would encourage war in the region. Bar-Illan is the director of the Jonathan Institute, an anti-terrorist foundation based in Jerusalem and New York.

As you read, consider the following questions:

1. Why does Bar-Illan disagree with the idea of negotiating with rioting Palestinians?
2. What events does the author predict will occur if a Palestinian state is created?
3. What two events could bring peace to the region, according to the author?

David Bar-Illan, "Can Israel Withdraw?" Reprinted from *Commentary*, April 1988, by permission; all rights reserved.

"Think of the alternative," Henry Kissinger used to say when pressing Israelis and Arabs to modify their positions in the days of his shuttle diplomacy in the Middle East. It is a salutary admonition, since we tend to forget that the alternative to *bad* is not always *good*. It can be *worse*. It can be catastrophe.

Israel is in a bad situation. Not because it won the 1967 war and, as a result, added a million hostile Arabs to the population under its control; not because it suffers universal calumny for allegedly mistreating them; not because the higher Arab birth rate poses a demographic threat; and not even because the territory of the land of Israel is also claimed by Ishmael. Difficult as these problems are, they can all yield to rational resolution. What defies resolution and what makes Israel's situation truly bad is that 300 million Arabs consider the very existence of Israel an offense to their sense of history and destiny.

The Moderates Are Dead

Once upon a time there were Arab leaders, like King Hussein's great-uncle the Emir Feisal, who believed that the Jews should have a state on both sides of the Jordan, and that the Jewish and Arab national movements "complete one another" and should work together for a "reformed Middle East." Those Arabs are dead, and any Arab leader today who expresses remotely similar sentiments is assured of joining them in short order. There are, however, Arab leaders who were convinced by their defeat in 1967 that Israel could not be destroyed, and that its existence had to be tolerated. Indeed, so convinced were they that nothing short of a total reversal of that defeat could reawaken their hopes of wiping Israel off the map. Yet such a reversal is precisely what the whole world now appears to want. . . .

There is no doubt that the status quo has little to recommend it. If the "uprising" in the territories is a true reflection of the popular mood there, Israel has on its hands 1.3 million Arabs whose hatred is boundless and unremitting. Moreover, the massive and, in places, violent "peace day" demonstration within the pre-'67 borders, held in solidarity with the "uprising," may indicate that the hostility of the 700,000 Arab citizens of the state of Israel is, though better camouflaged, not less intense. So even if the demographers who predict that the Arabs of Israel and the territories will constitute 45 percent of the total population by the year 2000 are as wrong as demographers have been in the past, and even if the ratio of Arabs to Jews remains constant for the foreseeable future, a full one-third of the population will be chronically hostile, violent, and disruptive. Hardly a happy state of affairs. . . .

Faced with such hostility, some Israeli leaders on both sides of the political spectrum have recommended unilateral withdrawal from Arab population centers. "Let them stew in their own juice" is the common rejoinder to questions about the internal mayhem that would inevitably ensue. But the consequences of unilateral withdrawal would not be limited to internecine struggles. Unilateral Israeli action would be seen as surrender to riots, which could only lead to the conclusion that more riots would bring more retreat. It is not, after all, the pervasive presence of Israeli soldiers that creates disturbances. As anyone who knows the territories will attest, the Israeli presence is hardly in evidence there in times of calm, and the day-to-day administration has been steadily and rapidly transferred to Arab hands.

The simple truth is that incitement in the streets and the mosques is not against the Israeli army's presence in the towns themselves, but against Jewish rule of "Arab lands." If Israel forfeits its right to enter the towns and villages, they will be transformed from islands of occasional anarchy to bases of permanent terrorism: little Beiruts from which violence will radiate unhampered to the main roads, the Jewish settlements, and ultimately to the cities of Israel.

But if unilateral Israeli action is ruled out, what about a negotiated settlement?

In what has become a parody of the democracies-negotiating-with-themselves syndrome, most Israeli leaders have been gauging the viability of peace plans not according to Israel's interests and needs but according to what the Arabs would accept. In December 1984, Jordan's King Hussein, counting on an agreement with the Palestine Liberation Organization's Yasser Arafat, indicated that he would consent to direct talks with Israel on the condition that a PLO-approved delegation from the territories participated in the negotiations. At that point, Shimon Peres (who was then Prime Minister) rejected the alternative Soviet proposal for an international conference on the Middle East as a lethal trap intended to force Israel and the U.S. into untenable positions, and he passionately inveighed against it in his meetings with Reagan and Shultz. But when, a few months later, Hussein, under Syrian pressure, changed his position and insisted on an international conference as the only venue for talks, Peres became a passionate pursuer of the idea and tried to sell it to the same Reagan and Shultz. . . .

An Illusory Option

The "Jordanian option," favored by the Labor party, involves a trade-off of most but not all the territories for peace. The Allon Plan, still nominally part of the Labor-party platform, stipulates annexation by Israel of over one-fourth of Judea-Samaria (the "West Bank") and Gaza, including East Jerusalem. But recent pronouncements by Peres (who is now Foreign Minister) have made it clear that the dovish majority of the Labor party is willing to settle for much less: specifically, a return to the status-quo-ante-June 1967 with minor border changes; Jordanian rule in the territories, which would be demilitarized; security arrangements in the Jordan valley, preferably leaving Israeli settlements there; and a compromise on Jerusalem which would keep it municipally united but would cede the eastern part of the Old City, with the exception of the Jewish quarter, to Jordan. . . .

There is, however, one problem with the Jordanian option. It does not exist. The reason is not only that Jordan agreed in Rabat in 1974, and has reaffirmed many times since, that the PLO is the sole representative of the Palestinian people; nor is it merely that adding to the kingdom 1.3 million citizens, among whom the pro-Hashemites are the weakest, would be a reckless gamble. Even more important is the drastic change since 1967 in the balance of power between Jordan and Syria. . . .

It therefore follows not only that the Jordanian option is a chimera but that no final peace agreement can be reached unless Israel relinquishes the territories. No Arab ruler can accept less than Egypt's Sadat did at Camp David in 1978—every inch of "occupied land"—or make a separate peace without Syria, and live. If, then, Israel signs a peace treaty, no matter with whom, it will have to withdraw from all the territories, including the Golan Heights, and there will be a Palestinian state in Judea, Samaria, and Gaza.

Civil War in a Palestinian State

To some Israelis, mainly on the Left but also among Likud members, a Palestinian state is preferable to the "Jordanian option." They contend that only by satisfying the national aspirations of the Palestinians can peace be achieved, and that these aspirations can only be satisfied by allowing the Palestinians a state of their own in the territories.

But the assumption that a Palestinian state would lead to peace ignores the nature, dynamics, and goals of the various Palestinian groups that would be vying for power there. After all, vicious internal struggles generally follow revolutions, "wars of liberation," and national upheavals even when national identity and cohesion are mature and deep-rooted. But while *Arab* nationalism goes back to the 19th century, the particularization of Palestinian nationalism began only about two decades ago. (Thus, between 1948 and 1967, when Jordan ruled Judea and Samaria and Egypt ruled Gaza, no talk was heard of a separate Palestinian state there.)

It is, of course, possible to develop passionate nationalistic feelings even in the short span of twenty years. Yet it is unrealistic to expect that the loyalties to the various sponsoring regimes of Palestinian nationalism, or the intensely antagonistic ideologies and grandiose ambitions within the movement itself, can be superseded by unity, national patriotism, and peaceableness. The murderous struggle for power between the Abu Musa and the Arafat factions of the PLO following the organization's departure from Beirut is but a foretaste of what could be expected once the spoils of sovereignty were at stake. . . .

Mortal Danger

To return to the 1967 borders would put Israel in mortal danger. Demilitarization of the West Bank would not be meaningful. It is a half-hour drive from Jericho to Jerusalem, and it takes 48 hours to mobilize our reserves—the basis of our strength, our ability to deter war.

Moshe Arens, *The New York Times*, January 24, 1988.

The whole Lebanon condition would thus be shifted to the new Palestinian state, with Israel a much readier target. Lebanon borders on the sparsely populated rural north of Israel and has a Christian and Shi'ite population on its southern frontier which accommodates an Israeli security belt. But a Palestinian state in Judea-Samaria and Gaza would cut through Jerusalem and flank the city on three sides, touch on Tel Aviv's suburbs, and have a long border, nine to fifteen miles from the sea, with Israel's most thickly populated areas. Palestinian militias, now armed not with gasoline bombs and stones but helicopters, missiles, artillery, and automatic weapons, all quickly imported through ports in Gaza and airfields elsewhere, would have Israeli pedestrians within rifle range, 80 percent of Israel's population and two-thirds of its industry within Katyusha range, and Zion square in Jerusalem and Ben-Gurion airport within mortar range. Israel would be reduced to responding with retaliatory ground raids, the way it did against Jordanian-held territories in the 50's and 60's—or with air raids, as it does in Lebanon today. . . .

A Syrian Invasion

In the meantime, if the history of other "wars of national liberation" is any guide, the winners of the internal PLO struggle would be those with Soviet sponsorship or, in this case, the backing of the Soviet proxy, Syria. In other words, the most radical forces within the PLO would come to the fore. And once such a faction established its power base, Syria would be invited to bring stability to the area, which it considers as much a part of "Greater Syria" as it does Lebanon. (The PLO version of the resolutions at the Amman conference refers to "the struggle of the Palestinian people." In the Syrian version, it is the struggle of "our people.")

Without the Golan Heights, Israel would not be able to prevent a Syrian invasion through the Galilee and northern Jordan. To meet the Syrians, who would by then have achieved strategic parity with Israel, the Israelis would have to fight their way up the mountains of Samaria through the by-now well-armed Palestinian forces, replenished by airborne Syrian divisions landed in Palestinian airfields. Israeli Arabs, swept up in the excitement of Palestinian nationalism, armed with weapons easily smuggled from the independent Palestinian state next door, and convinced—not baselessly—of an Arab victory, could ambush Israelis going to the front line. . . .

Fighting for its very survival, it would probably be able to stop the Syrians. Yet those who blithely talk of Israel's ability to defeat all the Arab armies, let alone one or two, and who believe that the miracle of the 1967 war could be easily repeated, are ignorant of the changes that have taken place in the balance of power in the region, particularly in the case of Syria. They also ignore the fact that Egypt regards its defense pact with the Arab countries "against Israeli aggression" as taking precedence over its peace treaty with Israel. And what would be a more clear-cut case of "aggression" than Israel's attacking the budding Palestinian state just because it invited Syrian troops to help bring stability to the area?

Staggering Costs

If Israel were to lose, the Arabs would finally have achieved their hope of "wiping the Jewish state off the map." But even if Israel won, the human cost would be staggering. No one seems to remember now that Israel prepared for 40,000 dead in the 1967 war. It was a reasonable expectation, obviated by a combination of extraordinary circumstances which no longer exist. Even if no chemical weapons were used, Syria's state-of-the-art short- and medium-range missiles; its huge air force, larger than Israel's, with Mig 29s; its 4,500 tanks—a larger force than the U.S. has in Europe; its anti-aircraft command-and-control system connected directly to Moscow; and the "cover" of the Soviet navy based in its port of Tartus—all this would make tens if not hundreds of thousands of Israeli casualties inevitable. . . .

Thus, to state that "peace, not territory, is Israel's security"; to suggest that peace requires only that the Israelis act with courage, wisdom, and generosity, and respond to Arab violence as if it were a misunderstanding in Scandinavia East; to expect that a reformed Arafat or a born-again Abu Nidal will preside over the one and only sanctuary of coexistence and cooperation in the Arab world— is to insult history and to mock common sense.

Vital Mountain Passes

Perhaps people believe that Israel can have "strong and secure borders" without controlling Judea and Samaria (called "the West Bank" by Jordan).

They are mistaken.

Israel without the administered territories is a strategically crippled country, an Israel that is a liability and a burden to her Western allies. . . .

Retaining "the West Bank" area means control of vital mountain passes and strategic depth between the Jordan River and Israel's highly populated and industrialized coastal plain.

Jedidiah Cartwright, *Liberty Report*, October 1987.

Is there, then, no hope for peace? A wiser administration of the territories, on the pattern established under Menahem Milson in the early 80's, might still restore a peaceful, if fragile, *modus vivendi*. Much could also be done about the 350,000 refugees still living in camps in the territories, who provide the main cannon-fodder for unrest. A cynical world has for forty years shed crocodile tears over them, but has forbidden Israel to "change their status" by moving them into decent housing. A rehabilitation project might succeed even now in countering the agitation and incitement. . . .

Real peace can come only in the event, now not very likely, that a very large number of Jews from the Soviet Union, South and North America, and Europe immigrate to Israel. A massive settling of Judea and Samaria would then make Israel's presence there irreversible, eliminate the current feeling of uncertainty (as abhorrent to political stability as a vacuum is to nature), reconcile the local population to autonomous life under Israeli rule, and finally convince the Arab states to resign themselves to the existence and indestructibility of Israel and give up the war they have been waging against it since the day of its birth.

Another, even less likely, development which might bring peace would be the rise of democratic governments in Jordan and Syria. As in the case of Germany and France, governments truly reflecting the will of the people can bury age-old enmities and render borders a secondary consideration.

An Insoluble Situation

Failing such eventualities, the world will have to get used to the idea that the Israel-Arab conflict, like the conflicts in Northern Ireland, the Basque region, Cyprus, Sri Lanka, the Punjab, and others, is insoluble for the foreseeable future. Bad as this is, the only real alternative is worse.

"A more resolutely Jewish Israel, as opposed to a secular-socialist one, is a far more congenial ally for America."

Israel Should Become More Religious

Mordechai Nisan

Gush Emunim is an umbrella organization that includes several groups which form a highly-influential fundamentalist movement in Israel. In 1968 Gush Emunim established the first Jewish settlements in the newly-captured Arab West Bank and since then has been a consistent opponent of ceding Israeli-held territory to Arabs. In the following viewpoint, Mordechai Nisan supports the policies of the Gush Emunim movement. He believes that Israel can recapture its vitality and affirm its spiritual underpinnings by basing its policies on Jewish teaching. Nisan lectures on the Middle East at Hebrew University in Jerusalem.

As you read, consider the following questions:

1. According to Nisan, what profound weakness in Israeli society did the 1967 war reveal?
2. What does the author describe as the goals of the Gush Emunim movement?
3. What arguments does Nisan make to refute the contention that by becoming more religious Israel will be less democratic?

Mordechai Nisan, "The Search for the Israeli Ethos," *Global Affairs*, Summer 1987. Reprinted with permission.

The crisis in Zionism can no longer be hidden or ignored. Despite its birth in the Enlightenment spirit of progress, which seemed to make Israel a vibrant success story in the 1950s and 1960s, Israel is now passing through a kind of post-modern sobriety, if not pessimism, about the country's capacity to recapture its early youthful élan. Today the revolutionary doctrine of secularism, as a Zionist war cry against Judaism, is winding up its brief but brutal history in *Eretz-Israel.* What happened to it can provide a thread leading to unearthing a different kind of Israel for the future. . . .

The dissolution of a coherent national ethos began to become pitifully apparent at the moment of military victory and popular exuberance in 1967. The paradox of physical strength coincident with spiritual atrophy surfaced in the political and social planes of Israeli life. Older Zionist axioms like "Hebrew labor," "*halutziut*" (pioneering verve), Jewish settlement, socialist construction, and the like had become petrified slogans. The capture of Judea and Samaria, the historic hearth of the land, the locus of prophets and priests, the mountains of defense and the valleys of tears, did not elicit an active and determined response. The policy of "territories for peace" implied the area's commercial value as barter in peace-making negotiations with some potential Arab partner. At the juncture, therefore, *Eretz-Israel* had clearly ceased to act as an agent of national self-fulfillment. The Jews stood at a distance and awaited developments. . . .

Alienated in the Jewish Homeland

The crisis of the spirit, expressed in the loss of a native Jewish ethos in Israel, was radically exposed by the halting, confused Israeli reaction to the sudden territorial homecoming to the core of pristine national history.

The subversion of Jewish sensitivity to the Temple Mount in Jerusalem and the Cave of the Patriarchs in Hebron was part of a more profound self-alienation from the people's very Jewishness. This was not perceived in the immediate days after 1967. It would take another war and other developments to expose the extent of the spiritual dislocation in the national psyche. . . .

Suddenly after the 1973 war, with national morale down and economic difficulties beginning, as the world demanded Israeli territorial withdrawal and veritable political capitulation to the Arabs, the country saw the birth of a popular, pioneering movement called *Gush Emunim* that set out to populate—better, to redeem—the areas of Judea-Samaria in the name of Jewish national rights. Youthful religious activists demonstrated that they would be able, borrowing a phrase from Lionel Trilling, "to recruit the primitive strength that a highly developed culture has diminished." Bearing a kind of cosmic defiance, and submitting to pain associated with heroic ventures, the dedicated patriots of Gush Emunim tenaciously pursued the old vision of Zionist settlement against a diffident government, a hostile Arab population, and an angry world. They clearly thrust aside the amenities of materialistic society and the comforts of urban life. Wedded to a Jewish faith, they carried their earnest campaign into the mountains, implying that their actions would close political options. They wanted to assure that the Zionist option in *Eretz-Israel* would never again be closed. By 1987 they could point proudly to the following facts: over a hundred Jewish settlements, with some sixty thousand inhabitants, integrated into the multiple grids of national life centered in Jerusalem and Tel Aviv. . . .

Jewish Soil

Ultimately Israel must reveal its deepest national secret: an abiding belief that Judea and Samaria are rightly Jewish soil to begin with, comprising the very heartland of the Jewish national home. From biblical patriarchs, matriarchs, prophets and kings to Maccabees, Pharisees and Sadducees—and continuing uninterrupted through two millennia of Diaspora—the Jewish people have been linked not so much with Tel Aviv and Haifa as with Hebron, Shechem (Nablus), Shiloh and Jerusalem. . . .

There is no choice but to argue the case for permanent annexation—or, more appropriately, reunification, the completion of the national population transfer begun when the Arab world expelled its Jews to Palestine.

Don Aharoni, *Los Angeles Times*, January 29, 1988.

From the point of view of religious Jews, Israel's purpose was never in doubt. It signified the era of providential redemption as enunciated by the biblical prophets and rabbinic sages of millennia ago. The return to the land was central to a historic process of Jewish state-building that incorporated broader themes: national redemption and universal redemption. These paramount Torah-based themes were, however, dislodged from Jewish consciousness and policy by the secular deviation that characterized the modern Zionist enterprise. Not David Ben-Gurion, not Golda Meir, certainly not Yitzhak Rabin or Shimon Peres or Yitzhak Shamir, not even Menachem Begin, could truly reflect and embody the *Jewish* philosophic core of the Israeli chapter in this era of redemption. But with the secular phase in abeyance, at last it may be added, the Jewish phase could raise the torch of national authenticity on high. Its central themes would include legitimizing the *Halacha* (Jewish law) as the arbiter of national life, from marriage and identity, to culture and policy-making; entrenching traditional religious educational orientations as opposed to the vacuous secular "state" institutions; and evoking pride of presence in the massive settlement of the core region of the homeland, Judea and Samaria, and this in the teeth of Arab opposition and global denunciation. It seemed that a Jewish revolution was in the offing, a revolution of the spirit if not yet one of society. In retrospect Begin's premiership that began in 1977, following a surprise electoral victory by Likud against Labor, constituted the historic threshold. The religious idiom, in the person of a sentimental traditional Jewish leader, would now enter the political arena.

The Forces of Secularism

But as the new spirit sought out new forms, the forces of secular establishment power rose to withstand the challenge. With a virulent animus against things Jewish, a campaign of defamation with no holds barred was undertaken. A universe of discourse was consolidated, the appropriate moral stance was assumed, and the attack was launched with a vengeance. Juxtaposed to realism was fantasy; to wisdom, emotion; to sanity, insanity; to modern, medieval; to enlightened, archaic; to peace, war. The epithets were hurled with a fury, as the struggle for Israel's soul ensued.

The controversy over Judea and Samaria and Israeli military rule there focused much of the rearguard action to repel the Jewish offensive. Peace Now, a collection of leftist groups formed in 1978, condemned Jewish settlement because, in their pious moralizing, "it corrupts the soul of the people of Israel." Knesset member Mordechai Bar-On, formerly chief education officer in the Israeli army, paraded around the ancient Jewish city of Hebron with placards written in Arabic deriding any Jewish presence there (presumably dead Jews like Abraham the Patriarch could remain). Police Minister Haim Bar-Lev was a willing accomplice of the Arab effort to dismantle a Jewish settlement on the outskirts of Nablus, by providing a written statement in 1979 that questioned the military value of the spot from *Israel's* point of view. In openly siding with the adversary, Bar-Lev was not deviating from a well-trodden leftist path. . . .

The tone of the attack became outright vicious as Likud's territorial vision and Gush Emunim's commitment continued to carve out the new settlement map. Orthodox Jews and their views were rejected as "fundamentalist" and "colonialist." . . .

These manifestations of Jewish self-criticism and enemy-identification are part of a dogged effort to delegitimize the rising Jewish tide in Israeli national life. The retention of the post-1967 areas will be, at root, a nationalist, rightist, and religious victory; simultaneously, it will be the first major defeat for the secular, leftist, and liberal forces in the country. This has historic significance in the Israeli body politic: It is not just, though it certainly is, a Likud achievement and a Labor loss. In principle, this political and territorial resolution of the issue means that the losers could not come up with a spiritual response to the 1967 victory. They offered no ideological message, and their political policy ran aground dismally. As a result, a pallor of gloom hovers above the left-liberal, secular camp. The country is becoming a land of self-estrangement for them. It no longer speaks to them, its melodies are not theirs, its spirit foreign to their sensibility. Life has lost its savor and many are leaving for the West, for America, which is more emotionally congenial to their tastes. Such people have sadly become strangers in their own country, as losing power meant losing purpose.

Nothing To Refresh the Spirit

In a remarkable book called *The Socialist Phenomenon,* Igor Shafarevich has shown that peoples die in history when their spiritual world is gone—no religion, rituals, and faith—and nothing remains to refresh their spirit.

Mordechai Nisan, *Global Affairs,* Summer 1987.

A vivid measure of human purpose and believing in the future is always reflected in the rate of childbirth and family size. The religious segment of the Israeli population is running a much higher reproduction rate than the secular segment, and this is not due to higher income levels or the like. The family unit is socially strong, deriving from the authority of a traditional culture and the confidence in the destiny of the Jewish people. In contrast, the family unit and the parental role were severely jarred by socialist doctrines, for example in the kibbutz environment of separating children at an early age from their parents. No doubt the secularist ethos of individualism likewise curtailed the possible role of family in acculturation of the youth.

But most severe in this connection is the decay of any spiritual purpose for many Israelis today. It could be simply said that atheistic socialism, in principle or in the Zionist experience, leaves the mass of people ultimately emotionally shipwrecked. The radical utopian dreams collapse and the actors involved become spiritually atrophied. . . .

The Democracy Argument

Building on a negative onslaught against the Jewish turn in Israeli life had no major impact on the fundamental spiritual trends. The fury of the attack was lacking a philosophic theme, an admission of pained desperation without intellectual content. . . .

At this point, specifically in 1984, the opportunity arose to generate a positive alternative to the Jewish message. An *ersatz* democratic ideology, bound as are all ideologies to particular historical circumstances, began to surface in Israeli intellectual, educational, and political circles. It dawned on the secular-left that the very victory of Likud on the territorial question now exposed the nationalist camp to the grave charge of fostering an undemocratic political regime, due to the persistent denial of equality and citizenship to 1.5 million Arabs resident in Judea-Samaria and the Gaza Strip. Israeli control was incompatible with the principles of democratic government, the democratic attribute being, so Abba Eban would proclaim in a 1982 article, Israel's "crowning glory." Certainly he was reinterpreting the Zionist adventure and modern Israeli statehood, for which the Jewish attribute was the "crowning glory." But he undoubtedly assumed that casting the issue in universally acceptable democratic semantic terms would help legitimize the losers' position and delegitimize that of the victors. At last, then, Israel's Jewish raison d'être stood challenged by another idea, with an emotive tenor of justice and morality, backed by global approval, deriding the narrow, tribalistic Judaic ethos of Jewish singularity in and over *Eretz-Israel.* The secular-left had a new flag and charged into battle with renewed vigor. Perhaps the Gush-Likud interlude, with its traditionalist meaning, would pass from Israeli history like a bad nightmare. . . .

Let it be said that the political regime of Israel since statehood has been based on Western democratic lines, including equal citizenship, a multiparty system, and representative government. It has functioned as such ever since, in spite of Arab warfare and terrorism within the country and across its borders. Security measures curtailed limitless, unconstrained freedoms in the internal Arab sector, from 1948-66 in particular, but still the egalitarian principle was never abandoned. . . .

At root, Arab culture is uncongenial to the cultivation of a democratic ambiance in concert with Jewish culture. The religion of Islam taught Muslim superiority over Jews, and Arab dignity waxed painfully within Hebrew-speaking Jewish Israel after 1948. The authorities did not impose military service upon the Arab citizens, and this skirting of the question of loyalty and participation highlighted the lack of ideological consensus between Jews and Arabs on the fundamental issue of the state's purpose. . . .

The National Jewish Ethos

The challenge to an authentic Jewish-defined Israel that would posit the ethnic-religious principle as legitimizing power was now opposed by a binational, pluralistically defined Israel that posited a universal egalitarian principle as legitimizing power. Gone from the latter vision is the "chosen people" notion of the Jewish particularity among the nations. The elite mission of the Jews in history is now subsumed under the anonymity of crude numbers in statistical democratic terms of simply counting heads and votes. Gone also from the Israeli polity is the cohesiveness of a society tied by common memories and sentiments that carried the Jewish people for four millennia, now to be dissolved into the abstraction of an Israeli state for all its Israeli citizens (perhaps ultimately to include the Arab residents in Judea-Samaria and Gaza)—regardless of their differences in temperament and tradition, language, religion, and ethnicity. What was to bind them all together for common efforts? No one in the mid-1980s dared ask such an honest question. But in the meanwhile the *national Jewish* ethos of Israel was thrust aside as antiquarian and discriminatory; instead, the *democratic* ethos was advanced as a modern and just alternative. . . .

Israel's Spiritual Redemption

As Israel's physical redemption achieves greater levels of achievement and recognition, its spiritual redemption remains retarded and even distorted at the psychic and philosophic core. Choosing democracy or socialism, liberalism and humanism, or any other modern ideology, merely delays the ultimate integrating experience when the Jews will reflectively consider Judaism and thus lay the inner struggle to rest.

At the same time, a more resolutely Jewish Israel, as opposed to a secular-socialist one, is a far more congenial ally for America. The Soviet-inspired statist economy of Israel is offensive to the spirit of freedom-loving people, Jews and Americans, and a giant impediment to the country's capacity for economic growth and ultimate economic independence. The anti-religious cast to early Zionism and its present offshoots is a corrosive moral factor in Israeli national life. In addition, the repudiation of the Bible and a traditional cultural ambiance—both dear to the Jewish and American peoples—is an affront to ancient history and, perhaps, future visions. . . . In summary, a more thoroughly Jewish-based Israel is not only a domestic requirement fulfilling an authentic national spirit, but also a policy orientation that converges with wider American interests both from a civilizational and strategic perspective. This fortuitous dovetailing is a historic opportunity that merits considerable study by all concerned.

"Fundamentalists generally reject Western models of democracy and citizenship."

Israel Should Not Become More Religious

Ian S. Lustick

Israel's 1977 elections marked the defeat of the liberal Labor Party, which had ruled Israel since the country was founded in 1948. The election signaled a rightward swing in Israeli politics and showed the growing power of the Israeli fundamentalist movement Gush Emunim. In the following viewpoint, Ian S. Lustick warns that fundamentalism endangers both traditional Zionism and the democratic underpinnings of the Israeli state. Lustick contends that because Gush Emunim members believe they are carrying out God's plan, they refuse to make the compromises that would give Israel peace and protect its security. Lustick is an associate professor of government at Dartmouth College.

As you read, consider the following questions:

1. What are the policies of Gush Emunim, according to the author?
2. Why does Lustick contend that the fundamentalists reject key Zionist teachings?
3. Why does the author argue that US policymakers should help Israeli moderates combat the influence of religious fundamentalists?

Ian S. Lustick, "Israel's Dangerous Fundamentalists." Reprinted with permission from FOREIGN POLICY 68 (Fall 1987). Copyright 1987 by the Carnegie Endowment for International Peace.

For most of this century, Zionism has been a social democratic movement. And for most of its history, Israel was essentially a social democratic state. Since the Six-Day War of 1967, however, and especially since the Yom Kippur War of 1973, that ethos has lost its central importance. Battling to reassert its vision of the Jewish state, social democratic Zionism faces unprecedented challenges from an ultranationalist, eschatologically based, irredentist ideology aptly characterized as Jewish fundamentalism. Kulturkampf [Cultural War] is not too strong a word for the struggle that is now under way. Its outcome will have profound implications for Israel's future and for the evolving relationship between Israel and its superpower partner, the United States.

Gush Emunim's Strength

The dynamism that underlay the shift toward fundamentalism has been concentrated in Gush Emunim (Bloc of the Faithful)—an umbrella organization including more than 10,000 devoted activists. Gush Emunim helped unseat the last Labor government in 1977 and subsequently infused Likud leaders, on the right of Israel's political spectrum, with much of its own vision of authentic Zionism. In many respects Gush Emunim, as an energized influential minority movement emphasizing pioneer values and a grand vision of Zionism, can be compared to the kibbutz movement of Israel's prestate era. Before 1948 the kibbutz movement, which never included more than 7 per cent of Israelis, and the socialist Zionist leadership associated with it provided the Yishuv (Jews living in Palestine) with the most salient models of Jewish patriotism, Zionist civic duty, and spiritual guidance. Gush Emunim, its settlers in the West Bank and Gaza Strip, and its charismatic and rabbinical leaders have provided highly salient models for the present generation of Israelis.

The men and women of Gush Emunim have made it their lives' work to ensure that the occupied West Bank and Gaza Strip are incorporated permanently into the state of Israel, thus hastening the fulfillment of Jewish destiny. For most of these activists, this ultimately includes establishing Jewish sovereignty over the entire biblically described Land of Israel, substituting authentically Jewish forms of governance for Western-style liberal democracy, rebuilding the Temple in Jerusalem, and implementing the divinely ordained, albeit long delayed, messianic Redemption. Fundamentalists insist that direct political action is the means to accomplish the rapid transformation of Israeli society according to uncompromising, cosmically ordained imperatives. In this insistence they must be understood as radically different from pietistic, largely non-Zionist, ultraorthodox Jews whose beliefs lead to withdrawal from society and political action only to defend their isolation from it.

The core of Gush Emunim's membership resides in many of the more than 130 settlements established in the West Bank, the Gaza Strip, and the Golan Heights since 1967, but recruitment extends to Israel's largest religious youth movement, Bnei Akiva, to a network of paramilitary field seminaries, to the religious education system, to new immigrants, and to many middle-class Israelis committed to expansive versions of Labor Zionism or Revisionist Zionism. Although officially nonpartisan, Gush Emunim is actively supported in national politics by half a dozen cabinet ministers and more than 35 per cent of the Knesset, representing 5 political parties. Although it is mainly an Ashkenazic (European and American) movement, electoral support for parties linked to Gush Emunim is strong among Israel's Oriental Jews, those who emigrated from, or whose parents emigrated from, Asia and Africa. . . .

Zionism's Purpose

The men who gave expression to the Zionist idea and made it come true did not see in Jewish nationalism a means of spiritual salvation. They wanted to establish a progressive Jewish society, but they did not seek to give the Jews new tablets of the Law. Theirs was a down-to-earth wish: to give the Jews a home—a house, not a Temple—so that they would be able to live in it in decency, preserve old traditions, develop their old-new language, create their new culture, continue their quarrels and serve as a welcoming shelter to their suffering brethren. They wanted the new dwellers of the old, forsaken home to become new liberated Jews and to act as orderly good neighbors among the older members of the family of nations.

Amnon Rubinstein, *The Zionist Dream Revisited: From Herzl to Gush Emunim and Back*, 1984.

Even as Gush Emunim seeks ways to institutionalize itself and its program, it already has created powerful myths for contemporary Israeli society. These myths, and the attitudes and policies they encourage, will mold Middle Eastern affairs for decades. Israelis now entering the army were born after the 1967 war. For them, the West Bank is Judaea and Samaria. The Green Line, which separated Israel from the West Bank and Gaza Strip from 1948 to 1967, does not appear on official maps of their country. For increasing numbers of these Israelis, what was absurd to many of their parents but is common sense to Gush Emunim—that the whole Land of Israel must be Jewish-ruled for Zionism to be vindicated—is common sense to them. And increasingly, what is absurd to Gush Emunim but was common sense to many of their parents—that land should be traded for peace with the Arabs—is absurd to them as well.

Despite its importance, most Americans and many Israelis share a dangerous ignorance of the beliefs that animate Jewish fundamentalism. If Americans do not appreciate how radically different the Gush Emunim world view is from their conception of what Israel is all about, they will continue to be surprised and exploited by Israeli actions that flow naturally from it. And if U.S. policymakers, or even leftist and left-center Israeli politicians, do not understand or take seriously Gush ideology, they will miss likely opportunities to divide and defeat the movement.

Fundamentalism's World View

There are good reasons why Gush thinking is not understood outside its own circles. The belief system does not encourage attempts to explain it to non-Jews. Nor did its most authoritative spokesman, Rabbi Zvi Yehuda Kook, produce a systematic presentation of his approach to Zionism and the redemption process. . . .

Until his death in 1982, Kook's leadership was unquestioned. Even now, ideological and tactical disputes among fundamentalists are commonly framed by the participants as disagreements over accurate interpretations of his opinions. The world view of Jewish fundamentalism is best revealed through the homilies and writings of Kook, analytic articles by those of his students prominent in Gush Emunim, and the works of two scholars—the late Rabbi Menachem Kasher and Harold Fisch. . . .

Jewish fundamentalist thinking is grounded in seven basic beliefs. Although expressed in terms consistent with Zionist rhetoric, in fact they represent categorical rejections of some key tenets of Zionist ideology.

Zionism arose simultaneously in both Eastern and Western Europe in the late 19th century. The analysis of the "Jewish problem" and its solution, propounded independently by Leo Pinsker in czarist Russia and Theodor Herzl in Austria, France, and Germany, was anchored in the bold conviction that anti-Semitism could be utterly eliminated if Jews were granted the opportunity to become a "normal" people. In the Hebrew phrase, Jews were to become *goy kekol hagoyim*, a nation like all the other nations. Living scattered among other peoples, a minority everywhere, the Jews appeared to Gentiles as a mysterious, even ghostly presence. Anti-Semitism was traceable to this abnormal mode of existence and to the fears and passions that, under the circumstances, Jews naturally provoked among Gentiles. By concentrating themselves as a majority in their own land, the structural abnormality of their collective life would cease. Jews would then develop a national culture and personality no different in their fundamentals from those of any other people, and anti-Semitism eventually would disappear.

Fisch articulates Gush Emunim's radical reversal of these Zionist propositions. The idea, he says in *The Zionist Revolution*, "that the Jewish nation is a normal nation and ought to be treated as such by the so-called international community. . . .is the original delusion of secular Zionism." For Fisch, authentic Zionism entails rejecting classical Zionism's use of other nations as models for how the Jewish people should behave. Jews are not and cannot be a normal people. The eternal uniqueness of the Jews is the result of the covenant made between God and the Jewish people at Mount Sinai—a real historical event with eternal and inescapable consequences for the entire world.

Messianic Politics

The Six Day War and the occupation of territories led to an awakening of a messianic view of Zionism among the National Religious. In this view Zionism, the establishment of Israel, and the liberation of Jerusalem, Judea, and Samaria are perceived as pivotal stages in an inexorable, deliberate process ending in a final Redemption. . . .

Messianic politics of this type lack the existential sense of danger that sometimes motivates people to recognize the need for compromise. When Israel signed its peace treaty with Egypt, many Israelis who identified with the religious Right viewed the treaty as a retreat from the process of Redemption. Yielding territories meant abandoning the fruits of the Six Day War and setting the wheels of Redemption several years backward. To those who believed, as Gush Emunim adherents did, that present-day history is by necessity the beginning of Redemption, anxieties about unending wars that lead to a peace treaty with the largest Arab state had no impact.

Moshe Halbertal, *Tikkun*, vol. 2, no. 2, 1987.

Not surprisingly, fundamentalists fully embrace Jews as an *Am Segula* (a chosen or "treasured" people). The implication is that the transcendent imperatives for Jews effectively nullify moral laws that bind the behavior of normal nations. Rabbi Shlomo Aviner, of the Ataret Cohanim Yeshiva in Jerusalem and one of Gush Emunim's most prolific ideologues, argues that divine commandments to the Jewish people "transcend the human notions of national rights." He explains that while God requires other nations to abide by abstract codes of justice and righteousness, such laws do not apply to Jews. To his people of Israel, God speaks directly. . . .

Many Zionists, especially on the left, not only have come to recognize the legitimate rights of Palestinian Arabs but even have noticed similarities between the historical experiences of Jews and

Palestinians. Jewish fundamentalist assumptions about the world, however, make it essentially impossible for them to see Jews and Palestinians in comparable terms. Nor can fundamentalists acknowledge any real tie between Palestinians, or any group other than Jews, and the Land of Israel. . . .

For all Israeli Jewish fundamentalists an irreducible attachment to the Land of Israel, in its entirety, is at the core of their world view. The priority accorded the land is reflected in a slogan popular with Gush Emunim, "The Land of Israel, for the people of Israel, according to the Torah of Israel." . . .

Borders of Cosmic Import

One implication of this belief is that questions of borders automatically assume cosmic proportions. The very discussion among Jews of the possibility of relinquishing land is abhorrent. To express the intimate bonds they feel to the land, fundamentalists commonly invoke images of the Land of Israel as a living being. Territorial concessions and the destruction of settlements then become "the severing of a limb from a living body," as Rabbi Chaim Druckman, a member of the Knesset and a disciple of Kook, said in 1982 in condemning Israel's withdrawal from the Yamit district of the northeastern Sinai peninsula.

A key element in Jewish fundamentalism, as in any fundamentalist movement, is its adherents' belief that they possess special and direct access to transcendental truth and to the future course of events. For Jewish fundamentalists, history is God's means of communicating with his people. Political trends and events contain messages to Jews that provide instructions, reprimands, and rewards. Combined with religious texts, political and historical analysis guides the continuing struggle toward redemption. . . .

Given the metaphysical essence of the Arab-Israeli conflict, the deep division within Israeli society between hawks and doves is, practically speaking, irrelevant to the prospects of peace or war. The internal contest over the future of the occupied territories is nonetheless of critical importance. It represents a test for authentic Zionism, which accepts the lonely destiny of the Jews as God's covenant people and embraces the "scandal of biblical reality," as Fisch put it, in its struggle with a Zionism that distorts Jewish history in a vain search for normalcy. In fundamentalist parlance, the "secular left" in Israel comprises modern-day Hellenizers whose doctrines of "meism" and "nowism" foster apathy and endanger the Jewish people's ability to survive in a hostile world. For Gush Emunim, only faith and a willingness for self-sacrifice, not pseudosophisticated political calculations, can support effective political action. A renewal of such faith will entail abandoning "cheap imitation of the culture of the West" and ignoring "world opinion," as Fisch asserted. . . .

The difficulty that a large share of fundamentalist activists have in accepting a consensus-building strategy toward the wider Israeli public makes the movement vulnerable. . . .

Gush Emunim's vulnerability is apparent in the burgeoning effort to assert Jewish rights over the Temple Mount in Jerusalem, a site also holy to Moslems that they call Haram el-Sharif (Noble Sanctuary). Such a move is seen as a prelude to the removal of the Moslem shrines and the reconstruction of the Temple. In recent years, leading rabbis have used archaeological finds as a basis to declare that previous religious restrictions against Jewish entry onto the Temple Mount need no longer be applied, at least with respect to most of the area. For vanguardists, the commitment to "speak the truth" and the image of irrevocable change that might follow the Judaization of the site are compelling reasons to demand change in the status quo there. The Temple Mount issue has emerged from the realm of fringe utopianism to occupy a central place in the political activity of Gush Emunim. . . .

On the anniversary of the Israeli occupation of East Jerusalem in June 1986, 12,000 fundamentalists marched in protest to the Temple Mount to witness a sound and light show called "The Temple Mount—Heart of the People." Amid violent clashes, a detachment of soldiers and police succeeded in preventing 100 demonstrators from forcing their way onto the site. . . .

The Movement's Dilemma

The Temple Mount issue represents a terrible dilemma for Gush Emunim. On the one hand, no single trend within the movement contains more potential for precipitating radical change consistent with its overall world view. Nor is any event more likely to achieve a profound realignment of public attitudes within Israel, to precipitate a crushable Palestinian revolt in the occupied territories, to disrupt peace initiatives and destabilize the Egyptian-Israeli relationship, and to distance Israel, politically and culturally, from the entire gentile world than a government-supported fundamentalist move to Judaize the Temple Mount. On the other hand, nothing contains greater potential to destroy the unity of the movement, to deflect it from politically productive activities concerning most Israelis, or to provide its enemies with the means to isolate and defeat it than unauthorized and violent efforts by vanguardists to change its status. . . .

To exploit such opportunities, Israeli moderates must have a much clearer understanding of Jewish fundamentalism than they have displayed up to now. Such knowledge is needed equally by U.S. policymakers if they are to help prevent the explosiveness that surrounds Jewish fundamentalism from being unleashed on the region and the world. It is neither too early nor too late to prepare for managing the crisis that is bound to come. Without explicitly framing its policy as countering fundamentalist influence, Washington should stress, much more strongly than it has in the recent past, how central to America's special relationship with Israel is the cluster of democratic, libertarian, and universalistic values that the two countries have always shared. The United States should emphasize forthrightly the extent to which its friendship and support ultimately depend on these shared values—values that are, of course, unrealizable in the "completed" Israel envisioned by the fundamentalists. . . .

Promote Egalitarian Values

To help discredit the fundamentalist vision as a basis for a new Israeli consensus, the United States might begin a bilateral educational and cultural effort to promote the democratic and egalitarian norms to which the two countries traditionally have been committed. The program's most useful focus would be both countries' experience in the integration of historically oppressed, partially disenfranchised minorities—Jews, blacks, and Hispanics in the United States and Oriental Jews and Arabs in Israel. Since most Israeli Jews accept the fact of Arab citizenship within the Green Line and the principle of equal rights for all citizens, and, in contrast, since fundamentalists generally reject Western models of democracy and citizenship on equal terms for the "Arabs of the Land of Israel," such programs would help isolate Gush Emunim and highlight Jewish fundamentalism's radically antidemocratic beliefs. Much more effectively than largess or pseudorealpolitik, such a policy can strengthen the position of Israelis who must confront the fundamentalists and show their compatriots just how intolerably dangerous is the route to redemption that Gush Emunim is traveling.

"The Zionist movement's great achievement was precisely to lay the foundation for a secular, Hebrew democracy, not a 'Jewish state.'"

Israel Should Become a Pluralist State

Bernard Avishai

Israel's purpose as a state has been debated since the first Zionists began advocating a homeland for the Jews. In the following viewpoint, Bernard Avishai argues that Israel's purpose has been and is to establish a secular, pluralist democracy. The rights of non-religious Jews and of Moslem and Christian Arabs should be respected, he contends. Avishai lived in Israel for three years. He is associate editor of *The Harvard Business Review* and the author of *The Tragedy of Zionism.*

As you read, consider the following questions:

1. How has the "demographic argument" affected Israeli Jews, according to Avishai?
2. According to the author, why are Israeli citizenship laws discriminatory?
3. What parallel does Avishai see between Israel now and the American South in the 1950s? Do you think this is a valid comparison?

Bernard Avishai, "Israel, the Forty Years' Crisis," *The Nation*, April 23, 1988. Copyright © 1988 by The Nation Company. Reprinted with permission.

Greater Israel may not be possible as the Israeli right has envisioned it. But the response of Israeli Arabs to the uprising has raised some unsettling questions about "smaller" Israel—questions the Israeli left, especially the leaders of the Labor Party, have tended to disregard.

Israeli Jews have often said that they do not intend to return to the borders of the pre-1967 state. Israeli Arabs, in their support for the Palestinian uprising, have shown their unwillingness to return to the pre-1967 state of affairs—whatever the borders—back to an Israel that was the product of revolutionary Zionism. After 1967, after all, the dominant rejoinder of the Labor Party's left to Moshe Dayan's argument about "security borders" was not an argument in favor of reciprocal Palestinian and Israeli national rights. Rather, it was Finance Minister Pinhas Sapir's assertion of a danger to a Jewish majority in *Eretz Yisrael*. Sapir, who died in 1975, pointed out that the Arab birth rate, including that of Israeli Arabs, was much higher than the Jewish one. If the territories were not returned, he said, Israelis would soon be living in a country whose "Jewish character" was lost.

An Arab Majority?

Presumably, if Jews were in the majority, they would continue to have the historic right to turn the country into something Jewish. What if the Arabs were the majority? Would not protections for Jewish national rights be rescinded?

Political scientists close to Labor developed the argument further, taking Sapir's essentially cultural fears and putting them into the context of Israeli electoral politics. Shlomo Avineri, professor of political science at Hebrew University—who has chastised American Jews for not being Zionists in action—insisted that if the occupation continued, Israelis would be forced to choose between living in a Jewish state or a democratic one. He wrote that an emerging Arab majority might well mean a majority for P.L.O. leader Yasir Arafat in the Knesset. That demographic argument has been reinforced by the work of Haifa University geographer Arnon Sofer, who found that in 1985 there were 365,000 Jewish children under 4 years of age living in Greater Israel, and 370,000 Arab children.

Of course, all this begs the question of just what Avineri, Sofer and others actually mean by "Jewish character" when they speak of the Jewish state. There are problems with the term "majority" too. Israeli Jews are not a single block of people. They are themselves split into dozens of approaches to Jewish theology and history, modern intellectual styles, cultural and ethnic camps. . . .

While I was in Israel, a cousin of mine in Haifa—a man strongly in favor of territorial compromise—invited Professor Sofer to his house to speak before forty guests, some with annexationist views and some, like him, in favor of partition. Sofer made a forceful presentation of the demographic facts. My cousin was astounded to discover that people who were opposed to territorial compromise before his talk were even more opposed to it when Sofer had finished.

This was not perverse stubborness on their part. A majority of Israelis see and dread something that people on the left—those who think of the Jewish state merely as a state with a Jewish majority—often overlook. What, in practical terms, does living in the Jewish state mean? How does the demographic argument play in the Israeli Arab community?

Lasting Peace

Palestinians and Jews, free at last from discrimination and injustice, will forge lasting peace only in a democratic and secular society where elementary rights are accorded to all.

Palestine Perspectives, March/April 1988.

No Israeli nervous about demography—not Sapir, not Sofer, not even Avineri—ever seriously considered giving the Palestinians of the occupied territories the right to vote. Therefore, the growth of the population of West Bankers or residents of Gaza never really threatened to change the Hebrew atmosphere of Israel or the electoral balance of the Knesset, whatever the impact of the occupation on democratic values.

In contrast, many of the institutions and ideological principles supported by the Jewish state are deeply vulnerable to the claims of the 750,000 Arabs who are citizens of Israel. These people have demanded serious changes in the legal and bureaucratic structure of the state, changes having little to do with demographics. The Palestinian uprising has swelled the desire of Israeli Arabs for full, meaningful civil equality—in Hebrew, if necessary—and they see no reason why the state should fail to grant this equality simply because they constitute 17 percent of the population and not 51 percent. At the same time, there are perhaps 100,000 Arabs from the occupied territories working in Israel mainly in low-level jobs in construction and tourism, many of whom want to be treated as permanent residents.

Citizenship Rights

What changes? Though Israeli Arabs vote, Israel is legally held to be the state of "the Jewish people," not merely of its citizens. Traditional Jewish law is used to determine citizenship rights under the Law of Return: A Jew is anyone born of a Jewish mother or converted to Judaism by a rabbi. The Orthodox rabbinate has established jurisdiction in supervising marriage, divorce, aspects of child custody, burial—and food catering. Entrenched privileges have been accorded the Orthodox rabbinate and leaders of state-supported Orthodox educational institutions. Incidentally, a philosophical friend told me that there are now as many yeshiva students in Israel (partly supported by the state) as there were in Poland before World War II, some 30,000.

Old Zionist development institutions, which were not retired after the state was founded, still bestow economic rights on individual Jews—people whose nationality is legally designated as Jewish on state identity cards. The Old Zionist land development corporations, Keren Hayesod and Keren Kayemet, are in effect organs of the state land authority; the Jewish Agency is an organ of the Ministry of Immigration when it comes to disbursement of loans to new immigrants and settlements. So have the public corporations, agricultural settlements and welfare agencies of the Histadrut labor federation remained national Jewish institutions.

Israeli Arabs, the Druse excepted, do not serve in the army, as if military loyalty presupposes loyalty to the Jewish people and not to the democratic state of Israel. Israel has no integrated system of public education, no civil marriage, no Bill of Rights to protect non-Jews against discrimination in housing or employment and, indeed, no protections for secular Jews against the encroachments of Orthodox politicians.

No Return

Israeli Arabs will thus never settle for an unreformed Israel, which is precisely what Labor intellectuals have promised to get back to. The Labor Party is identified with the proposition that partition will rescue the Jewish state from fundamental Arab challenges. But it is now clear that even in the context of a peace process, even if a Palestinian state was to be established, there could be no return to the "Days of Binyamina" (as Chava Alberstein's nostalgic song evoked the years between 1948 and 1967): no return to the years when the principles, battle cries and costumes of the Zionist movement engendered a revolutionary Jewish national life.

To be sure, that was a stirring time for any Jew, a time of unfamiliar, heady patriotism, of pride in the harvest, the biblical land, the people's army. But the Israeli state apparatus created during these years was afflicted by compromises with rabbinic theocrats, by constitutional stopgaps, privileges for a labor aristocracy, separate administration of Arab villages—the seeds of the current inequalities. Meir Kahane has understood, evil genius that he is, that the demographic problem of *this* state can be solved most logically by expelling all Arabs. In Rabbi Meir Kahane's view—God knows how many Israelis now share it—such expulsions would only pick up where the 1948 war left off. . . .

I visited a friend on Kfar Yehoshua (a cooperative farm in the Jezreel Valley), a *moshavnik* and a Labor supporter literally from birth. "I would be for a Palestinian state today," he told me earnestly, "but that will not be the end of it. The Palestinians are a majority north of Safed, in the upper Galilee. They are a majority down the road, in the Little Triangle. Why won't *they* want a state?"

Because, I responded as best I could, Israel will not relinquish the territory, and the Israeli Arabs know it is strong enough not to. Besides, they are not demanding national rights for themselves. The creation of a Palestinian state will probably mitigate their national or separatist impulses. They could then enjoy Israeli citizenship and enjoy Palestinian nationalism vicariously. They are modern in Hebrew; they like the political and sexual freedom of Israeli civil life.

"What do you mean, 'citizens of Israel'?" he asked skeptically. "I know many Arabs: They are building contractors and farmers— we get along. But they'll never want to be citizens of a Jewish state! They'll never sing 'Hatikvah' [the Zionist anthem], they'll always be unhappy. We'll start with a Palestinian state, and then the Arabs here will want to go to the army, and they'll want Israel to be like any other state, a multinational state, like America. Then what will it have all been for?"

Right and Right

I believe in a Zionism that faces facts, that exercises strength with restraint, that sees the Jewish past as a lesson, but neither as a mystical imperative nor as a malignant dream . . . a Zionism that accepts both the spiritual implications and the political consequences of the fact that this small but precious land is the homeland of two peoples fated to live facing each other, willy-nilly, because no God or angel will descend to judge between right and right. The lives of both depend on the hard, tortuous and essential process of learning to know each other in the strife-torn landscape of the beloved country.

Amos Oz, quoted in *New Internationalist*, November 1987.

Some of this fear, I would still maintain, is the result of not having thought things through. If Kfar Yehoshua is any evidence, then the Zionist movement's great achievement was precisely to lay the foundation for a secular, Hebrew democracy, not a "Jewish state." The Hebrew language predominates in historic Palestine. Even young Palestinians in the West Bank and Gaza have, for economic reasons, been forced to acquire its rudiments.

Nor would Israel be much changed in the everyday sense if it were to become the more complete secular democracy—like "America"—that Israeli Arabs and a growing but small minority of Israeli Jews want. The Israeli Arab intelligentsia will still be drawn more to Hebrew literary culture than to the village. If you want to see how Israel is not a democracy, look at the way Arab writers live; if you want to see how it is, listen to the way they speak.

Israel at forty is hardly a revolutionary Zionist society. If Israelis were to acknowledge the post-Zionist Israel in which they live, Tel Aviv would still be steamy, the Hebrew University would offer the same courses, the lyrics of Matti Caspi's songs would still reveal a wry Yiddish wit, the Moroccan Jews would still celebrate the festival of Mamuna. Most Israeli Jews, including the largely middle-class, Sephardic supporters of the Likud, are hardly religious fanatics and would find themselves quite at home in a country where civil marriages were permitted and in which the buses—not just the soccer players—ran on the Sabbath.

Besides, the tremendous growth of the Israeli Arab population in the upper Galilee only underscores how foolish the Israeli state has been to squander its resources on populating the West Bank. The settlements are no security asset; Defense Minister Rabin has openly criticized the citizenry for making the army's job more difficult. . . .

The Attitudes of Israeli Youth

In spite of their admiration for America, few young Israelis think of liberal institutions and civil rights as nonviolent routes to settle disputes that would otherwise be intractable. In consequence of the occupation, most of them (and young Palestinians for that matter) have come to see Arabs as a dominated class, power as something that speaks from the barrel of a gun. Today, 60 percent of Israeli Jewish youth would reduce, not enhance, the rights of Israel's Arabs. Israeli soldiers and Palestinian rock-throwers are routinely in the grip of an atavism that outpaces political science.

As for my friend on Kfar Yehoshua, a serious, compassionate, utterly charming man: He has as much difficulty envisioning a pluralist Israel as white residents of Little Rock, Arkansas, had envisioning the New South in 1958.

240

"Jews must choose a Jewish state."

Pluralism Would Destroy Israel's Divine Purpose

Meir Kahane

Meir Kahane is a Brooklyn-born rabbi who has long been controversial both in the US and in Israel. Since 1984 Kahane has been a member of Israel's parliament, the Knesset. In the following viewpoint, he argues that Israel must be a Jewish state. Israel's divine purpose is to fulfill God's prophecy that after wandering for millennia, the Jews will return to their biblical homeland. In keeping with divine will, Kahane contends, Jews should encourage Jewish population growth and should deport individuals who are unwilling to live in an orthodox Jewish state.

As you read, consider the following questions:

1. What does the author believe should be the relationship between Israeli Jews and Jews in other countries?
2. Why does Kahane argue that Jewish population growth is necessary?
3. What is the real basis of the Arab-Jewish struggle, according to Kahane?

Meir Kahane, "Policies and Programs of the Authentic Jewish Idea," *"Kahane" The Magazine of the Authentic Jewish Idea*, March/April 1988. Used with permission of Kach International.

Editor's note: In keeping with his religious beliefs, the author of the following viewpoint does not spell out divine names. He uses the letters "G-d" to mean "God" and "L-rd" to mean "Lord."

The Jewish people is unlike any other. It is a Divine, special, holy and different nation, chosen by the Al-Mighty at Sinai to live a specific life under Jewish law and commandments. Jewish destiny—that which will be—depends on one thing only: Jewish adherence to their special mission of obedience to that Law. There must be a return to Jewish faith and observance, or tragedy will strike regardless of whether Right or Left guides the Jewish ship of state. . . .

The Jewish people was made to be different, separate, set apart from all the others. Not assimilation or amalgamation or integration with the nations is the Jewish role but rather the creation of a separate people, living in a separate state, and building a separate and special society. That is the Jewish injunction and that is the true meaning of the Jews as *"a light unto the nations."* The Jewish people must, thus, be isolated from foreign cultures that corrupt and destroy the authentic Jewish Idea.

And, of course, there must be an unrelenting campaign to make intermarriage and assimilation anathema, with no compromise on rejection of the concept of marrying out of the faith. In particular, no Jew who is intermarried shall be allowed to hold a Jewish leadership post.

And Jewish policy must also be one of isolation from a corrupting world political process. To that end, the Jewish state must leave the United Nations, a band of international desecrators of the name of the L-rd. No fear of isolation! We are a people that dwells alone.

Love of Jew for Jew

The Jewish nation is one. There are no boundaries that separate the Jews and the pain of one is the pain of all. There is an obligation to rush to save oppressed and suffering Jews, wherever they may be and in whatever way is necessary. The weak Jew who is threatened must be rescued by the Jew of strength. Jewish power, in such a case, is an obligation.

It is unacceptable to speak of internal affairs of any country in which Jews are threatened. In particular, while Jews remain in the Exile and are endangered by Jew-haters, it is the role of the State of Israel to do all in its power to defend them and to put an end to attacks on Jews. Israel was established as the Jewish state, as the trustee and guardian of Jews all over the world. It must live up to that obligation.

For the Jew, there are no permanent allies except the Jew himself and the Al-Mighty. For the Jew, Jewish interest comes first, for who will care about him, if not himself? Public Jewish funds must stop going to non-Jewish causes and a new order of priorities must be established that set Jewish education—the real and substantive kind—the Jewish day school, the *yeshiva*, as the most important of Jewish projects. Public Jewish funds must be set aside, not for community centers with huge numbers of non-Jews as members, but for Jewish defense, *aliya*—immigration to Israel—and Jewish centers that are truly Jewish and not just centers. . . .

To be Jewish is to be the Chosen of the L-rd and Jews must rid themselves of the guilt, self-hate and inferiority that grip so many today. Not guilt but pride; not self-hate but intense love; not inferiority but the knowledge that Jews have been chosen from all the nations upon the face of the earth to receive the Divine truth. Jewish pride! But combined with the humility of bowing to the will of G-d.

G-d Gave It to Us

There is one sublime reason why we should not give up a centimeter of land. *It belongs to us.*

If we have no right to Judea, Samaria and Gaza, then we indeed have no right to Tel Aviv. Abraham did not walk on Dizengoff Street nor did our ancestors live in the Israeli cities that were built in the 20th century. But Abraham, who lived in Hebron, and Jacob in Shchem, now Nablus, and David in Bethlehem are the sole legitimate reasons that Jews can lay claim to a Tel Aviv and the kibbutzim of the guilt-ridden left. The land belongs to us because the G-d of Israel, Creator and Titleholder of all lands, gave it to us.

Meir Kahane, *The New York Times*, February 2, 1988.

What is moral and ethical, what is just and merciful, must be based not on western and gentilized concepts but on Divine values that can be derived only from the sources of Jewish Law. The concept of the yoke of Heaven must be accepted and must be the only yardstick for Jewish values regardless of how they differ from western and gentile ones. Jews must become conceptually Jewish, with Jewish public funds allocated primarily for real substantive Jewish education that produces proud, knowledgeable and observant Jews. In the Exile this will put an end to the curse of the Melting Pot, the public school and the interfaith that Jewish leaders have foisted on Jews that have caused the loss of an entire generation. In the State of Israel it will put an end to the spiritual tragedy of the destruction of Jewish values among the young. . . .

Let there be an end to practices which numerically diminish and weaken the body of the Jewish people, who will be needed in coming generations to sanctify His name and build and sustain the Jewish state. In place of abortion anarchy, planned childlessness and other incremental and insidious forms of Jewish national suicide, let there be mass Jewish population growth in accordance with Jewish law. The social fabric of the Jewish people and the national policies of the Jewish government of Israel, alike, must encourage each Jewish mother and father to raise the maximum feasible number of Jewish children within the framework of *halacha* [oral law]. This will insure a population large enough to secure the Jewish people, populate and defend Eretz-Yisrael, and compensate numeric losses of the Holocaust and assimilation.

Eliminate Abominations

At the same time, let us end the disgrace of unwarranted Jewish abortion, which is nothing less than murder. Throughout Jewish history, the act of destroying the fetus in the womb has been singled out as one of the "abominations of Egypt" which Torah has enjoined us to suppress. Feticide, except where birth endangers the life of the mother, is forbidden by *halacha;* its practice must be eliminated in the Jewish state.

The State of Israel must eliminate those foreign abominations that desecrate the name of G-d and turn it into a gentilized, westernized country rather than the Jewish state it is meant to be. These include:

a) The disgrace of missionaries and pagan cults who destroy the Jewish soul. The Jew is, indeed, destroyed equally through the ovens of Auschwitz or through the loss of the Jewish soul to the missionaries and cults. They must be banned from Israel.

b) The disgrace of the Temple Mount where Moslem mosques are built on the holiest site in Judaism. A synagogue built on Islam's holiest site in Mecca would lead to world Moslem outcry. Jewish silence in the face of the desecration of Judaism's holiest site is inexcusable and a disgrace. The Moslems and their mosques must be removed from the site of the holy temples of Israel.

c) The disgrace of intermarriage and sexual intercourse between Jew and gentile. This has been an abomination and desecration since the birth of the Jewish nation and has always been forbidden and prohibited by Jewish governments. Once again, the laws of the Jewish state must put an end to it.

The entire land of Israel belongs to the Jewish people, alone. There are no other legitimate claimants. It is the holy land, the land of G-d, given by Him to His holy people for the purpose of creating a holy society, therein. Because of this, none but the Jew can have a role in the destiny and political affairs of the state. The non-Jew can live within the Jewish state only as a "resident stranger" who enjoys his personal, social, cultural, and economic rights but with no citizenship, no political representation, no membership in governmental service, and no say in the destiny of the country. Those who are not prepared to accept this, cannot remain.

Repatriate the Arabs

The Arabs living in Eretz-Yisreal must be repatriated. The Arabs of Israel, specifically, will never consider themselves as integral part of a country that is legally defined as a Jewish state. They can never feel love and empathy for it. Only those who have contempt for the Arabs cannot and will not see this. Only they believe that national pride, dignity and self-determination can be bought in exchange for economic benefits. The Arabs who refuse to live as resident strangers—and the numbers of these must be limited so as to endanger neither the security nor the economy of the Jewish state—must be given a choice of leaving willingly with full compensation for their property or being compelled to leave without compensation.

Keeping Arabs Out

Not just the PLO must be kept out of Judea/Samaria—and this to allow the Jewish people to build their Homeland for spiritual purposes and strategic well-being—but *any Arab force* must be kept out. . . . In truth, not Jordan, not Syria, not the PLO, not the UN must ever take control of the Samarian mountains or the Judean desert. The Zionist Return to Eretz-Israel will continue and its fruits will blossom, so long as this grand process of Jewish restoration remains unencumbered by any foreign force whatsoever.

Mordechai Nisan, *Outpost*, Summer 1987.

The High Arab birthrate, the low Jewish one, the drop in immigration to Israel and the rise in emigration from the country, threaten to create an Arab majority in the country (and the Galilee already suffers an Arab majority). An Arab majority will destroy Israel as a Jewish state as surely as bullets and bombs. The truth is that there is potential contradiction between the concepts of a Jewish state and a western democratic one. Jews must choose a Jewish state.

The transfer of Arabs will complete the exchange of populations begun in 1948, after which almost one million Jews fled Arab countries with no compensation. These Jews were integrated into the Jewish state of their brothers and sisters. Let the same be done for the Arabs of Israel by their brethren. Social support payments which the government of Israel has squandered on Arabs and other enemies, must be redirected to help needy Jews, and especially, Sefardi and oriental Jewish communities in various development towns and economically disadvantaged *shikunim* (neighborhoods) around Israel. From those Arabs who receive compensation, 10% will be taken off the amounts to compensate Sefardi Jews who received nothing when they were expelled from Arab countries.

The Jew is forbidden to give up any part of the land of Israel. The land belongs to the G-d of Israel and the Jew, given it by G-d, has no right to give away any part of it. All the areas past liberated, or areas which may be liberated in the future, must be annexed, made part of the State of Israel, and populated by Jews as rapidly as possible. Jewish settlement in every part of Eretz-Yisrael, including cities that today, sadly, are *Judenrein* (Jewish excluded), must be unlimited. Maximum continuous expansion of Jewish settlement must be encouraged by well-coordinated national policies binding upon all agencies of the State of Israel and all related Jewish institutions with authority or influence over urban and rural development, housing, agriculture, transportation and industrial investment.

"Palestine" Was Never Born

There is no "Palestine" or "Palestine people." They are Arabs, part of the Arab nation that lives in many countries, and to where the Arabs of Eretz-Yisrael must and will be repatriated. The Roman Emperor Hadrian changed the name of our land from Judea—the land of the Jews, to "Palestina"—the land of the Philistines, after crushing Bar Kochva's revolt. It was the Roman design to destroy the Jewish people by erasing the name of our homeland. Now the Philistines, the Roman Empire and even the Latin language are as dead as Babylon. But the Jewish people never died, and the Jewish state is alive and the Jewish army stands guard over it. Israel will live forever; "Palestine" never was even born.

The Arabs do not want peace. It is illusion and delusion to believe the Middle Eastern problem is a dispute over the *occupied lands of 1967*, or the creation of a "Palestine" that would exist next to Israel. Those who understand the Arabs and are free of contempt for them know the essence of the problem is the Arab belief that the Jews have stolen the entire land from them. Arabs went to war with Israel in 1956 and 1967 when the "occupied lands" of today were in their hands. Arabs turned down the United Nations' 1947 partition plan and went to war then, too. Arabs murdered Jews in the 1920's and 1930's when there was no Jewish state and no "Zionist occupation force."

There are no Arab moderates. Witness the Jordanian "moderate" who in 1967, in possession of the lands of Judea and Samaria (the so-called "West Bank") and East Jerusalem, went to war! The Arabs differ in tactics, not goals. Foolish Jews who call for concessions have already cost us dearly and we will pay terribly for those concessions that were made on the assumption that Arab "moderates" would seek peace with Israel and be its allies. Similarly, it is mad delusion to insist that Arab terrorists do not represent the "Palestinians." Of course they do, because the "Palestinians," as a whole, are committed to the destruction of an Israel they see as a robber state.

The true issue is the refusal of the Arabs to recognize a Jewish state of any size or shape for any permanent length of time. It is not an Arab-Israel issue but an Arab-Jewish one and it is more than a political dispute; it is a religious war. We should not be surprised that Christians and Moslems, who kill each other, join against the Jews or that a Pope meets with Moslem terrorists. The very existence of the Jewish state is proof of the truth of Judaism, a thing that neither Islam nor Christianity can accept. Peace is not possible under the above circumstances but Jews need not weep or wail. Zionism, from the first, was not created primarily for peace but for a Jewish state. Hopefully, it was believed, this could be accomplished by peace. But with or without peace, the primary goal was a Jewish state. . . .

The Jews of the Exile, including those of the United States, face a horrible growth of Jew-hatred that will be triggered by economic and social upheaval in the world. At the same time, they face the nuclear confrontation that will wipe out large areas of the Exile, but never that of a Jewish state that the rabbis of the Talmud guarantee can never become a third exile. Before it is too late, they must leave the graveyard and return to Israel. It is the obligation of Zionist leaders in the Exile to take the lead by emigrating to Israel.

Time Runs Out

Since the state of Israel arose, not because of Jewish merit, let it be clear that this beginning of the final redemption is merely the start of a process whose end will be determined by Jewish actions. If the Jew returns to G-d, that final redemption will come instantly and gloriously. If Jews, however, continue to be blind to Jewish reality, it will come only after terrible and needless suffering, G-d forbid. The choice is in Jewish hands.

Recognizing Deceptive Arguments

People who feel strongly about an issue use many techniques to persuade others to agree with them. Some of these techniques appeal to the intellect, some to the emotions. Many of them distract the reader or listener from the real issues.

A few common examples of argumentation tactics are listed below. Most of them can be used either to advance an argument in an honest, reasonable way or to deceive or distract from the real issues. It is important for a critical reader to recognize these tactics in order to rationally evaluate an author's ideas.

a. *scare tactics*—the threat that if you don't do or don't believe this, something terrible will happen

b. *personal attack*—criticizing an opponent *personally* instead of rationally debating his or her ideas

c. *categorical statements*—stating something in a way that implies there can be no argument

d. *deductive reasoning*—claiming that since a and b are true, c is also true, although there may not be a connection between a & c

e. *testimonial*—quoting or paraphrasing an authority or celebrity to support one's own viewpoint

The following activity can help you sharpen your skills in recognizing deceptive reasoning. The statements below are derived from the viewpoints in this chapter. *Beside each one, mark the letter of the type of deceptive appeal being used. More than one type of tactic may be applicable. If you believe the statement is not any of the listed appeals, write N.*

1. A full one percent of Israel's population was killed in their war of independence. If the US experienced similar casualties in a war today, it would mean the loss of two-and-a-half million people.

2. A Palestinian state between Jordan and Israel can only serve as a terrorist base from which both Israel and Jordan will be threatened.

3. Israel's record of genuine peaceful intent speaks for itself.

4. Terrorist organizations operate within Palestine. They have used threats and assassination against Palestinians inclined to negotiate with Israel. Therefore, victory over terrorism is essential to achieve peace.

5. Although the US was stronger than Vietnam, US military forces were nevertheless defeated. Likewise, Israel cannot count on military superiority to protect it against the fervor of Arab nationalism.

6. If the six-mile-wide security belt on Israel's northern border is given up, the Galilee will be exposed to shelling and terrorist incursions.

7. Palestinian nationalism is illegitimate because, as novelist Leon Uris said, Palestinians are "people who don't have the dignity to get up and better their own living conditions."

8. Nationalism is in large measure a matter of emotions or a state of mind, and it cannot be denied by those outsiders who find it inconvenient.

9. Israel argues against Palestinian nationalism at its own peril. The histories of South Africa, Northern Ireland, and Lebanon show that suppressed nationalisms can be a powerful force that is dangerous to ignore.

10. If Israel returns to its pre-1967 borders, the surrounding Arab nations will sweep down like a vulture and destroy it.

11. Israel can oppose Palestinian nationalism because PLO leader Yassir Arafat is a terrorist.

12. If Israel does not give up the occupied territories, there will be nuclear war in the Middle East.

Periodical Bibliography

The following articles have been selected to supplement the diverse views presented in this chapter.

Alon Ben-Meir
"Israel and the Palestinians," *Vital Speeches of the Day*, April 15, 1988.

Yoseph Ben-Shlomo
"In Defense of West Bank Settlement," *Harper's Magazine*, September 1987.

Meron Benvenisti
"Israel's 'Apocalypse Now,'" *Newsweek*, January 25, 1988.

Mitchell Cohen
"Occupying Each Other," *Commonweal*, April 22, 1988.

Robert I. Friedman
"Jewish Outposts Could Upset Jerusalem's Delicate Balance," *The Washington Post National Weekly Edition*, February 17, 1988.

Robert I. Friedman
"No Land, No Peace for Palestinians," *The Nation*, April 23, 1988.

Thomas L. Friedman
"My Neighbor, My Enemy," *The New York Times Magazine*, July 5, 1987.

Yehoshafat Harkabi, interviewed by Salim Tamari
"Choosing Between Bad and Worse," *Journal of Palestine Studies*, Spring 1987.

Arthur Hertzberg
"Israel: The Tragedy of Victory," *The New York Review of Books*, May 28, 1987.

David Kimche
"Political Schizophrenia Tears the Nation at 40," *World Press Review*, July 1988.

Moshe Levinger
"'Arabs Don't Want Peace,'" *U.S. News & World Report*, April 4, 1988.

Lance Morrow
"Israel," *Time*, April 4, 1988.

Donald Neff
"Israel at Forty," *Christianity Today*, April 22, 1988.

The New Republic
"Israel's Mad Settlers," May 2, 1988.

The New York Times
"Imagine a Palestinian State," April 28, 1988.

A.M. Rosenthal
"The News from Jerusalem," *The New York Times*, April 29, 1988.

James M. Wall
"Sowing Hate, Raping 'the Yellow Wind,'" *Christian Century*, April 13, 1988.

Chronology of Events

1881:   Russian pogroms force thousands of Jews to move west. Leo Pinsker founds the Hibbat Zion movement which urges persecuted Jews to settle Palestine as a national homeland.

1882:   A student society establishes Rishon le Zion, the first Zionist settlement in Palestine. Several other colonies are founded soon after.

1897:   Theodor Herzl convenes First Zionist Congress which designates Palestine as an appropriate Jewish homeland. Less than ten percent of Palestine's population is Jewish.

1915:   Sir Henry McMahon enlists the support of the Arabs in Britain's World War I effort against Turkey by promising British approval of a unified Arab nation. Arab nationalists later argue this promise includes Palestine; the British maintain Palestine must be an exception to Arab rule.

1917:   British Foreign Secretary A.J. Balfour declares Britain's support for a national homeland for the Jewish people in Palestine.

1920-1948:   Britain rules Palestine under agreement with the League of Nations. The British Mandate approves limited immigration for Jews.

1929-1939:   Arabs rebel violently against British rule; Jews and Arabs fight each other for the right to live in Palestine.

1930:   The British government, reacting to Arab riots against Jewish immigration, publishes the Passfield White Paper which advocates restriction of Jewish immigration and land sales in Palestine.

1937:   A British Royal Commission headed by Lord Peel, reports that Arab and Jewish national aspirations are irreconcilable and recommends the partition of Palestine.

1933-1939:   Hitler takes power in Germany and begins segregating Jews. In these six years, he forbids marriage between Jews and Germans, demands that Jews wear yellow stars and encourages the destruction of synagogues and Jewish property.

1939:   The British tighten limits of Jewish immigration into Palestine.

1939-1945:   During World War II, six million Jews are killed by Nazis. The Jewish population in Palestine reaches 608,000 by 1946.

1945-1948:   Zionist organizations wage a campaign of violence to end immigration restrictions in Palestine; thousands of Jews enter Palestine illegally.

November 29, 1947:	United Nations (UN) General Assembly votes to partition Palestine into Jewish and Arab states with Jerusalem being an international city. Arabs reject the plan.
May 1948:	Israel's first Prime Minister, David Ben Gurion, proclaims the State of Israel. Five Arab League states invade Israel soon after.
June 1948:	United Nations mediator Count Bernadotte calls a truce after 37 days of fighting. The Israeli army, smaller than the Arab forces but well organized, holds back the Arab invasion on five fronts but loses the Jewish section of Jerusalem.
July 1948:	Fighting resumes for ten days before a second truce with Israeli forces retaking the Jewish quarter of Jerusalem and pushing north past the Lebanese border.
December 1948:	The Israeli forces capture still more territory ouside the original UN partitions. More than one-half million Palestinians flee Israel to refugee camps in neighboring Arab states.
August 1949:	Israel and the Arab nations sign armistices but Israel refuses to return the land gained in the war and the Arab states refuse to recognize the State of Israel.
1950:	The Law of Return grants every Jew the right to immigrate to Israel.
January 1, 1950:	Israel names Jerusalem its capital despite protest from Arab states and the UN.
May 1964:	Arab leaders convene in Jerusalem and agree to the establishment of the Palestine Liberation Organization. The Palestine National Charter calls for the PLO to engage in armed struggle to "liquidate the Zionist presence in Palestine."
February 1966-May 1967:	A leftist coup brings a Soviet-supported regime to power in Syria. When the Syrians initiate a series of terrorist attacks on Israel, Israel responds with air strikes along the Syrian border. The Soviet Union encourages Egypt to enter the conflict and prevent further Israeli retaliations.
May 1967:	Egyptian leader Gamal Abdel Nasser orders UN emergency forces to withdraw from the Sinai peninsula, declares a state of emergency along the Gaza Strip, and closes the Strait of Tiran, blocking the Suez Canal to shipping both to and from Israel. Israel and the US warn Egypt to remove blockade; the US Sixth Fleet moves toward the Middle East; the USSR warns it will help resist aggression in the Middle East.
June 5-10, 1967:	Six Day War. Israel attacks Egypt, Jordan, and Syria and captures the Sinai, Gaza Strip, West Bank, and Golan Heights. One million Arabs living in the captured territories come under Israeli rule.

November 22, 1967:	UN Security Council Resolution 242 calling for peace in the Middle East is adopted. The resolution asks that Israel return land acquired in the Six Day War and that Arabs respect Israel's boundaries.
1968-1970:	Egypt and Israel engage in a "war of attrition" over the blocked Suez Canal, with the Soviet Union supplying arms to Egypt and the US providing weapons for the Israelis.
October 6, 1973:	Yom Kippur War. Egypt and Syria, in a two-front attack, surprise Israel on the holiest day of the Jewish calendar and advance into Israeli-occupied territory before Israel forces them back. Tensions between the US and USSR escalate; both countries seek cease-fire.
October 22, 1973:	Security Council Resolution 338 calls for immediate cease-fire in Yom Kippur War and establishes a peacekeeping force.
November 11, 1973:	Israel and Egypt sign a cease-fire after engaging in the first high level discussions since the 1949 armistice.
April 11, 1974:	Three Arab terrorists attack a four story residential building in Qiryat Shmona in an effort to sabotage peace negotiations for the Yom Kippur War. The guerillas kill 18 Israelis before an explosion, touched off when a bullet from Israeli troops outside strikes an explosive laden backpack, kills them.
1974:	The Arab states meet in the Rabat Summit Conference and agree to recognize the PLO as the sole legitimate representative of the Palestinian people.
October 1974:	The United Nations General Assembly invites the PLO to participate in debate over Palestine. At the meeting, PLO leader Yassir Arafat addresses the General Assembly while Israel announces it will never deal directly with the PLO. The UN grants the PLO the right to limited participation in all UN meetings.
September 1975:	Israel and Egypt sign an interim peace agreement in which Israel agrees to return 6250 square kilometers of captured Sinai territory. As part of the agreement, the US agrees not to negotiate with the PLO unless the PLO recognizes Israeli sovereignty.
November 1975:	The UN General Assembly adopts a resolution equating Zionism with racism.
November 11, 1976:	UN Security Council objects to Israel's establishment of settlements in the territories it has occupied since the Six Day War.
November 9-21, 1977:	To promote renewed peace talks, Egyptian President Anwar Sadat visits Israel. This is the first time an Arab leader has visited the State of Israel.
March-June 1978:	UN troops move into southern Lebanon to enforce a cease-fire called by Israel. Israeli troops withdraw after establishing the presence of a pro-Israeli Christian militia backed by the UN forces.

September 5-17, 1978:	Camp David summit meeting between Carter, Sadat, and Israeli Prime Minister Menachem Begin leads to an Egyptian-Israeli peace agreement and the return of Sinai to the Egyptians. Most of the Arab states, the PLO, and the Soviets denounce the agreements.
June 1982:	Arab assassin kills the Israeli ambassador to Great Britain; Israel retaliates with the full-scale invasion of Lebanon.
July-September 1982:	Fighting in Lebanon escalates as Israel moves into Beirut and demands that the PLO leave the city. US Marines help patrol the PLO evacuation.
September 14, 1982:	Israeli forces in Lebanon stand by while Lebanese Christian Phalangists massacre 300 Palestinian refugees in the Sabra and Shatila camps. The ensuing public outcry forces Israel's Defense Minister Ariel Sharon to resign.
May 17, 1983:	Lebanon and Israel sign an agreement to withdraw Israeli forces from Lebanon. Israel refuses to completely withdraw until Syria also withdraws.
April 1985:	An Israeli gunboat intercepts an Arab vessel attempting to land on the Israeli coast near Tel Aviv. After a firefight, the Israeli ship sinks the Arab's boat, killing 20 Palestinians and capturing eight.
September 1985:	Terrorists kill three Israeli tourists in Cyprus. Israeli warplanes respond with the bombing of PLO headquarters in Tunisia.
July 26, 1986:	Morocco's King Hassan holds a surprise meeting in Morocco with Israeli Prime Minister Shimon Peres. The move draws intense criticism and diplomatic reprisals from other Arab nations and Hassan resigns as president of the Arab League.
December 1986:	Allegations of Israeli involvement in the Iran-Contra scandal arise in the US press. The reports indicate Israeli arms merchants Al Schwimmer and Jacob Nimrodi, with the complicity of the Israeli government, arranged for the sale of American-made Israeli missiles to Iran in return for hostages. The Israeli government denies involvement in the affair.
December 8, 1987:	Four Palestinians are killed when an Israeli army truck rams their car after they attempt to run a military roadblock in Gaza.
December 9, 1987:	During the funeral for four Palestinians killed in Gaza the day before, Israeli troops clash with mourners. One Palestinian is shot and killed in an event which marks the beginning of widespread Palestinian protests and rioting.
December 23-25, 1987:	Israeli troops arrest over 1,000 in Gaza and the West Bank suspected of involvement in Palestinian rioting.

January 3, 1988:	Israel announces it plans to expel nine Palestinian activists for their leadership role in the December uprising. An Israeli soldier shoots and kills a Palestinian woman. Both incidents spark renewed unrest.
January 19, 1988:	Defense Minister Yitzhak Rabin announces a new Israeli policy of using "might, power and beating;" arming soldiers with clubs rather than live ammunition to deal with Palestinian rioting.
March 13, 1988:	The Unified National Command, underground leadership of the uprising, calls for Palestinians to resign from government posts and to punish "collaborators"; those cooperating with the Israeli government. Approximately 500 West Bank and Gaza Palestinian police officers resign.
April 6, 1988:	A 15-year-old Israeli girl is accidentally killed by a Jewish settler in a confrontation between Israeli settlers and Palestinians on the West bank. She is the first non-military Israeli Jew to die in the Palestinian uprising which began December 9, 1987.
April 16, 1988:	Khalil al-Wazir, second to Yassir Arafat in the PLO chain of command and believed to have helped direct the Palestinian uprising, is assassinated in his Tunisian home by a commando unit of the Israeli Defense Forces.
April 28: 1988:	The number of Palestinians killed by Israelis in rioting since December 9 reaches 168; 60 more died from beatings and tear gas.
August 1988:	King Hussein of Jordan announces the severing of legal and administrative ties to the West Bank. Jordan ceases to pay the salaries of the 24,000 West Bank teachers, doctors, religious officials and municipal employees it has maintained there. The status of the 750,000 Palestinians holding Jordanian passports grows doubtful as responsibility for the West Bank's economic and municipal functions shifts to the PLO.

Organizations To Contact

The editors have compiled the following list of organizations which are concerned with the issues debated in this book. All of them have information or publications available for interested readers. The descriptions are derived from materials provided by the organizations themselves.

American Friends Service Committee
1501 Cherry St.
Philadelphia, PA 19102
(215) 241-7000

The organization works worldwide to relieve human suffering and to find new approaches to world peace and justice through nonviolence. It provides information on these issues to government policymakers. Its Peace Education Division publishes *Peace Education Resources,* a catalog of publications that includes literature on Israel and the Middle East.

American Israel Public Affairs Committee (AIPAC)
500 N. Capitol St. NW, Suite 300
Washington, DC 20001
(202) 638-2256

AIPAC is a registered government lobbying organization that provides information and services on American foreign policy in the Middle East. It seeks to maintain and improve goodwill and amity between the US and Israel. AIPAC provides training seminars for college students and publishes the AIPAC Monograph Series.

American Jewish Committee
c/o Institute for Human Relations
165 E. 56th St.
New York, NY 10022
(212) 751-4000

The Committee conducts a program of education, research, and community services. It fights against bigotry and for civil and religious rights. It publishes the monthly journal *Commentary,* the bimonthly *Present Tense,* and numerous articles, pamphlets, reprints, bibliographies, and a publications catalog.

American Jewish League for Israel
30 E. 60th St.
New York, NY 10022
(212) 371-1583

The League is a Zionist organization whose objectives are to rebuild the state of Israel, strengthen its ties with American Jews, and intensify Jewish life outside of Israel. It publishes a monthly *News Bulletin.*

American Zionist Federation
515 Park Ave.
New York, NY 10022
(212) 371-7750

The Federation is an umbrella organization that coordinates the sixteen national organizations that constitute the American Zionist movement. The Federation conducts a Zionist information and education program to create a greater appreciation of Israeli society and culture among American Jews. It publishes the periodic *Issue Analysis* and the quarterly *Spectrum*.

Americans for Middle East Understanding
475 Riverside Drive, Room 771
New York, NY 10115
(212) 870-2336

The organization works to foster better understanding in America of Middle Eastern peoples and cultures, the rights of Palestinians, and the forces shaping American policy in the Middle East. It publishes books on the Middle East, the bimonthly newsletter *The Link,* and an annual book catalog.

Americans for Progressive Israel
150 5th Ave., Suite 911
New York, NY 10011
(212) 255-8760

The group sponsors educational seminars, speakers, and tours. It supplies information on Israeli farm communes (kibbutzim), the Israeli labor movements, and the Israeli peace camp to students and community organizations. It also publishes the bimonthly socialist magazine *Israel Horizons* as well as translations of Israeli articles.

Americans for a Safe Israel
114 E. 28th St., Suite 401
New York, NY 10016
(212) 696-2611

The organization provides and disseminates information on conflict in the Middle East. It believes that a strong Israel is important for American security interests. Its publications include books, pamphlets, news updates, articles, videos, and the quarterly magazine *Outpost*.

Association of Arab-American University Graduates (AAUG)
556 Trapelo Road
Belmont, MA 02178
(617) 484-5483

AAUG is an educational and cultural organization dedicated to fostering better Arab-American understanding. To this end, it organizes conferences and seminars, provides speakers on topics concerning the Arab world, supports human rights and civil liberties in the Middle East and elsewhere, and publishes books and periodicals including *Arab Studies Quarterly*.

Consulate General of Israel
Department of Information
111 E. Wacker Drive
Chicago, IL 60601
(312) 565-3300

Israeli consulates officially represent the government of Israel in major US cities. This diplomatic presence seeks to maintain understanding and good relations between the citizens of the US and Israel. The Consulate's Department of Information provides pamphlets, studies, reports, and maps published by the government of Israel.

257

Givat Haviva Educational Foundation
150 5th Ave., Suite 911
New York, NY 10011
(212) 255-2992

Givat Haviva is comprised of socially and politically progressive Jews and non-Jews who work for better relations between Jews and Arabs. Its goal is an egalitarian Israeli society of Jews and Arabs. It publishes a semiannual *Givat Haviva Newsletter.*

Hadassah
50 W. 58th St.
New York, NY 10019
(212) 355-7900

Hadassah is the Women's Zionist Organization of America. It provides medical, educational, social, and fundraising services in the US and Israel as well as operating numerous community centers. Its numerous publications include the monthly *Hadassah Magazine* and the quarterly *Hadassah Headlines* as well as a catalog of educational publications.

The Institute for Palestine Studies
PO Box 25697
Washington, DC 20007
(202) 342-3990

The Institute is a private Arab research organization designed to promote a better understanding of the Palestine problem. It publishes reprints, monographs, and anthologies in English, French, and Arabic, as well as the quarterly *Journal of Palestine Studies.*

Jordan Information Bureau
2319 Wyoming Ave. NW
Washington, DC 20008
(202) 265-1606

The Bureau provides travel, cultural, and economic information on Jordan. It publishes factsheets, speeches by Jordanian officials, government documents, the quarterly magazine *Jordan,* and the bimonthly *Al Urdun.*

Kach International
PO Box 425
Midwood Station
Brooklyn, NY 11230
(718) 646-7301

Kach International is a Zionist organization whose primary goal is to bring the Kach political party, under the leadership of Israeli Knesset member Rabbi Meir Kahane, into power in Israel. Kach International opposes intermarriage between Jews and Gentiles, assimilation of non-Jewish culture by Jews, and political compromise with the Arabs. It publishes the monthly *KACH Newsletter* and the bimonthly *Kahane Magazine.*

Middle East Research and Information Project (MERIP)
PO Box 43445
Columbia Heights Station
Washington, DC 20010
(202) 667-1188.

The Project provides information, research, and analysis of US involvement in the Middle East and the Middle East's political and economic development. It publishes the bimonthly magazine *MERIP Middle East Report*.

Palestine Human Rights Campaign (PHRC)
220 S. State St., Suite 1308
Chicago, IL 60604
(312) 987-1830

The PHRC works for peace and justice for Palestinian refugees. It monitors human rights violations against Palestinians living under military occupation. PHRC publishes books, reports, and the *Palestine Human Rights Newsletter*.

Palestine Research and Educational Center
9522-A Lee Highway
Fairfax, VA 22031
(703) 352-4168

The organization conducts research and educational programs on Middle Eastern affairs with a focus on Palestinian issues. It publishes pamphlets, monographs, and a bimonthly magazine, *Palestine Perspectives*.

United Jewish Appeal (UJA)
99 Park Ave.
New York, NY 10016
(212) 818-9100

The United Jewish Appeal is the principal US fundraising organization for Jewish needs overseas. It cooperates with other Jewish organizations to provide humanitarian programs and social services for Jews worldwide. It publishes *The Whole UJA Catalog*, including campaign and fundraising manuals, the quarterly, *UJA Life*, and a biweekly news update, *Campaign Hotline*.

The West Bank Data Base Project
c/o The Jerusalem Post
120 E. 56th St.
New York, NY 10022
(212) 355-4440

The West Bank Data Base Project is an independent research group that studies and analyzes demographic, legal, social, economic, and political conditions in the West Bank and Gaza territories presently administered by Israel. It publishes its research in yearly *Studies Series*.

Bibliography of Books

Edward Alexander | *The Jewish Idea and Its Enemies*. Brunswick, NJ: Transaction Books, 1987.

Geoffrey Aronson | *Creating Facts: Israel, Palestinians, and the West Bank*. Washington, DC: Institute for Palestine Studies, 1987.

Shlomo Avineri | *The Making of Modern Zionism*. New York: Basic Books, Inc., 1981.

Bernard Avishai | *The Tragedy of Zionism*. New York: Farrar, Straus & Giroux, 1985.

Bishara Bahbah | *Israel and Latin America: The Military Connection*. New York: St. Martin's Press, 1986.

Benjamin Beit-Hallahmi | *The Israeli Connection: Who Israel Arms and Why*. New York: Pantheon Books, 1987.

David Ben Gurion | *My Talks with Arab Leaders*. New York: The Third Press, 1973.

Meron Benvenisti | *The West Bank Handbook*. Boulder, CO: Westview Press, 1986.

Yehuda Z. Blum | *For Zion's Sake*. New York: Herzl Press, 1987.

Hyman Bookbinder and James G. Abourezk | *Through Different Eyes*. Bethesda, MD: Adler and Adler, Publishers, Inc., 1987.

Michael Comay | *Zionism, Israel, and the Palestinian Arabs*. Jerusalem: Keter Publishing House Jerusalem Limited, 1983.

Michael Curtis, ed. | *A Middle East Reader*. Brunswick, NJ: Transaction Books, 1986.

Michael Curtis, ed. | *Antisemitism in the Contemporary World*. Boulder, CO: Westview Press, 1986.

Abba Eban | *Heritage: Civilization and the Jews*. New York: Summit Books, 1984.

Saad El-Shazly | *The Arab Military Option*. San Francisco: American Mideast Research, 1986.

Simha Flapan | *The Birth of Israel: Myths and Realities*. New York: Pantheon Books, 1987.

Eytan Gilboa | *American Public Opinion Toward Israel and the Arab-Israeli Conflict*. Lexington, MA: Lexington Books, 1987.

Yosef Gorny | *Zionism and the Arabs, 1882-1948*. Oxford, UK: Clarendon Press, 1987.

Stephen Green | *Living by the Sword: America and Israel in the Middle East*. Brattleboro, VT: Amana Books, 1988.

Stephen Green | *Taking Sides: America's Secret Relations with a Militant Israel*. Brattleboro, VT: Amana Books, 1987.

David Grossman | *The Yellow Wind*. Translated by Haim Watzman. New York: Farrar, Straus & Giroux, 1988.

Grace Halsell | *Prophecy and Politics: Militant Evangelists on the Road to Nuclear War*. Westport, CT: Lawrence Hill & Co., 1986.

Yehoshafat Harkabi	*The Bar Kokhba Syndrome: Risk and Realism in International Politics.* Chappaqua, NY: Rossel Books, 1983.
Arthur Hertzberg, ed.	*The Zionist Idea: A Historical Analysis and Reader.* New York: Atheneum Books, 1969.
Jane Hunter	*Israeli Foreign Policy: South Africa and Central America.* Boston: South End Press, 1987.
Israeli Attorney General's Office	*The Karp Report: An Israeli Government Inquiry into Settler Violence Against Palestinians on the West Bank.* Washington: Institute for Palestine Studies, 1984.
Israeli Department of International Relations	*Labour and Employment in Judea, Samaria, and the Gaza District.* Jerusalem: Ministry of Labour and Social Affairs, 1985.
Vladimir Jabotinsky	*The War and the Jew.* New York: The Dial Press, 1942.
Milton Jamail and Margo Gutierrez	*It's No Secret: Israel's Military Involvement in Central America.* Belmont, MA: Association of Arab-American University Graduates, 1986.
The Jewish Agency for Palestine	*The Jewish Case Before the Anglo-American Committee of Inquiry on Palestine.* Jerusalem: The Jewish Agency for Palestine, 1947.
Paul Johnson	*A History of the Jews.* New York: Harper & Row, 1987.
Stephen Karetzky and Norman Frankel	*The Media's Coverage of the Arab-Israeli Conflict.* New York: Shapolsky Publishers, 1988.
James Everett Katz	*The Implications of Third World Military Industrialization: Sowing the Serpents' Teeth.* Lexington, MA: Lexington Books, 1986.
Walid Khalidi	*From Haven to Conquest: Readings in Zionism and the Palestine Problem until 1948.* Beirut: The Institute for Palestine Studies, 1971.
Aaron Klieman	*Israel's Global Reach: Arms Sales as Diplomacy.* Elmsford, NY: Pergamon-Brassey's, 1986.
Bruce R. Kuniholm and Michael Rubner	*The Palestinian Problem and United States Policy.* Claremont, CA: Regina Books, 1986.
Walter Laqueur and Barry Rubin, eds.	*A Documentary History of the Middle East Conflict,* fourth edition. New York: Facts on File, 1984.
Charles S. Liebman and Eliezer Don-Yehiya	*Civil Religion in Israel.* Berkeley: University of California Press, 1983.
Judah L. Magnes	*Palestine: Divided or United?* Westport, CT: Greenwood Press, 1983.
Thomas Mallison and Sally V. Mallison	*The Palestine Problem in International Law and World Order.* London: Longman Group, Ltd., 1986.
Lee O'Brien	*American Jewish Organizations & Israel.* Washington, DC: Institute for Palestine Studies, 1986.
Wesley G. Pippert	*Land of Promise, Land of Strife: Israel at 40.* Waco, TX: Word Books, 1988.
Steve Posner	*Israel Undercover: Secret Warfare and Hidden Diplomacy in the Middle East.* Syracuse, NY: Syracuse University Press, 1987.

Cheryl A. Rubenberg	*Israel and the American National Interest*. Chicago: University of Illinois Press, 1986.
Amnon Rubenstein	*The Zionist Dream Revisited*. New York: Schocken Books, 1984.
Edward Said and Christopher Hitchens, eds.	*Blaming the Victims: Spurious Scholarship and the Palestinian Question*. London: Verso Books, 1988.
Ze'ev Schiff	*A History of the Israeli Army*. New York: Macmillan Publishing Company, 1985.
Harris O. Schoenberg	*A Mandate for Terror: The United Nations and the PLO*. New York: Shapolsky Publishers, 1988.
Peter Shearman and Phil Williams, eds.	*The Superpowers, Central America and the Middle East*. Elmsford, NY: Pergamon-Brassey's, 1988.
Alan J. Steinberg	*American Jewry and Conservative Politics*. New York: Shapolsky Publishers, 1988.
Edward Tivnan	*The Lobby: Jewish Political Power and American Foreign Policy*. New York: Simon & Schuster, 1987.
Milton Viorst	*Sands of Sorrow: Israel's Journey from Independence*. New York: Harper & Row, 1987.
Samuel F. Wells Jr. and Mark A. Bruzonsky, eds.	*Security in the Middle East*. Boulder, CO: Westview Press, 1987.
Michael Wolffsohn	*Israel: Polity, Society and Economy*. Atlantic Highlands, NJ: Humanities Press International, 1987.
Claudia Wright	*Spy, Steal, Smuggle: Israel's Special Relationship with the US*. Belmont, MA: Association of Arab-American University Graduates, 1986.
Ronald J. Young	*Missed Opportunities for Peace*. Philadelphia: American Friends Service Committee, 1987.

Index

movement for, 215-216, 223
with Arabs
  as beneficial, 205-207, 209, 210
    con, 214-217
with PLO
  as harmful, 190-196
    con, 197-203, 207, 209
religion in, 238
  Judaism should be dominant,
    220-226, 241-247
  should be secular, 235-240
  should be weakened, 227-234
respects individual rights, 94, 191
    con, 60, 84-89, 139
shares Western values, 129, 130,
    133, 171, 225
  as bad, 243
    con, 136
should remain Jewish, 226, 241-247
supports peace negotiations,
    192-193
US alliance with, 226
  and military bases, 102, 113
  and pro-Israel lobby
    as legitimate influence, 121-127
      con, 115-120
  based on moral interests, 132-133
  benefits of, 102-103
    as exaggerated, 108-114
  deters Soviets, 104-105, 107
    con, 110-112, 139-140
  should be strengthened, 101-107,
    128-133
    con, 108-113, 134-140
war of independence of, 174-176,
    180, 191
see also Jewish state; occupied
  territories

Jamail, Milton, 155
Jewish state
Arabs in
  Jews must coexist with, 47-49
  rights of, 38, 42, 49
  should be a minority, 35-36
    con, 37-42, 48
as impractical, 25-31, 41-42, 44
as necessary, 17-24, 33-36
benefits of, 19-20, 23
in Palestine Mandate, 24, 26-28
  as needed, 32-36
  British policy toward, 19, 33, 39,
    71
  should be binational, 43-49
  would deny Arab rights, 37-42
steps in creating, 22-23
will eliminate anti-Semitism, 18,
  20-21

con, 33
Jewish
culture, 36
  as becoming stronger, 45-46
  as becoming weaker, 19, 30-31
  must be revived, 242, 243
  persecution of, 19, 21, 28, 33
history in Palestine, 33, 40, 44, 45,
  47, 63-64
history of Arab relations, 39-40
spiritual problem, 27, 34-35
population in US, 120, 126-127
Jordan
and the PLO, 195, 205, 214-215
as Palestinian homeland, 67, 192
  con, 200-201
Israeli negotiations with, 193-194
Joseph, Seymour, 58

Kahane, Meir, 238, 241, 243

Lebanon
Israeli involvement in, 195
1982 war in
  impact of, 113, 200
  US response to, 135, 194-195
Lenczowski, George, 132
Lewin-Epstein, Noah, 79
Lustick, Ian S., 227

MacArthur, Douglas II, 136
McCarthy, Colman, 157
Magnes, Judah L., 43, 47
Manor, Yohanon, 183
Marlette, Doug, 88
Muhsin, Zuhair, 67

Natshe, Rafiq, 66
Nisan, Mordechai, 220, 224, 245
Nordau, Max, 23, 27

occupied territories
administration of, 71, 78, 83, 214
Arab birthrate in, 208, 213, 236,
  237, 245
civil rights in
  are protected, 73
  are violated, 78-79, 86-89
economy of
  Israel exploits, 79, 80, 81-83
  Israel has improved, 73-74, 76
education in, 74-75
Jewish settlements in, 86-88, 114,
  246
riots in, 91, 93-94, 207, 213
security in
  as legitimate concern, 92, 214
    con, 85-86, 89